Praise for *The Divided Church*

"Sometimes it feels like the mainline church is coming apart
at the seams. Although Shriver and Hutcheson stand
at different ends of the church, they have clearly found a tie
that binds us all together."
DR. CRAIG BARNES, *The National Presbyterian Church*

" 'The problem with a quarrel,' said G. K. Chesterton,
'is that it interrupts a good argument.'
In *The Divided Church*, two obviously decent and thoughtful
Christians, themselves divided on questions of great moment,
strive to move the several churches from quarrel to argument in
the hope of reconciliation that will be reconciliation in the truth."
THE REV. RICHARD JOHN NEUHAUS, *Religion and Public Life*

"This is an honest, wise and hopeful book about the most
threatening problem in American Protestantism.
All who are concerned about and involved in the conflict between
the liberal and evangelical constituencies in the churches
should read and heed it."
DR. JAMES LUTHER MAYS, *Union Theological Seminary*

"This is the conversation that has too long gone unspoken!
It comes to no easy conclusions. But whatever your position may be,
I dare you to read this book without finding yourself in active,
creative dialogue with both Peggy Shriver and Richard Hutcheson.
You'll be better for it."
DR. JOHN A. HUFFMAN JR., *St. Andrews Presbyterian Church*

"To be a witness to the peace and wholeness that is possible
through an encounter with Christ, Christians themselves need to
be examples of the joy and reconciliation we advocate.
Hutcheson and Shriver are wise and weathered church leaders who
confront us with the broken body of Christ and walk us
through practical steps toward trust and a shared vision."
DR. VICTORIA ERICKSON, *Drew University*

"If Michelin produced a guide for liberals and conservatives to
come to the same restaurant, this would undoubtedly be it.
Looking carefully at the hungers which have led to this division,
the authors provide the menu that will delight all people
of good will. It won't be as easy to sit down as some think,
for a mature way of looking over the dishes is required.
However, this book is essential reading for everyone who wants to
come to the table of Christian unity. It's tough advice sometimes,
but it leads us to the absolutely important
five-star banquet of love."
DR. RICHARD RAY, *Pittsburgh Theological Seminary*

THE DIVIDED CHURCH

Moving Liberals
& Conservatives
from Diatribe
to Dialogue

RICHARD G. HUTCHESON JR.
& PEGGY SHRIVER

InterVarsity Press
Downers Grove, Illinois

InterVarsity Press
P.O. Box 1400, Downers Grove, IL 60515
World Wide Web: www.ivpress.com
E-mail: mail@ivpress.com

InterVarsity Press® is the book-publishing division of InterVarsity Christian Fellowship/USA®, a student movement active on campus at hundreds of universities, colleges and schools of nursing in the United States of America, and a member movement of the International Fellowship of Evangelical Students. For information about local and regional activities, write Public Relations Dept., InterVarsity Christian Fellowship/USA, 6400 Schroeder Rd., P.O. Box 7895, Madison, WI 53707-7895.

ISBN 0-8308-2223-2

Printed in the United States of America ♾

Library of Congress Cataloging-in-Publication Data

Hutcheson, Richard G., 1921-
    The divided church : moving liberals & conservatives from diatribe
    to dialogue / Richard G. Hutcheson Jr. & Peggy Shriver.
        p.   cm.
    Includes bibliographical references.
    ISBN 0-8308-2223-2 (pbk. : alk. paper)
    1. Evangelicalism.   2. Liberalism (Religion).   I. Shriver, Peggy
L.   II. Title.
BR1640.H875   1999
277.3'0829—dc21   99-35002
                                                                                                          CIP

17	16	15	14	13	12	11	10	9	8	7	6	5	4	3	2	1
12	11	10	09	08	07	06	05	04	03	02	01	00	99			

Acknowledgments

Perhaps our first word of gratitude should be to the Holy Spirit, if we may be presumptuous enough to think that Dick Hutcheson was so nudged when he wrote Peggy Shriver suggesting a daring dialogue or that she was moved to accept. We can more easily document the role of James Lewis and the Louisville Institute for the Study of Protestantism and American Culture, funders of our proposal to interview active church members regarding polarities in the church and how to approach them constructively.

It would serve little purpose to enumerate here *all* the persons with whom we have had contact in preparation for this book or all the sources of information, books, organizations and groups, meetings and forums for testing ideas. Many of them are documented along the way for the reader. In order to provide full freedom of expression, we decided to identify persons quoted from our interviews and Ecunet exchanges by their relationship or responsibility in a particular church tradition rather than by name. We are deeply appreciative of the thoughtfulness and time so many busy people gave when answering our inquiries.

Recognizing that we can list only a portion of those who contributed in a variety of ways, we mention first of all our spouses, Ann Rivers Hutcheson and Donald W. Shriver Jr., who accepted our occasional preoccupations and frustrations with the kind of Christian forbearance we urge in this book. We thank our editor, Cynthia Bunch-Hotaling, for seeing the promise in our manuscript.

Special appreciation of their time and insights goes to the following: James E. Andrews, Edwin David Aponte, J. Martin Bailey, Ned Benson, George Buchanan, John M. Buchanan, Robert Bullock, Joan Salmon

Campbell, Robert Campbell, Marjorie Carpenter, Joyce Cleveland, David Cockcroft, George Cottay, Robert Cramer, Michael Cromartie, Virgil Cruz, Robert Davidson, Gary W. Demarest, Joseph Dempsey, James Dollar, P. C. Enniss, William J. Fogleman, James A. Forbes, Kent Gilbert, Stephen Hayner, Roberta Hestenes, Masaya Hibino, John A. Huffman, Douglas Jacobsen, Nancy Jennings, Britt Johnston, Paul Johnston, Robert C. Lamar, Bruce Larson, John H. Leith, Robert Longman, Mary Ann Lundy, Richard Mathisen, Daniel Matthews, Mary Charlotte McCall, Patricia McClurg, David McShane, David K. Miller, Gary W. Miller, Elizabeth Moore, Sara B. Moseley, Stephen Mott, Barry P. Murr, Brian Nelson, Douglas W. Oldenburg, Charles Plant, Jovelino Ramos, Larry L. Rasmussen, Edmund W. Robb, Cecil M. Robeck, Rick Roderick, M. Anderson Sale, Paul Schmidt, David Shearman, David Sikkink, Joseph Small, Christian Smith, Max L. Stackhouse, George B. Telford, Gary Torrens, William Vance Trollinger Jr., Barbara Wheeler, Edward White, Philip Wickeri, Jeff Wildrick, Louis Wilkins, Robert Wuthnow and Louis H. Zbinden.

Preface

· · · · · · · · · · · ·

To Live in Christian Community
with Those Who Differ

*Polarization is symptomatic of an erosion in both camps of the self-evident sense of
the sacred, of the reality of the sense of God. . . . Perhaps both liberals and
conservatives are less "intolerant and rigid" than insecure, clinging to a life raft
because the ocean is so vast and the storm is threatening.*
PASTOR OF A LARGE METROPOLITAN CHURCH

This book is the attempt of two people, one perceived as a liberal and the
other as an conservative evangelical,[1] to deal jointly with the liberal-evangelical impasse in today's church. Conscious that the divisions in our
churches are many and complex, we try to write with some awareness of
these complexities. Our chief focus, however, is the liberal-evangelical (or
progressive-orthodox) tension. It is our hope that insights about one set
of tensions may be beneficial in addressing others, especially as they
interact.

Both authors of this book have been troubled for a number of years by
the "walls of hostility" within our shared denomination, the Presbyterian
Church (U.S.A.). But we see the problem as a far broader one. In the
ecumenical circles of the National Council of the Churches of Christ in
the U.S.A., similar barriers exist both within and without the conciliar
movement. Independently we have each written about these concerns
before, given speeches about them and participated in consultations and
efforts within our churches to try to understand them.

Each of us in our personal lives has moved and grown in a different
direction from where we started. One of us grew up in the Midwest,
small-town America, in a Dutch enclave that embraced almost exclusively

the Reformed tradition with a strong evangelical emphasis. Throughout a number of stages, including marriage and several geographic shifts, she has gradually enlarged her sense of the church and gained a deep appreciation of ecumenism and the gifts that each tradition brings to the others.[2] This has been expressed through her more than twenty years as a staff member in the National Council of the Churches of Christ in the U.S.A.

The other author, the son of a minister, grew up in a religiously conservative home. By the time of his graduation from Yale Divinity School he considered himself a liberal theologically, and for a number of years he identified with the Presbyterian denomination's liberal leadership. Gradually, through many years as a navy chaplain, denominational executive and pastor of a congregation, he moved in a more conservative direction and came to identify with the evangelical wing of his denomination.[3]

In a way, we have both experienced a shift within the church community in which we are most at home and trusted—he into a more evangelical community and she into an ecumenical, liberal one. Yet neither of us rejects our roots, although we have some critical distance from them as well as from our new "home." It is perhaps deceptively easy for us to discuss the tensions of the church together, because we share a lot of common ground. One of the problems we perceive in our churches today is a distrust of people who come out of a different religious culture from our own and a distrust of what they say and do. Since each of us has different communities of trust, we hope that more people will read a book written jointly than one written by either of us alone. We are trying to speak to the various separated communities in the church at once.

But we also mean to help people of differing perspectives hear one another. Thanks to a generous grant from the Louisville Institute for the Study of Protestantism and American Culture, we have been able to interview a number of church leaders to gather helpful viewpoints and insights. We have chosen leaders across a spectrum of perspectives in a variety of locations and denominations. We have interviewed clergy and a number of active laity: men and women; Anglos, Hispanics, Asians and African-Americans; leaders of ecumenical and parachurch groups; and seminary professors of several denominations. We have attempted throughout to keep a balance of participation from those across the theological spectrum. We have been in close contact with the Religious Research Association (of which one author has been a recent president), Professional Church Leadership of the National Council of Churches (with which one author is on staff) and the Institute on Religion and Public Life (with which one author has been affiliated). Interviews have been conducted with a past president of the National Council of Churches, one of the founders of the Institute on Religion and Democracy, and a staff member of the Ethics and Public Policy Center.

Our interviews have been face to face, each of us separately interviewing different persons in nearly all instances. We have both recorded and taken notes of the interviews, and then we have reviewed one another's tapes and taken notes from them. As a consequence, we have each heard all the interviews. We designed together a set of questions for a structured interview that we both agreed to follow. With some interviewees we were able to follow our structured interview questions quite closely, sometimes probing further where it seemed appropriate. In some instances the person interviewed volunteered so much helpful information and perspective that questions were answered before we asked them and other unanticipated avenues of discourse added insights. Our questions encompassed the following themes:

☐ the terms that appropriately "label" the polarization within the church and which label has been accepted for oneself; whether this polarization is real and serious and, if so, whether discussing it is helpful or hurtful

☐ the incidents, situations and related stories in which polarization has been lessened or reconciliation effected and which actions by either side were helpful; similarly, those situations in which polarization has grown worse and which actions by either side contributed to the worsening of the crisis

☐ the actions that have been or that might be taken by persons on the other side to improve relationships and cause healing; also those actions that are harmful and polarizing; the putting of oneself into another's shoes to see how one might be helpful as well as how one might be hurtful

☐ the trust between those who differ, how that trust is established and what one might learn from people with a different outlook

☐ the role of moderate congregations and how they should be characterized; whether they, or some others within the church, function as mediators

☐ guidance, advice and suggestions for leaders on both sides; additional questions or comments not covered in the interview; historical insights and biographical data

A number of books, analyses, current journals and studies, to which we have frequently referred throughout these pages, have informed our work. Where we have taken a cupful of wisdom, an ocean remains.

One resource we used, Ecunet, takes advantage of the computer technology that allows persons linked by modem to "meet" with one another over a chosen topic of conversation. We set up an online meeting on the subject of the "polarized pews" and posed several key questions to which we invited response. Over several months there ensued a lively conversation, to which we will on occasion refer. The limits of such a technique for research purposes is that Ecunet users are a self-selected and computer-literate group of people and therefore do not constitute either a random or a carefully balanced sample. But they are legitimate and well-informed voices within the church, and they expand the number of concerned Christians to whom we can listen and from whom we have learned. We are grateful for their participation. We discovered in the course of conversation via modem that this was a very special interchange among Christians from a broad spectrum of religious viewpoints and denominations. They have become friends through this new technology that allows candid, caring, searching, playful interaction. Their theological differences can be explored, even in this somewhat "public" manner, with honesty and fidelity to one another's feelings and their own faith stance. Would that more church Bible classes and workshops could achieve as much community face to face as have some of these long-time computer friends who may never have seen one another!

Another way we have gathered perspectives has been through focus groups of pastors and of lay people, the participants of which we have interviewed together and individually. We have also gathered data through conversation and observation at various church meetings we have attended over a period of several years. At informal meetings we have introduced the subject of our study and listened to the resulting discussion. Papers presented at the Religious Research Association and the American Academy of Religion on these issues have kept us informed of recent scholarship. One author moves in an ecumenical environment, the other in an evangelical one.

Through all of these approaches we have encountered serious and careful response. Each has taught us new things, and each has often confirmed something we have heard elsewhere. Naturally, we have listened to a wide range of views. We have not sought to count supporters to promote a particular perspective or idea. This is not a statistical study, and any attempt through this material to take a precise reading on where the churches stand today would be a misuse of the data.

What we have sought is wisdom, perspective, insight, hopeful ideas and stories from which we can learn how better to live with one another in the church and how to be faithful witnesses. Statistically speaking, one good idea or incident doesn't add up to much, but one good idea or incident can be worth more alone than a host of mediocre suggestions. There are a number of studies that produce illuminating statistics, however, and we draw upon them when appropriate without trying to replicate the statisticians' efforts ourselves.

We do not claim to have resolved our differences on every point addressed in this book. One of us presses more eagerly for keeping many nuances of the two basic poles of difference (orthodox-progressive or evangelical-liberal) in mind throughout the book than does the other, who sees the nuances as perhaps blurring the clarity of that basic polarity. Another area of tension has been the place of sociological analysis (which both of us value) in relation to the church's own tools of biblical and theological analysis. We believe the insights gleaned through this research should be of interest to the entire church, especially the pluralistic mainline denominations in which such sharp divisions exist.

So much has been written about the tensions in our churches—their relationship to culture, the fundamentalist upsurge, the decline of the mainline, the vigor of evangelicals, the church-state issues in a democracy in which culture wars rage—that a strong argument can be mounted for *not* writing another book on this subject! Our chief justification for this volume is its attempt to convey a candid exchange of views and some clues to how some of us manage to live in Christian community among those with whom we differ. The two of us do not stand outside the dialogue but are ourselves part of it. No book can do much more than suggest how orthodox and progressives or evangelicals and liberals with many variations might more knowledgeably attempt such a journey together. But if a few people find further insight and encouragement to carry on the challenge, it will be more than worth our effort.

Part 1

· · · · · · · · · · · · ·

How Strong
Is the
"Tie That Binds"?

1

·············

The Polarized Pews

Two Viewpoints

Ted and Carol Manning (not their real names) moved to Vienna, Virginia, in the suburbs of the nation's capital in the early 1990s. Before their move they had been members of a congregation affiliated with the Presbyterian Church in America, a small, strongly conservative denomination. Now they began attending Vienna Presbyterian Church, a congregation of the mainline Presbyterian Church (U.S.A.). They were welcomed warmly. They quickly became involved in one of the congregation's outreach projects, preparing and serving food for the hungry in downtown Washington. Though the church was considerably larger than their old one, they were pleased with the congregation's worship. Their family's needs were met by a broad range of Christian education and nurture programs.

They joined a new-member class. That year, however, there was much talk about a report on human sexuality that was to be presented to the denomination's General Assembly, which was scheduled to meet in June. The report proposed a radical departure from classic Christian values related to sex and marriage. Nationwide attention was focused on its virtual acceptance of homosexuality, premarital sexual relationships and even adultery under some circumstances. For the first time in history the national news media—*Time* and the *NBC Nightly News* as well as the *Washington Post*—were following closely an issue before a Presbyterian General Assembly. And all the attention to this report reminded the Mannings that there were other points taken by some in the denomination, in addition to the one on sexuality, with which they disagreed. At the end of the six-week membership class, when the rest of the group joined the church, they did not join.

They continued, however, to participate in the work and worship of Vienna Presbyterian Church, which, like most mainline congregations, had both liberal and conservative members. That June the General Assembly resoundingly rejected the human sexuality report, while calling for continued study of the issues raised. The media furor quickly died down.

Despite their misgivings the Mannings became more and more comfortable in their new church home. In time they made their decision and asked to become members of the congregation. They requested, however, that in receiving them the Session note in its minutes that they were joining "with reservations."

How do you join a Presbyterian church "with reservations"? The only requirement for membership is "profession of faith in Jesus Christ as Lord and Savior." Did they have reservations about that? Absolutely not. Their reservations concerned other matters.

It is entirely appropriate, under the Book of Order, for a member of the Presbyterian Church to disagree with all or any part of the pastor's sermons, the confessional standards or the Book of Order itself and to reject *in toto* all actions of the denomination's General Assembly, as long as that member affirmed faith in Jesus Christ. Was not that enough?

No. It was a matter of principle for the Mannings that the Session minutes list them as joining "with reservations."

The Session, accustomed to diversity, was willing to cooperate. But how could this be managed? Among the categories of membership listed in the Book of Order are baptized, active, inactive and affiliate members, but not members "with reservations." Could members "with reservations" vote in congregational meetings? Could they teach a Sunday-school class? Were they eligible to be elected and ordained as elders or deacons?

For readers interested in the resolution of this dilemma, let it be said that a compromise was reached. The Mannings were received into full, active membership. They were invited, however, to write a letter to the Session specifying any reservations they had about the congregation or the denomination, and their letter could be included in the Session minutes. They agreed to the compromise, but in the end they did not write the letter.

Of deeper and more enduring interest, however, is the larger dilemma underlying both the Mannings's attempt to join a local congregation "with reservations" and the struggle over the Christian view of human sexuality that dominated religious news coverage while they were preparing for church membership.

All the traditional mainline American denominations are deeply polarized between liberal and conservative wings, each further divided over the variables of race, sex and social concerns. Princeton University sociologist Robert Wuthnow, in his 1988 book *The Restructuring of American Religion,*[1] suggested that the liberal-conservative split cuts across nearly all American churches. It has become a more important structural feature of American religion than denominational divisions are, he says. Wuthnow's analysis, though widely applied, dealt chiefly with mainline denominations: the Episcopal, Methodist, Presbyterian, Reformed, Lutheran and American Baptist churches, the United Church of Christ and the Disciples of Christ. These churches are inclusive in membership. Each spans a wide theological range, from liberal to conservative.

But the phenomenon Wuthnow identifies goes far beyond the mainline churches. It characterizes the Southern Baptists, whose polarization between conservatives and moderates has dominated that denomination's internal power struggles for more than a decade. (Although both sides are on the evangelical end of the wider Protestant spectrum, they remain deeply divided from each other.) The phenomenon can also be seen in Roman Catholicism. Even though American Catholicism has a very different background and worldwide context from Protestant denominations, it too is deeply divided between liberals and conservatives or traditionalists. (The term *evangelical* may not be appropriate here.) Even the Mormon Church (the Church of Jesus Christ of Latter-day Saints) has a small liberal presence. And denominations that are theologically unified still see themselves as part of a deeply divided religious community in America.

We are personally involved in the dilemma of pluralistic churches. How, we asked, can polarized denominations—to a considerable extent immobilized by their internal divisions—or local congregations of such denominations move toward reconciliation? How can members of such diverse churches not only live together in peace and mutual love but jointly engage in carrying out the mission of the church?

We share a belief that people on or sympathetic with either of the conflict's sides are authentic and devout Christians committed to the church of Jesus Christ. We agree that finding ways of lessening polarization and moving toward mutual respect and reconciliation should be a high priority. We seek not to devise solutions of our own but to learn from people actually struggling with the turmoil of church life today.

The data-gathering phase of the project went along without a hitch. But when the time came to agree on interpretations and conclusions, the going became tough. We had known from the beginning that we would not only learn from the stories of others but that our own experience would in some ways model the struggle of the church. And this proved to be true. We learned that in subtle ways we saw things differently. At times the same taped interview conveyed different messages to each of us. Although our starting point was the same and there was much on which we agreed, there were also things on which we strongly disagreed.

In the midst of struggling to reach agreement on what to say in the pages of this book, we recognized that for our own purposes we needed to clarify our personal assumptions as well as our respective perceptions of the two wings of the church we seemed to represent. So we agreed that Dick Hutcheson would commit to paper his perception of the evangelical wing of the church, with which he identifies, and that Peggy Shriver would do the same for the liberal wing.

The result was a major step toward mutual understanding for us. We believe it will also clarify for our readers, at the beginning of this enterprise, who we are, where we come from and what we mean when we speak in this book of *liberals* and *evangelicals*. Perhaps it also illustrates some of the imprecision and ambiguity of these terms.

A View of the Liberal Christian Spirit (by Peggy L. Shriver)

Since my birth I have been surrounded by persons and family who are deeply Christian, and I readily claimed my baptism as a young person. I spent a number of my early years in a church environment that had strong evangelical elements in it. There has never been a time when I did not think of myself as a seriously committed Christian, although throughout my college years I subjected my faith to probing scrutiny in light of everything else I was learning, and vice versa. That spirit of exploration, of testing, of willingness to learn from what God may be teaching us in all times and places has never left me, and gradually I learned that it had a name—liberalism.

Like many other liberals who are active and involved in the church, I have deep rootage in the evangelical truths of Christianity, and this heritage continues to flower in my life even as it is exposed to the sun and shadows of the rest of my experience. To be a liberal is to believe that in all aspects of life "we have to do with God." The sovereign God infuses all of life with meaning, and the surprising revelation of God's holy presence may come to us through anyone or in the most unlikely places. The most surprising and uniquely rewarding sense of God's presence is in the life of Jesus Christ.

It is Scripture, of course, that schools our eyes to see and our ears to hear the sacred moment, to recognize the presence of the Holy Spirit, to understand how God has spoken uniquely through the life and person of Jesus Christ. Christians have always needed the Bible to orient themselves to God's great drama. They need it to locate themselves in the story of God's relationship with humanity and the rest of creation, and they need it to acquaint themselves with Jesus Christ so that they can respond to his invitation into the life intended for God's people. Christian liberals (except perhaps for a few) do not reject the Bible, as some people accuse them of doing, but they read the Bible with an awareness that differs from fundamentalists and some evangelicals in at least the following ways:

Liberals view experience as both insight and limitation. One of the important contributions of science and the Enlightenment has been the recognition of the role of individual self-consciousness in our very understanding of Scripture. We live in a particular time, are influenced usually by one dominant culture, have been shaped by particular traditions and have a slant on history because of our race, our nationality, our gender, our geography, our educational training, our experiences. Even the meaning of words is affected by these givens and by the choices we make. Some people have become so acutely aware of the difficulties in communication posed by these and other differences that distinguish us one from the other that they despair of communicating any kind of shared truth at all. This so-called postmodern condition afflicts us to some degree as we discover that the truths we believe to be "self-evident" are not evident to many of our neighbors.

Liberals emphasize the important role of the church in interpreting Scripture. Liberal Christians do not despair that we bring ourselves, our times and our cultures to Scripture and that we therefore have somewhat different understandings of what God is saying there. Instead, we are called to humility before that fountain of truth; we know that though our thirst may be slaked by small sips, someone else has found an abundance of living water that we also need. The Christian community, the church, allows us to move beyond the limitations of our own individual cultural captivities and to learn from one another. The global church helps its various parts to discover what is of God and what is derived from our unique geographies and experiences (and perhaps should be subject to God's judgment).

Jesus, in the Gospel of John, urges "that the church may be one." Liberals sense the inadequacy of their own understanding apart from the rest of the church. These two motivations—the goals of unity and completeness—urge us to participate in the ecumenical movement. Even if we achieved wholeness as "the household of God," yet still lacked full comprehension of God, our witness to the world would have more integrity and truth. Our need of one another is clear. When some of us choose to seek our own special revelation apart from one another, as our super-individualistic society encourages us to do, we become sadly limited. Grief, shame and loss should and often do attend our failure to achieve full community within the church—from Roman Catholic and Orthodox to conservative evangelical and fundamentalist. But the impulse to be truly ecumenical keeps at least our modest conciliar efforts alive.

Over the past thirty years the liberal wing of the church has been paying special attention to the interpretive word of persons whose circumstances bring perspectives on the Bible that many of the rest of us are not equipped to hear. Women have done some of the most refreshingly insightful studies of the Bible in recent years, they allow long-overlooked passages to come to life when read with an attention to women's experiences. Similarly, theologies of liberation—of the African-American experience, of persons who have felt excluded from the people of God for a variety of reasons, such as homosexuality—require us to hear the Word anew. And such unique interpreters need to hear from each other and from the rest of us, because all of us are incomplete in our attempt to encompass God's revelation through the Holy Word. Some Christians are encouraging us to "listen to the earth," too, as we read Scripture.

Liberals avoid an idolatry of the Bible. God is in Scripture, but Scripture is not God. We receive the Word with fear and trembling, with the faith that God is in the Word and with the humility to know that our insight alone is not sufficient to an absolute knowledge of that Word. Both liberal and evangelical Christians, progressive and orthodox, have come to appreciate to varying degrees the historical, critical tools for studying the Bible. Many a hard word was spoken between Christians, however, before "higher criticism" was acknowledged as helpful.

Sometimes the dissection of Scripture seems like the tearing apart of a lovely rose, petal by petal, until only dead fragments and a slight fragrance remain. Yet having done so, one brings a profound knowledge of the essence of that "rose" to the appreciation of other "flowers" of Scripture. We bring our experience and the testimony of others as we return to that dissected passage again and again.

Liberals are open to the leading of the Holy Spirit. Far more important to our understanding of the Bible is the Holy Spirit's role in opening our hearts and minds to truth against which we may be opposed. I know how painfully many people wrestled with the Bible to try to sustain their racial prejudices, only to be overcome sometimes at last by the Spirit's instruction. Recently we have engaged in a search in Scripture for the appropriate role of women in the church and in society, and we have uncovered divergent messages, as we are now doing with the emotionally charged subject of homosexuality. Being open to the guidance of the Holy Spirit could lead us where we do not want to go, and courageous faith is necessary. "God has yet more light to break forth from his Holy Word," as pastor John Robinson said to the Pilgrims of 1620, which is our reason for returning again and again to the Bible.

Liberals try to act faithfully within ambiguity. Most of us would like to act on a sure thing, to know that all the facts are in before we take a position. We would like to exclude conflicting data so that we can take an unambiguous position. Liberal Christians, after all has been taken into account, still try to remain open to possible revision, to a better understanding of God's revelation, to an experience that reveals more clearly both the disclosure and the hiddenness of God. This includes not only the issues that Christians face in attempting to act "in good faith," but also the very person of God, who even in Jesus is not fully knowable to us. We live in a continual conversion to God's self-disclosure, an unfolding revelation of God's nature. Our self-deceit about God is always having to be stripped away. It is humbling. Sometimes it is unnerving, and this uncertainty makes poor evangelists out of many liberals. Yet we do have an obligation to share as winsomely as we can the "truth that is in us."

Liberal Christians look first to the Bible to learn about God and God's will for our lives. We believe, however, as did the psalmist, that God reveals himself also through the mighty acts of history, by judging and chastising us through the deeds of nations, by challenging us afresh with the needs of distant neighbors and by urging us to help shape the beginning of the kingdom of God on earth. God has filled us with curiosity about our natural environment and has given us minds to explore the macro and micro universe. The efforts of science to explain the natural forces of the world require our attention too. The task of relating scientific knowledge and the revealed knowledge of faith has barely begun, and it is a hazardous effort. But we believe God speaks to us through both external and internal history, as H. Richard Niebuhr describes in *The Meaning of Revelation.*[2]

Niebuhr, a respected voice among liberal Christians, also stresses the interdependent, interactive quality of being a human self in a "common memory and common hope."[3] The church becomes for Christians the community of common memory and hope. Most of us liberals rely on the church to help us avoid the pitfalls of an atomistic individualism. One way of speaking of communities of hope and memory is through tradition.

Praising God through worship, nurturing and cultivating the spiritual life and religious understanding of the faithful, engaging in Bible study and theological thinking together, caring for one another's needs and reaching out to the larger society in witness and concern for its needs are widely recognized as basic to the church's mission. Evangelicalism and liberalism are each outgrowths of the Second Great Awakening, and their roots are intertwined. But liberals, having both engaged and embraced insights from the Enlightenment, have tried to maintain responsibility for world missions while at the same time giving respectful space and hearing to other faiths and to modern science. Sometimes this has produced creative tension, but it has also made some liberals very cautious about the way they evangelize, if they evangelize at all.

We try to present our Christian faith to the world as a precious gift available to all who will receive it, but we are uncomfortable with the kinds of evangelism that try to scare people into faith or that insult their differing religious convictions. Jesus' loving compassion to all people is the clue to evangelism, I believe. The search for justice in society is a witness to divine love and, when done in the spirit of Christ, is evangelism. The portrayal of evangelism and social action as competitive purposes is a false dichotomy. Either purpose alone leads to hypocrisy. While evangelicals sometimes neglect social justice in their evangelism, liberals sometimes miss the moment for proclamation during their social action. We need each other to correct our omissions!

The progressive liberal spirit, which has sought a collaboration with God in the unveiling of his kingdom on earth, has taken a beating throughout this bloody twentieth century. Progress toward that kingdom seems undermined by two grueling world wars, the Holocaust and other massive killings, the nuclear cold war, Vietnam, environmental degradation and persistent world poverty and human suffering. We look not only at individual sins, therefore, but also at social systems to find the evil in them that must be challenged as we labor, following Jesus' teaching, toward the kingdom of God.

The tension between emotion and reason. Throughout the history of the church universal, there have been significant differences among Christian groups in the importance they've given to emotion and reason. For some Christians the lack of emotional fervor in worship is a sign of a lack of religious commitment, whereas others would argue that if you cannot give an intelligent summation and reason for the faith that is in you, then you lack conviction. It is an endless quarrel that is often tied more to personality than to religion. Sometimes liberals express fervor more easily about social justice, where they have taken a clear stand, than about the tenets of Christian faith, to which they have a constrained allegiance as they remain open to further enlightenment. Evangelicals are sometimes in quite the reverse position. Yet reasoned religion without heart is as empty as emotional religion without reason. That at some time or other we all lack good reasoning or emotional depth in our faith is a fair judgment. Too much of our reasoning and emotional fervor has been exerted against those who, in our opinion, have too little. Evangelical and liberal cultural styles tend to differ, and this tension is one of the areas of difference. It may also be an example of God's wisdom in giving us to one another!

The tension regarding the three faces of God. The concept of the Trinity is a human effort, a contribution of the Christian community's "memory and hope" that has enabled us to speak about the nature of God revealed to us through Jesus Christ and the Holy Spirit even though much is still incomprehensible. The unity of God in three persons is looked at suspiciously by Muslims, for example, who are inclined to reject Christianity's claim to be monotheistic. Different parts of the church seem more at home with one person of the Trinity than another. Liberals tend to place more emphasis upon the Godhead and the Holy Spirit than upon the saving role of Jesus, while evangelicals seem to begin with Jesus and follow his steps toward God. The language of salvation seems more appropriate on the lips of evangelicals than on those of liberals, who are more likely to speak of God's sovereignty, purposes, justice and love. It is not so much a matter of exclusion as of starting point, but each tends to see the other as having ignored aspects of Trinitarian theology especially important to themselves.

Jesus Christ is absolutely essential to the unveiling of some aspects of God's nature otherwise hidden from us. God is not an abstract idea but a person introduced to us through the Son, who always points away from himself to God. Jesus makes us humbly realize our humanity in the presence of God, but he also assures us that God does not turn away from us. In the person of Jesus, God's intention for humanity is realized.

We liberal Christians do seem to vary in our descriptions of Jesus and of what he has accomplished through his life, death and resurrection. Some of the more fundamentalist theories of the atonement imply that God is a harsh judge who must have a pound of flesh as payment for our sins, even if it comes from God's own son. Other theories have a magical quality of expungement. Liberals resist attempts to describe how Jesus Christ as the Lamb of God has taken on the sins of the world and saved us, but we also need assurance in Christ that we have been forgiven by God. It seems that fundamentalists, in their need for a reasoned way of explaining the atonement, have developed terminology and a theological formula. Christians who deviate from their formula are suspect.

The Holy Spirit is highly regarded by nearly all Christians, although when we talk about the Spirit we often seem to be speaking of the immediate presence of God or even of the presence of the resurrected Jesus. I confess that as a liberal I experience the Holy Spirit both as God and as Jesus and almost never as a separate person and that I do not feel constrained to settle on a firm, final definition of what seems ineffable. The experience of God's Spirit is essential, but the exact interpretation of the presence of the holy seems impossible and humanly presumptive.

The tension between liberals and liberationists. The "scandal of particularity" of God's entry into humanity through the life and times of Jesus has long been a subject of theological discussion. Liberals see in Jesus Christ the meeting point of God with all of humanity and that Jesus in his singular personhood becomes the symbol for what is universally human. This view is under siege not from evangelicals, but from groups who claim their particular humanity is in some very special relationship to the Creator. Black theology and other liberation theologies see the "preferential option for the poor" in the Bible as giving them special insight and access to the Great Liberator and Judge. Their special distinction is at cross-purposes with our understanding of God's kindness toward universal humanity. Liberationists who speak for the marginalized, the poor and the unheard are in tension with liberals on this. Women also have difficulty defining simultaneously their own personhood both apart from men and with them in a common humanity. As a liberal woman, I claim my personhood as a child of God first, however, and my gender second.

Just as we must understand that evangelical Christians are not necessarily fundamentalists even though they hold many beliefs in common with them, so must we allow liberals to be distinguished from liberationists. Liberals appreciate, as I said above, the insights into Scripture and the contributions that come from liberation theology, but liberation theology is not a substitute for their liberal stance. We can learn from such a perspective without its becoming our own. Indeed, liberation theologians from the Third World would argue that privileged North American Christians cannot really claim as their own the liberation theologies that have emerged from the blood and tears of oppressed peoples in other cultures. Theologies of particular peoples are precisely that—theologies of particular peoples— and these groups have important things to say to the rest of us, as do we in dialogue with them. The liberal espousal of a universal humanity can lapse only too easily into a radical individualism in which community becomes merely a collage of cultures that threatens a belief in our common humanity. Then postmodernism can step forward to declare there is no transcendent reality, rationality or value system.[4]

The temptations faced by liberals. Liberal Christians face certain inherent temptations. There is a tendency to make liberalism itself, rather than God, the object of faith, so that openness and diversity become our true points of reverence. It is also, unfortunately, quite possible to betray that very openness by conveying an unyielding posture in the name of openness. When liberalism strays too far from its evangelical roots and biblical revelation, it feeds only on itself and eventually loses its life and vision. In the compassionate search for justice, the liberal can fall into the idolatry of promoting one perspective or one justice goal, making it a god and ignoring other purposes and needs of the church. Because a liberal keeps listening to what God may be saying today, it is easy to ignore the wisdom of tradition, to hear what one wants to hear or to decide that all truth is so relative to individual experience that we have no good news to share.

Without having exhausted even for myself the meaning of being a liberal, to say nothing of how other liberals would add to and change subtly these themes, I would briefly summarize the liberal position as follows:

Nothing is more central to the liberal Christian spirit than the awareness that the living God is active in our midst, requiring us to respond afresh in a community of faith that cherishes God's revelation through Jesus Christ, through Scripture and through the church. Many of us find the image of a pilgrimage or a journey helpful in describing our response in faith to God, who beckons us into a more profound knowledge disclosed to us through Jesus, the Holy Spirit, the Word, the world, the tradition and our own self-conscious experience. It is rigorous and invigorating, humbling and stretching. Liberalism requires a strenuous faith in the midst of uncertainty and ambiguity.

A Perspective on the Evangelical Wing of the Church (by Richard G. Hutcheson Jr.)

I grew up in the home of a minister who was broad of mind and who took "liberal" positions on race relations long before the civil-rights movement of the 1960s. He acted on his convictions and at times suffered for his actions. Though my father was a much-loved pastor, after his death I discovered in his papers a collection of "hate letters" written in response to sermons or actions having to do with race relations. He was, however, an orthodox Christian for whom Scripture was totally authoritative and who believed strongly in the classic faith of the Westminster Confession and Catechisms.

At the beginning of my sophomore year in college I gladdened my father's heart with a decision, during an on-campus religious-emphasis week, to enter the ministry. But in the course of my college studies I encountered for the first time all the crosscurrents of biblical criticism, the social gospel and Enlightenment secularism that had been roiling the waters of American Christianity since the late nineteenth century. My Bible professor, an enormously winning and persuasive recent Ph.D. from Yale Divinity School, opened my eyes to a whole new religious world.

As graduation neared, I horrified my father with an announcement that I planned go to seminary at Yale—a citadel of liberalism. He began a frantic rescue operation. He hauled me off to his own denominational seminary for a conference with its staunchly conservative president, who warned me against all the perils of liberalism. But I persisted.

At Yale Divinity School I was a radical liberal who saw Jesus chiefly as an exemplary ethical teacher. It was only through the grace of God, the urgent need for World War II chaplains (fortunately in regions far from middle Virginia) and the fact that my father was an influential member of the presbytery, that I managed to be ordained.

The realities of day-to-day ministry in the crisis-oriented environment of the navy soon began to reawaken for me some basic verities of classic Christianity. After ten years as a chaplain, during a period of graduate study at Union Theological Seminary in New York—another bastion of liberalism—I was jokingly referring to myself as a neofundamentalist. I continued, however, to identify with the liberal postwar Protestant leadership, which in my view was rescuing the church from the "dark ages." It was this identification, evident in public statements and writings, that brought me in the 1970s to a second career in the denominational establishment, despite the liberal suspicion engendered by the fairly high rank I had reached in my first career as a navy chaplain.

In the early eighties I wrote a book called *Mainline Churches and the Evangelicals.*[5] At that time I was employed by the General Assembly of the former Presbyterian Church in the United States (southern) as chairman of its Office of Review and Evaluation. The job of my office (in which my coauthor had served with me in the late seventies) was to monitor and evaluate the performance of all denominational agencies and to report my findings directly to the General Assembly each year. I had became convinced through that experience that one of the most critical problems facing the church was the growing polarization between its liberal and evangelical wings. The book reflected such a conviction.

At that time the term *evangelical* (or *neoevangelical*) was just coming into common use for designating the more conservative wing of the denomination. Despite my long identification with the liberal, ecumenical wing of the church, I did not find myself uncomfortable with those in the denomination who were beginning to call themselves evangelicals and did not regard them as the enemy. I was writing, however, from what I called a "mainline perspective."

The evangelical literature I was reading as I researched the book opened up a new scholarly world for me. It was clear that I regarded myself as an outsider as I traced the development of the evangelical movement and tried to describe it in that book. I introduced my summary of evangelicalism this way: "Presumptuous as it may be for an outsider to attempt to delineate the movement, there are certain themes common to the writings of most of today's evangelicals distinguishing them from the separatist fundamentalists. From a mainline perspective, the following would seem to be the major characteristics of the new evangelicals."[6]

Somewhat to my surprise, the book (which was featured in the Word Book Club and was fairly widely read in mainline church circles) was received more enthusiastically by evangelicals than by liberals—which perhaps revealed more about where I stood than I realized at the time. Few evangelicals took issue with the way I described them. Much of that description focused on the difference between fundamentalists (of which there are few if any in the mainline churches) and evangelicals. And this is still a necessary distinction, particularly in view of the tendency of some liberals to lump all conservatives together and dismiss them as fundamentalists.

The summary at the end of my chapter on "the evangelical renascence," from which I draw here,[7] still reflects accurately my own perception of the evangelical wing of the church. Only one thing has changed significantly: I now recognize that this describes reasonably accurately my own perspective. This is the wing of the church with which I now personally identify.

Evangelicals hold to the authority of Scripture. The principle of the reliability and final authority of the Scriptures in matters of faith and practice is central for evangelicals. Evangelicals are not, however, agreed on the nature of biblical inspiration. Historical criticism is accepted to some extent by many [I would now say most] of them. There is, however, a difference in tone between the liberal and evangelical approach to criticism. The liberal tends to approach the task from the scientific side—criticism is a given, and the liberal looks for the religious values still to be found in the Bible despite its human and historic conditioning. The evangelical approaches from the biblical side—the authority of the Scriptures is a given, and the question is how criticism can help to understand it.

Evangelicals, by definition, support evangelism. Evangelicals are united in giving a central place in their concept of Christianity to a personal faith in and commitment to Jesus Christ as the only savior from sin. There is, therefore, a strong emphasis on the conversion of sinners. "Evangelizing the world for Christ" tends to be the primary goal.

Evangelicals expect converts to live godly lives. They believe in sanctification conceived as a distinctively Christian life following rebirth. They are, however, less likely than fundamentalists to define that Christian life in terms of prohibitions against such things as drinking and dancing or in terms of a traditionalist sexual code.[8] [I would now carefully define this final clause as referring to a puritanical rigidity in relations between the sexes. Commitment to the traditional biblical sexual code focused on marriage has been strongly affirmed by evangelicals in the struggles over permissive sexuality and the ordination of homosexuals.]

Evangelicals want to influence their communities. Many, though not all, are deeply involved in social concerns. Some, who may be quite fundamentalist in theology, see commitment to social action as the single most important difference between evangelicals and fundamentalists.

Evangelicals do not shun science. Evangelicalism is marked by a friendliness to science, which is no longer seen as the enemy. One prominent evangelical spokesman distinguishes between fundamentalism and evangelicalism in terms of the rejection by the former of the modern scientific-historical world view derived from the Enlightenment and the acceptance by the latter.[9]

Evangelicals are not anti-intellectual. Evangelicals insist on a rational faith and reject the anti-intellectualism of some fundamentalists. They have studied the classic liberal and neo-orthodox theologians and have found much to affirm in the writings of the neo-orthodox, particularly those of Barth.[10]

Evangelicals support some ecumenical movements. While their attitude toward ecumenism is ambivalent, they do not completely reject ecumenism as do the fundamentalists. They are not primarily interested in conciliar ecumenism, and they stress the importance of doctrinal unity for organic unions. They do, however, talk about and practice a functional ecumenism and are often deeply involved in noninstitutional ecumenical undertakings.

Evangelicals have various millennial positions. New evangelicals tend to reject dispensational premillennialism, particularly the dispensationalism associated with the Scofield Reference Bible. They do not reject the second coming of Christ.

Evangelicals are moderately conservative. Perhaps the greatest difference between evangelicals and fundamentalists is in tone, style or spirit. Evangelicals reject the narrowness, defensiveness and extremism of fundamentalism. They reject its anticultural, world-denying characteristics.[11] They reflect a more open, listening and reconciling spirit than do their fellow conservatives of the extreme right.[12]

It is clear from the above summary that there is considerable diversity within the evangelical community. It ranges from a near-fundamentalist conservatism (particularly in theology) on the right to a near-liberal openness to modernity, respect for differences and commitment to social justice as evangelicalism approaches the center of the church's spectrum.

One additional, central characteristic of evangelicals in the mainline churches might also be mentioned: the concept of renewal. This implies a belief that the church, under the leadership of the liberal establishment that has been dominant in the latter half of the twentieth century, has lost its spiritual vitality and is in need of renewal. The evangelical groups in the mainline churches identify themselves as "renewal groups." The term *renewal* has been closely associated with charismatic or Holy Spirit movements in mainline denominations. Though a minority of evangelicals are charismatics, their emphasis on renewal as a spiritual process dependent on the work of the Holy Spirit has influenced the whole evangelical movement.

No description of the evangelical community in the church can encompass all its diversity. It is, however, an identifiable wing of Protestant Christianity. It sees itself as reasonably unified and coherent and finds itself engaged in a struggle with what it perceives as a reasonably unified, coherent and identifiable liberal wing.

2

. . . .

Appreciation of
the Other Side

E arly on we discovered that stating one's own position is never
enough to bring mutual understanding. Being able to define yourself rather than having others define you is important and brings clarity.
But the problem is not simply that one doesn't know what the other
believes. Reconciliation begins with some positive act of reaching out in
acknowledgment and appreciation of the other.

We therefore agreed that each of us would write a summary of those
aspects of the *other* wing that he or she personally admires and appreciates.

An Appreciation of Evangelicalism (by Peggy L. Shriver)
It is the conviction of the authors of this book that liberals and evangelicals
need each other in the church, that the excess of virtue in each wing needs
to be curbed by the other and that the deficiencies of each have some
corrective by the other. In that spirit I would like to point to several

aspects of evangelicalism that, as a liberal, I admire and which I would not want to have lost from the church.

A clear sense of the essentials of faith. Evangelicals hold to the core of the Christian faith and are not as tempted as liberals are to substitute a primary concern for "ultimate concern." The wholeness of the gospel is therefore monitored faithfully by evangelicals, and all Christians can benefit from the balance that this reminder of its wholeness provides. Liberals know alienation from our neighbor and from God is the basic human condition that our faith addresses, and evangelicals are not shy about calling it *sin*. Liberals also believe that divine love and justice have been made available to humanity to overcome our brokenness and our alienation—and evangelicals readily call this *salvation*.

By concentrating upon the fundamentals, evangelicals are less inclined to embrace the new or to assume that it is likely to be better than the past. Liberals have been sobered by the failures of modernity, the lack of progress in much that progressives have fostered and the intractability of many of the social problems we confront. Many liberals have engaged in a renewed spiritual search for the sustaining power within the tradition and within Scripture to enable them to "keep on keeping on." Evangelicals find traditional church language easier to use than do liberals, but what they both feel deep in their hearts may not be all that different. Our challenge—to interpret the Christian message to people outside the faith in a way that today's secular person can hear and understand—is laid before both progressive and traditional Christians.

A passion for the centrality of the Bible. I prefer to say that evangelicals hold strongly to the *centrality* of the Bible instead of saying they have a passion for biblical *authority* because the latter statement implies that liberals do not have such passion. We have different approaches to receiving that authority, and the approach of the liberal has a complexity that makes reading the Word less a comfort than an effort to grasp its meaning. The evangelical, who is by no means "simple" in reading Scripture, leaps more readily to quoting the Bible, savoring its message and making unequivocal application. Perhaps we liberals sometimes make it too difficult!

I'm describing a kind of piety that lives in daily commerce with the Word of God, something which some liberals also practice but which evangelicals are more likely to do. Such grounding in Scripture, such pervasive infiltration of the biblical word into "all that we ask or think" is a significant witness to those with a more occasional contact.

Evangelicals and fundamentalists rightly insist, as Lloyd J. Averill observes in his very helpful book *Religious Right, Religious Wrong*, "that the central significance of the Bible is that it records not a human search but a divine initiative; not a persistent effort to bridge the gap between the finite and the infinite from the human side, which ends as often as not in some kind of idolatry, but the account of God's own persistence in reaching out to men and women in spite of their frequent spiritual obtuseness and arrogance."[1]

The courage to testify. There have been times and places where the message of faith might "go without saying," but fewer and fewer places today are so culturally infused with Christianity that we can assume people already know what we mean when we say we are Christians or Methodists or Baptists. Many evangelicals, by being fixed on the essence of the faith, by being scripturally grounded and by having a strong sense that without the saving Word a person is absolutely lost, are equipped to testify in a society that is often hostile to their message. Although the way the testimony is expressed in some instances and settings makes liberal Christians uncomfortable, they can still admire the courage of the one who testifies. Liberals are reminded to strive harder to find ways of expressing their own convictions selflessly and with respect for the hearer. Although liberals do not want to coerce people or preempt what is rightly the work of the Holy Spirit, they may neglect the importance and necessity for everyone to make choices—of commitments, of conviction, of truths by which to live an abundant life.

Personal caring. One danger of an intellectualized liberalism rightly concerned about the structures and systems of society that grind people down unjustly is to ignore the individual hurting person. Evangelicals, often impatient with the studies and legislative agenda of liberals, frequently engage in social programs that tend to the sick, the weak, the unemployed, the grieving. Liberals who think they are alone in concern for social justice do not remember the Grimké sisters, the concern for racial justice led by Oberlin students and faculty or the past efforts to alleviate poverty by evangelicals in New York City and the current programs in many evangelical congregations to which many of our interviewees attest. Rather than argue over meeting immediate need or addressing root causes, we would do well to acknowledge the importance of both.

I, along with many other liberals, am grateful for these contributions made by evangelicals to our human community of faith that is the church, and it is my prayer that we all can so live with one another that the best of each of us may strengthen the best in the other, diminishing the failings in us all.

An Appreciation of the Liberal Tradition (by Richard G. Hutcheson Jr.) I share with many evangelicals a deep appreciation of certain aspects of the liberal tradition within Christianity. Perhaps the most treasured contribution of that tradition is its openness to and respect for differing viewpoints, including differing interpretations of Scripture.

The acceptance of multiple interpretations. This is a point at which liberal and conservative traditions are in tension. The conservative Christian, rooted in belief in an omnipotent God who reveals the truth through Scripture and convinced that "the plain teaching" of Scripture is clear on most points, is tempted to be dogmatic on issues of truth. If the Bible speaks plainly on a particular issue and the Bible is truth revealed by God, then contrary opinions are erroneous and not to be tolerated. The conservative needs the liberal insistence that Scripture is always interpreted by human beings and that God alone has absolute truth.

Just as conservatism, at the one extreme of the spectrum, becomes dogmatic and intolerant, so at the other end of the scale liberal openness to differences can become a human-centered relativism, recognizing no absolutes at all and lacking conviction of any kind. In Christianity this becomes a kind of universalism that claims no uniqueness for biblical revelation. But authentic faith lies in the tension, not in the extremes. Evangelicals, who belong to the conservative tradition, are in continuous need of the liberals' emphasis on respect for differences, their openness to the presence of varying interpretations of Scripture and their ability to live with diversity.

It may be true, as evangelicals sometimes charge, that in recent church fights liberals have been just as close-minded and intolerant as conservatives. But essentially close-mindedness is the inherent conservative danger, and openness is an inherent liberal characteristic, which evangelicals urgently need.

The pursuit of justice. A second major gift of liberalism to evangelicalism is its emphasis on social justice. An earlier conservatism saw the social gospel as a departure from spiritual Christianity. Many evangelicals still believe that the extreme left wing of liberal Christianity has substituted a secular kind of social justice for the church's basic spiritual mission. Some still see evangelism and social justice as opposites. But this is not really the case. Liberal Christianity has reminded evangelicals of the great biblical call for social justice, beginning with the Old Testament prophets and reaching fulfillment with Jesus' mission of good news to the poor, release to the captives, healing of the blind and liberty for those who are oppressed. Thanks to this liberal emphasis, evangelical Christianity today insists on both evangelism and social justice.

The effort toward ecumenism. As an evangelical I am also deeply grateful for the ecumenical movement that has been central in Protestant liberalism—so central, in fact, that many prefer *ecumenical* to *liberal* as the term most accurately describing that wing of the church. The evangelical Protestant tradition at its best has not been exclusivist. From the beginning it has been denominational, with each denomination recognizing others as authentic parts of the church universal. Classic evangelical movements, such as the Great Awakenings of the eighteenth and early nineteenth centuries, were transdenominational events. The modern conciliar ecumenical movement had evangelical missionary roots. The first ecumenical council was the 1910 World Missionary Conference in Edinburgh. But today's conciliar ecumenical movement has been largely the product of liberal Christianity.

Much of modern evangelicalism is based on a functional ecumenism across denominational lines. But the organized ecumenism of the National and World Councils of Churches is also needed by the evangelical as well as the liberal wing of the church. Informal relationships between like-minded Methodists and Episcopalians are not enough. The Methodist and Episcopal churches need to be in relationship with each other. Though one may disagree with some of the actions and directions taken by the NCC and the WCC—and I, like many evangelicals, have done so—if we did not have such councils I believe we would have to invent them. I am convinced that evangelicals need to commit themselves to the *renewal* of the ecumenical councils rather than a departure from them, just as they are committed to renewal within their denominations. Evangelicals need liberals to keep alive the spirit of ecumenism.

The importance of scholarship. I am also grateful to the liberal tradition for its emphasis on human rationality and on the necessity for religious scholarship. A wide-ranging evangelical scholarship is a relatively recent development. In an earlier period the safeguarding of sound doctrine and fear of error led to a narrowly limited conservative scholasticism that was closed to insights from science, culture or scholarship in a broader sense. The evangelical revolt against this kind of fundamentalism was in large measure a result of the classic liberal emphasis on scholarly inquiry and investigation.

The contemporary evangelical movement in Christianity would not exist apart from the influence of these and other aspects of liberalism on conservative Christianity. Authentic Christian discipleship lies not in ideological purity alone, but in the tension between competing claims of sometimes-opposing perspectives.

The Path Ahead

We are strongly aware that to speak of the church—as we have just done—in terms of the liberal and evangelical wings we in some sense represent is an over-simplification of reality. In the next chapter, as we examine some sociological insights into the present state of the church, we will look at some of the complexities of our divisions. In chapter four, as we turn to the church's own perspective, we will focus on some of the scriptural insights on which there is wide agreement.

In later sections of the book we will of necessity speak primarily of liberals and evangelicals, in order to deal with the very real problems of polarization. We will try to do so, however, with an awareness of both our social and cultural complexity and our basic unity under a common Lord and Savior.

3

....

Sociological Help in Understanding the Splits

There are two kinds of people; those who divide everybody into two kinds of people and those who do not.
ESSAYIST ROBERT BENCHLEY VIA
ECUNET PARTICIPANT PAUL SCHMIDT

The problems that beset the mainline denominations have not gone unnoticed. Religious researchers, social-science analysts, journalists, seminary professors, church leaders, church members—all have taken a turn at probing the wounds to seek some remedy for them. This chapter will be able to examine just a few of many attempts to diagnose and to prescribe for ailing churches.

Enlisting the tools and insights of the sociology of religion, however, is itself subject to some debate. We, the authors, found ourselves in some tension over the value of these insights. The tendency of liberalism is to see God's hand at work in the attempts by academicians and religious researchers to understand the nature of the division and to understand these attempts as being in conversation with scriptural and ecclesiastical traditions. The evangelical prefers to look primarily within the church's own tradition and Scripture for the insights to inform the church's self-understanding.

Sociological-historical analysis uses tools and perspectives distinct from the church's own tradition. We have agreed, however, that such analysis is useful, especially as it engages in dialogue with the biblical and church traditions. The church is responsible for dealing with its own problems in terms of its own faith. But the work of sociologists and historians, many of whom stand within the community of faith themselves, helps us Christians to see ourselves as others see us. This chapter, therefore, tries to summarize some of the most helpful insights of such observers.

To describe divisions or polarities, we must use some nomenclature and typology. As Peter L. Berger observes in *The Heretical Imperative*, "The regrettable fact is that nobody trying to make sense of modern theology (or, for that matter, any other area of intellectual endeavor in which there have been large numbers of different expressions) can *fail* to attempt some sort of typification; otherwise the sheer diversity and complexity of the phenomenon will frustrate any effort at understanding."[1] There is no lack of effort to diagnose and typify, which this chapter amply demonstrates.

One of the most alarming symptoms has been the long, slow decline in membership among Methodists, Presbyterians, United Church of Christ, Lutherans, American Baptists, Episcopalians and, to a lesser degree, some other communions. Robert Bellah and his coauthors report that "between 1970 and 1986, among the old and well-established Protestant churches, the Presbyterians and Episcopalians lost more than one-fifth of their members and the Methodists and Lutherans more than one-tenth of theirs—losses that are proportionately larger when measured as a percentage of the expanding U.S. population."[2] The trend has continued since 1986, and recent figures indicate that mainline Presbyterians, for example, have lost more than a fourth of their members since the late sixties.

As more liberal mainline denominations were losing members, more evangelical and fundamentalist churches could point to increases in membership. But it was not simply a transfer of congregants from one church to the other. Far more liberals have been lost to secularism than have been claimed by conservative churches, say researchers Wade Clark Roof and William McKinney.[3] A spate of studies has tried to understand the nature of the problem, so as both to avoid unwarranted claims or attacks and to try to match solutions to actual conditions. Although no clear remedy has emerged from thousands and thousands of research hours and dollars, at least some awareness of the complex interaction of many factors has resulted.[4] That does not keep some conservatives from claiming growth as evidence of their distinct spiritual vitality, nor does it assuage a liberal sense of malaise, unease or defensiveness.

In no denomination has the contemporary sense of malaise been more extensively examined than in the Presbyterian Church (U.S.A.). At the beginning of the 1990s a major sociological-historical study of the denomination was published in seven volumes, totaling 2,300 pages, under the general title *The Presbyterian Presence: The Twentieth-Century Experience*.[5] Sponsored by the Lilly Endowment and edited by Milton J. Coalter, John M. Mulder and Louis B. Weeks (all of whom were at Louisville Presbyterian Theological Seminary at that time), the series was intended as a case study in the decline of mainstream Protestantism—institutionally, numerically and in cultural impact and internal confusion. Sixty-five scholars took part in the study.[6]

Pluralism and diversity are obviously major themes of the series, particularly when they are part of the rift between conservatives and liberals. Much attention is also given to cultural developments such as disestablishment, racial and ethnic diversity and changes in gender relationships. Clearly the series judges that the denomination is experiencing severe problems, membership decline being one of them.

A similar denominational study, also funded by the Lilly Endowment, was conducted through Christian Theological Seminary (Disciples of Christ) in Indianapolis. Edited by D. Newell Williams, it was entitled *A Case Study of Mainstream Protestantism: The Disciples' Relation to American Culture*, 1880-1989.[7] Numerous other similar denominational studies confirm these concerns.

Denominational Ecology

One helpful insight of these denominational studies, lifted up by Dorothy C. Bass of Chicago Theological Seminary, applies to most U.S. denominations: "denominational ecology." Just as we have come to understand the interdependence of living organisms as a system in nature, so we can see that our organizational structures have an ecology too. Denominations, which are a unique American religious construct, have depended upon Sunday schools; groups for women, men or youth; Bible-study groups; magazines and other church publications; and church-related colleges, seminaries, conferences, camps and other institutions to feed and maintain the denomination. Each denomination or communion has some similar institutions and practices yet also some differences that constitute its particular ecology in relation to other denominations. In an ecological system, when one part of the system weakens, the whole is diminished. Consider the health of many of the items on this list in most denominations today!

Furthermore, each denominational system lives within a larger social system that in earlier times supported it with blue laws and public schools sympathetic to its beliefs and customs. In turn the denomination borrowed from wisdom and experience in the larger society—such as adopting the efficiencies of the corporate business world. Today's denomination, lacking the vigor of feeder and maintenance structures needed to build a loyal membership, also lacks the outward support of the larger society. National media, higher education, governmental legislation in a diverse population and the courts all tend to look upon religion today with caution if not outright suspicion or hostility. Mainline denominations, accustomed to a comfortable leadership position within American society, have undergone painful and reluctant adjustment.

More religiously conservative churches, particularly those with a fundamentalist outlook, have in some measure seen themselves as "strangers in a strange land" all along and therefore have not had to make such an adjustment to a new sense of marginality. They have nourished their ecclesiastical ecological system with kindergarten-through-high-school Christian schools, colleges, television networks, national rallies, conferences and publishing houses that produce video as well as printed media. Their ecology has been supported also by conservative parachurch groups of many kinds.

For a variety of reasons, individual Christians, as they move today from place to place, are likely to choose worshiping congregations that shift them into several different denominations. Lacking a strong denominational, ecological support, they make choices that further weaken the denominational structures that build loyalty. It becomes a cycle of debilitation, for the next generation feels even less denominationally attached and may leave the church altogether. Some even question the survival of denominations (we will discuss this more in chapter thirteen). Thus mainline denominations feel beset within and without. It is in this context that this book looks at one of the aspects of religious life today that weakens, if not fractures, denominations—the polarization of liberals and evangelicals.

Cultural Cleavages

American denominations, of course, have had a long history of cleavages and polarizations, as documented in Peggy Shriver's denominational sketches, *Having Gifts That Differ.*[8] The most striking instance was the slavery issue in the Civil War period. So divided were the churches at that time that major denominations—Methodist, Baptist and Presbyterian—split, with northern and southern branches remaining separated until well into the twentieth century.

Other polarizations have included the "old side-new side" and "old school-new school" divisions in historic Presbyterianism and the ethnic divisions that characterized earlier Lutheranism and still separate many Orthodox. Issue-oriented polarities have included controversies over revivalism in the late eighteenth and early nineteenth centuries, prohibition in the late nineteenth century and science and evolution as symbolized by the Scopes "monkey trial" of the early twentieth century. But church historian Martin Marty suggests that the most enduring and persistent divide has been that between two "continuing parties" in American Protestantism. Citing earlier work by Josiah Strong as the basis of his analysis, he labels them "private" and "public" Protestants, with respective emphases on personal faith and piety and on social justice.[9]

In *The Struggle for America's Soul*, sociologist Robert Wuthnow argues that the major divisions in American religion now revolve around an axis of liberalism and conservatism rather than the denominational landmarks of the past. The new division parallels the ideological cleavage that runs through American politics. It divides religious practitioners from one another over questions of social welfare, defense spending, communism, and the so-called moral politics of abortion, sex education, gender equality, and prayer in public schools. But this division is not only political; it is deeply religious as well.[10]

Wuthnow is concerned that this cleavage is moving our churches from religious pluralism to religious polarization, and he sees the erosion of denominational loyalty and "boundaries" as contributing toward such polarization.

An institutional form characteristic of this new religious landscape is the parachurch organization, or special-purpose group, formed to support a particular liberal or conservative cause. Since 1945 some five hundred new groups have been founded, compared with the total of four hundred in existence in 1945.[11] Alliances of liberals or conservatives across denominational lines are now more important structures than the denominations themselves, argues Wuthnow.

University of Virginia sociologist James Davison Hunter, in his 1991 book *Culture Wars: The Struggle to Define America*,[12] carried Wuthnow's analysis beyond religion and politics, placing it in the larger context of the whole of American culture. America, he says, is the battleground for two "competing moral visions," polarizing tendencies within American culture that Hunter (avoiding the classic liberal-conservative terminology) labels "progressive" and "orthodox." These two impulses are struggling to define America. They permeate the whole range of American culture, secular as well as religious, although it is in the religious arena that major battles are being fought. It is to the religious world that Hunter turns repeatedly for evidence and illustrations.

Hunter has highlighted the extremes of religious right and religious/secular left but has done little to define the cultural middle, which he acknowledges is where most Americans stand. Indeed, Hunter deplores "the eclipse of the middle," and he sees media as having intensified the polarization in society by playing to the sensational: *"Middling positions and the nuances of moral commitment, then, get played into the grid of opposing rhetorical extremes."*[13] In his epilogue he urges Americans in the middle to speak up—but the overall impact of his book is to interpret contemporary American culture in terms of the warring extremes.[14]

Wade Clark Roof and William McKinney interpret the strength of the extremes by their description of the "collapse of the middle" in *American Mainline Religion; Its Changing Shape and Future.*[15] In their thorough and thoughtful review, they examine the legacy of the sixties and find a flourishing of religious fringes to right and left, but a "languishing at the center." Many young religious liberals experimented with new religions and spiritualities, seeking an inward journey to self-enlightenment, while those conservatively inclined sought stability, reassurance and authority in tradition. "But those in the middle—the more liberal, culturally accommodating versions of Protestant, Catholic, and Jewish faith—were in a state of collapse. Pulled from all sides, the liberal religious center was unable to hold. Gaps had widened between religious and secular world views and between those in pursuit of self and inner truth and those who sought to restore a more theocentric and traditional religious order."[16]

Roof and McKinney have assembled some very helpful data in their book, materials that have been given considerable attention by the churches they are describing. However, the rhetoric of "collapse" may perhaps be more eye-catching than accurate. As participants in that broad center, we can testify to the painful necessity of rethinking the role of now disestablished churches in a diversified religious environment where they cannot any longer claim to be central. We find helpful the interpretation of mainline decline in *The Good Society:* "The crucial point in such trends is that the erosion of mainline religion's strength has been a matter more of ethos than of numbers. It remains numerically strong but with a growing consciousness of itself as a beleaguered cultural minority, caught between the widening freeways of the secular city and the rising bastions of the religious right, and divided from within by conflict between spirit-filled evangelicals and dispirited if still stubbornly principled liberals."[17] Having for many years counted upon the cultural environment to support their religious views, these once-mainline churches must rapidly learn to speak with authority in a culture that no longer gives them an authoritative voice.

Some current scholarship is taking a radical second look at this basic two-party analysis of American Protestantism and suggesting that the complexity of these various definitions calls into question a "basic polarity." Douglas Jacobsen and William Vance Trollinger Jr., with the aid of the Lilly Endowment, have brought together over a three-year period a broad spectrum of religious leaders and scholars in a project entitled "Re-forming the Center." In their resulting published volume they say,

> The reality is that the two-party model does not and can not do justice to the bewildering complexity of American Protestantism. Not only were and are there numerous Protestants who do not truly fit within either party, but

the fault lines within Protestantism are both multiple and constantly shifting, hence ensuring that conflicts did not and do not reflect a single bifurcated division.[18]

Other Cleavages

The various dimensions of the cultural cleavages we have examined illustrate the sheer complexity of the problem. Our interviews with numerous church leaders remind us of other potent divisions—splits over theology, politics, gender issues and ethnicity, to name some of the most important. A layman long active in denominational leadership put it graphically: "The problem is, I think, three-dimensional. If you took a cut across it you could take a liberal-conservative cut. But you could cut it in an infinite number of ways."

Racial or ethnic splits. The divisions between people of different races and ethnicities within society are paralleled, as one would anticipate, within and among Christian denominations. Most of the "establishment mainstream" denominations have made efforts to become more inclusive of other racial and ethnic groups than found in their historic European ancestry, especially in recent years. So have evangelical churches and parachurch groups. Christians who are members of ethnic or racial minorities have been "wooed" by both sides of Hunter's polarities, and they are often caught feeling more comfortable with the faith stance of the orthodox but attracted to some of the social programs of the progressives.

A minister of Hispanic background has for a number of years staffed a denominational ministry to ethnic minorities and a similar program within a major ecumenical agency. In his view people of various ethnicities should not be too readily "typecast" in either polarity. In a letter that documents these assertions he states the following:

1. Not all important issues generate mobilized support.

2. Some issues touch some constituencies more than others.

3. No unanimous support can be built for any issue.

4. On some liberal-versus-conservative issues, members of racial or ethnic minorities are found on both sides.

Peacemaking and homosexuality issues, this minister suggests, have attracted little support among nonwhite Christians. Perhaps this is because the nuclear-war concern seemed remote from the violence already in their lives and because the gay movement assumed too easily its rights as a natural extension of the civil-rights movement. Immigration issues and "English as the official language" movements tend to attract much more natural support from Hispanic Americans and Asian Americans than from African-Americans or Native Americans. Often consensus is not reached among these groups because of disagreement over strategy and tactics, which is often the case among European Americans too. In the abortion issue, which is a strong divider of orthodox and progressives in our secular culture as well as in religious communities, members of ethnic minorities support the pro-life and the pro-choice sides and "none of the above," says this minister.

In one of the Re-forming the Center conferences, held at Messiah College in 1995, Edwin David Aponte presented a paper on Hispanic-Latin Protestant churches in relation to the liberal-evangelical split in U.S. churches. These two-party categories do not fit the complex reality, tensions and genius of Hispanic Protestantism, Aponte claimed. Examining Philadelphia's Hispanic community, he said personal piety and social ministry go hand in hand; Hispanics have learned that ministry to individuals also needs to address problems in public systems. The tensions within the largely Anglo mainline denominations are imposed upon their Latino/Latina mission churches, which find many of the tensions irrelevant. The churches should rather explore the cultural restructuring that is taking place in our society—class (including access to power), race, ethnicity and gender. Aponte suggests the mainline denominations should watch to see which models being constructed by Hispanic Protestants might enlighten our understanding of the emerging America.

Gender. The emergence of women as a vocal, critical and renewing force within the churches must be acknowledged as representing another important set of divisions, which although not fully elaborated here are well known and written about elsewhere. In an earlier time many women were reasonably content with an active involvement in the church that still left the decision-making responsibilities and leadership roles, including those in ministry, to men. They felt they had more than enough work to do with Sunday schools, dinners, circles, missionary societies, fundraising activities and the like. They even wanted to get the men more engaged in the work of the church. Many felt that it was inappropriate for women to be leaders, especially as clergy, and they were content to be subordinate to their husbands and male leaders as some Bible passages suggest. This attitude still prevails in pockets of the mainline and evangelical churches. It remains strong in many small sect groups and in churches with a fundamentalist stance. Yet even in Roman Catholicism, in which hierarchy stands firm on its tradition of exclusively male ordination to the priesthood, leaders are facing continuing challenges from some parishioners and many women religious on this issue, particularly in the United States.

Many contemporary women are restless within these limitations, partly because they are not so restricted in other aspects of their lives. The book *Defecting in Place*, by Miriam Therese Winter, Adair Lummis and Allison Stokes,[19] documents in vivid detail the anger and anguish of women who feel denied leadership roles in their churches. In the past forty years the mainline churches have made some significant changes that open the doors of leadership at all levels of denominational life, including ministry in nearly all of them. Seminary student bodies are now often one-third to one-half women. Many problems and frustrations remain, however, as a recent detailed study from Hartford Seminary reveals in a book on women in ministry, *Clergy Women: An Uphill Calling* by Barbara Brown Zikmund, Adair Lummis and Patricia Chang.[20] The struggle of women with differing expectations and hopes for their church involvement has produced tensions that contribute to several of the other divisions recounted here, including an exacerbation of the liberal-evangelical divide. An Evangelical Women's Caucus and similar caucuses of women within mainline denominations have been significant contributors to changing policies in church structures, and they continue to press for further change.

The current debate among women over the men's religious movement known as Promise Keepers shows wariness and ambivalence on the one hand and appreciation of its goals on the other. Some fear that the Promise Keepers' goal to reemphasize male responsibility in families will lead to renewed dominance over women. Supporters of Promise Keepers assert that it leads to a mutual responsibility between companions.

Clergy versus laity. The layman who suggested above that there are "many ways to cut" this debate went on to add that "a cut in which I see one of the fundamental problems is the clergy-lay division." He is concerned that this is a problem to which seminaries are not paying attention in their training of clergy.

A rector of a historic Episcopal church in Manhattan relates this tension within his denomination, in which wealthy families no longer predominate, to a class struggle. Often the tension is a matter of "taste" or the destruction of the "privileged church" as it is taken over by the nonprivileged. Because the priests often side with the poor, ethnic minorities and women seeking a place within the church, there is a strong clergy-laity struggle with a serious gap between the two groups. There are, of course, also elegant, reserved and educated clergy, he adds, who side with the wealthy in their attempt to hold onto an Episcopal Church that chiefly serves their status in society.

The head of a conservative lay organization within a mainline denomination agrees that he faces clergy-laity polarities, though of a different kind than the Episcopal rector described. The organization he heads was established to champion the cause of the laity in what was perceived as a clergy-dominated church. It regards lay people as generally conservative and most of the clergy as far more liberal. He says the clergy criticize his organization without even knowing it.

Congregation versus bureaucracy. Comparable in some ways to the clergy-lay division was the analysis of a southern seminary professor, who found the most significant polarization to be between "those for whom the church is the worshiping, believing congregation and those who think the church is in the bureaucracy."[21] "The book that has been clinically exact in describing it," this professor said, was one by Jeffrey Hadden, *The Gathering Storm in the Churches.*[22] Hadden's book, now more than thirty years old, appeared at a time when mainline Protestantism was at a twentieth-century high point in membership and apparent influence. (The numerical decline across mainline denominations is usually dated from about 1968.) This book forecast with considerable accuracy the course American Christianity has taken in the years since its publication.

According to Hadden there are three aspects of the church's malaise. The first is a crisis of belief, in which traditional doctrine vies not only with other theologies but with other views that may take precedence over it. Second, there is disagreement as to the function of the church—whether it exists to change society and further human development or for the glory and worship of God and the proclamation of the faith. Finally, Hadden outlined an authority crisis: clergy have long been vested with authority to run the church as they see fit, but laity are discovering that they have grave reservations about the way clergy have handled their authority.[23]

Overall, Hadden described the crisis more in terms of the growing gap between laity and clergy than in terms of congregations versus bureaucracy. He made it clear, however, that the capture of church bureaucracies by clergy intent on radical change was a central concern. Bellah and his colleagues have added a significant nuance, citing the work of Wuthnow: "The controversy did not rage between clergy and laity but between a coalition of college-educated laity and clergy supporting these causes [civil rights, anti-Vietnam war, grape boycotts], and less educated, often older lay people with more conservative political and cultural views."[24]

The seminary professor who cited Hadden noted that Protestantism got along without bureaucrats until the late nineteenth century. The real mushrooming of bureaucracies has come since World War II. They are now, he says, "totally out of touch with the grassroots of the church."

Large church versus small church. Similar to the tension between bureaucracy and local churches is a polarity between large and small churches, said some respondents. Large churches tend toward evangelical theology and culture, while small and middle-sized churches tend toward the progressive or liberal. There are, of course, exceptions to this categorization. How the "tall-steeple church" pastors relate in regional judicatories to the representatives of small and middle-sized churches is a matter for careful scrutiny.

The struggle for power. Two leaders—one a denominational leader, the other a former ecumenical-council president—see the struggle for power as the very human touchstone for many differing perspectives on issues within church and society. The former ecumenical leader feels that liberals have become too cavalier and conservatives too judgmental, that both are fighting for control of the church and that few issues are worth the strain upon the church's unity these struggles engender. One concern that she regards as worth testing the tensile strength of the church has to do with nationalism and a global perspective, however. Baptizing nationalism is a conservative tendency that she feels is so antithetical to the God of universal love and so dangerous that it must be challenged. She would agree with the assertion in *The Good Society* that we can only accurately describe and meaningfully respond to a diverse world that we cannot control "if we develop a richer, better grounded, more cosmopolitan understanding of our core ideals."[25] Learning to live together in love and making room for many diverse ideas and their mutual exploration can prepare the church for the big, important battles, she believes.

The polarity within our churches does not come from liberals and conservatives, declares the senior denominational official in a sweeping statement, but rather from the lust for power and control, a disease found in both sides. The danger is not schism but stalemate, a paralysis of vision and mission. But, ultimately, telling the truth to one another, correcting the mistakes and illegitimate uses of power and recognizing that all truth does not reside in one's own perspective are elements necessary for maintaining a healthy church at all levels, he says. His hopes are that the church will gain a new balance, recognize that the national structures have overbalanced the local church systems and learn to construct a new sense of church community, which is the first task of leadership.

Divisions based on personality type or human needs. One lay leader (whose insights on the endless variables of the church's polarities were mentioned earlier) sees a basic and fundamental divide between those who are "true believers" and those who tolerate ambiguity. True believers are easily offended and seek each other out. Put another way, polarization occurs in the local church on almost every issue and such people are driven to find a community that agrees with them, forming groups that ultimately divide the denomination.

Separate religious "cultures." A national survey of church leaders conducted in 1988 and 1989 by Hartford Seminary's Center for Social and Religious Research and reported by William McKinney and Daniel V. A. Olson adds yet another dimension to our understanding of church polarities. Studying questionnaires sent to a broad representative sample of church leaders, McKinney and Olson verified the theological stances one might anticipate as dominant in a spread of denominations. Of most interest for us, however, is the evidence of separate "cultures" among theological liberals, moderates and conservatives. McKinney and Olson listed sixty-five writers and religious activists and requested that respondents identify ten who have been particularly influential on their thinking about American religion. Carl F. H. Henry was cited by 39 percent of the conservatives, 4 percent of the moderates and 1 percent of the liberals; Billy Graham was named by 79 percent of the conservatives, 18 percent of the moderates and 3 percent of the liberals. Rosemary Radford Ruether, on the other hand, was listed by 1 percent of the conservatives, 12 percent of the moderates and 28 percent of the liberals. Robert McAfee Brown was influential among 6 percent of the conservatives, 35 percent of the moderates and 48 percent of the liberals. Only church planner Lyle Schaller was named significantly by all three (47 percent, 50 percent, 32 percent), followed by Henri Nouwen (12 percent, 48 percent, 47 percent) and Martin Marty (12 percent, 47 percent, 40 percent).

A similar sense of "separate thought worlds" was evident in church leaders' reading patterns. *Christianity Today*, an evangelical journal, was read by 59 percent of the conservatives, 21 percent of moderates and 6 percent of liberals, whereas the liberal *Christian Century* had a 10 percent conservative, 48 percent moderate and 54 percent liberal readership. Similarly, while 52 percent of conservatives, 21 percent of moderates and 9 percent of liberals read *Reader's Digest*, the *New York Times* is read by 7 percent conservatives, 27 percent moderates and 40 percent liberals in this sample.

This reinforces the experience Peggy Shriver had as she regularly skimmed dozens of church magazines in preparing editions of the National Council of Churches' *Ecu-Link*. When reading the evangelical *Christianity Today* or *Leadership*, she entered a different thought world—with a different set of leading characters, events, book reviews, even advertisements—than when reading *Christianity & Crisis* or *One World*. Not only are the leading thinkers different, but the reported church seminars and conferences and news stories tend to vary significantly. These are almost distinct cultural worlds, and these differences of culture (styles of prayer and worship, for example) add barriers to those who would attempt to have a more unified church.

This view was elaborated by Barbara Wheeler, president of Auburn Seminary and director of its Center for the Study of Theological Education, after she spent three years in part-time residence and interaction within an evangelical seminary. She says,

There is an evangelical culture; it is prodigious, pervasive among the many varieties of white evangelicals, including most fundamentalists, and very powerful. Today's evangelicals are culture-makers. . . . They produce an astounding number of leaders and celebrities who are widely recognized in the evangelical community—writers and pastors as well as media figures. They support hundreds of less prominent roving minstrels and inspirational speakers. They found new denominations and, even more importantly, create and expand nondenominational organizations at a very fast rate: big foreign mission and youth ministry agencies; less visible networks of prayer, fellowship and self-help groups.[26]

Wheeler further notes that one of the current weaknesses of mainline Protestantism is its failure to develop such cultural elements that are necessary for a religious tradition to survive: a piety, a whole way of life and shared practices, virtues and models of Christian adequacy in today's world—in short, a religious identity. We are also "bodied beings" and need something to look at, listen to and touch, and mainline Protestants lack such cultural artifacts, she claims. We, however, would maintain that there is a mainline Protestant culture of which Wheeler is a part; but it is less defined, more diverse (in fact, diversity is one of the prized elements of that culture) and does lack commonly shared "paraphernalia."

It is clear that there are a number of "ways of cutting it" when looking at the complex polarizations in the church. These must be borne in mind as we examine the church's basic evangelical-liberal polarization, which can be better understood in relation to these other tensions.

Societal Changes and Clashes

Divisions reflecting societal change. The Episcopal rector quoted earlier for his opinion on clergy-lay tensions feels the church is being caught up in the vertigo of change that has affected the larger society. He has a great sympathy for the fearful who see their ordered universe collapsing in a vast pool of tentativeness. We are almost at the end of the Enlightenment era, he says, and there are new assumptions about science, economics and racial diversity—radical, axiomatic changes. Whether you are conservative or liberal, you now have to be tentative about almost everything. The center is no longer there; it has no clear reality. There are no fundamental truths, there is no "old science," says the rector. God seems to be growing too. There is a fundamental shift in the axioms of culture, and neither conservatives nor liberals have the answers. Myths no longer work. Although we live using the past as our reference point, we find that much in life today has no clear reference point in the past. The rector cites changes in women's roles, new assumptions about sexuality and so on. Like Berger, this Episcopal clergyman finds much of our distress rooted in modernity itself.

Our current society requires forced social experiment, claims a Lutheran seminary professor. Everything is changing, is in flux, as socialism collapses abroad and society's sense of community collapses at home. There is massive suffering on the horizon, and the churches must be both a haven and a community engaging in pioneering creativity. Religion supplies the social glue for a culture in trouble, claim neoconservatives, but many different caucus groups in our pluralistic society are suspicious of that concept. Polarization comes in times of deep change, and religion may then be counterproductive, supporting the shadow side of the status quo, the caucuses claim. The question is how much diversity can culture stand? We must do better than simply forging a compromise among interest groups as we face the challenges of the future in such key concerns as poverty and environmental degradation, this professor argues.

A middle judicatory executive, though he may not see the social changes in quite the same sweeping terms as does the Episcopal rector or the Lutheran professor, detects within his own denomination a division in world-views that needs to be taken into account when analyzing polarities. He describes many middle-class members as either having a business perspective that has allegiance to the old conservative, industrial business world or else identifying with the information-media world that is often liberal and highly critical of America's role in the global society. He claims that even some business industrialists consider the American dream almost dead—but this church leader sees different responses to such an obituary. Liberals are angry about what they see happening around them, while conservative businesspeople are defensive and struggle to maintain at least a facade of the dominant American society they cherish. Stances taken by a denomination may emanate from the information-age view and take little account of the lay person who lives in that industrial business world, he observes. These are sometimes socially determined liberal-conservative polarities that have little to do with one's religious stance.

Class. Sociologist Berger, a Lutheran professor at Boston University, has long maintained that mainline Protestant churches have reflected and legitimated the middle-class culture of America.[27] In earlier days this was a positive analysis, since middle-class culture was to a large extent the product of mainstream Protestantism. However, Berger's more recent and widely influential New Class hypothesis lays the groundwork for a more negative understanding of the effect of the culture on the church:

> In America (and, incidentally, in all other advanced capitalist societies) the middle class has split. Whereas previously there was one (though internally stratified) middle class, there are now two middle classes (also internally stratified). There is the old middle class, the traditional bourgeoisie, centered in the business community and the old professions. But there is also a new middle class, based on the production and distribution of symbolic knowledge, whose members are the increasingly large number of people occupied with education, the media of mass communication, therapy in all its forms, the advocacy and administration of well-being, social justice and personal lifestyles.[28]

The new middle class, says Berger, "is on the left; in America this means 'liberal,' in current terminology. . . . Its class interest is in government rather than the market." The old middle class, he says, "has opposing interests. Therefore it tends toward the political right; in America this constitutes a 'conservative' tendency."

The symbiotic church-society relationship with middle-class culture has not changed, says Berger. But the split of the middle class is reflected in the polarization of the churches.

> The mainline Protestant churches . . . reflected the cultural break lines, and with a vengeance. In not a single denomination, of course, are members of the new middle class in a majority. But the clergy and officials of the mainline churches belong to the new middle class by virtue of their education, their associations and their "reference group." . . . In denomination after denomination, people who represented the new culture took over the bureaucratic machinery and thus the public face of the community.

Traditional authorities, says Berger, were unable to understand, let alone stop, this process. And laypeople did not try. Instead, they "voted with their pocketbooks and their feet: they reduced their contributions, and, in large numbers, they left." To a considerable extent, he says, "the evangelical resurgence since the mid-1970s developed as a 'resistance movement' against the new culture."

A similar approach is the starting point of St. Paul School of Theology Professor Tex Sample (a United Methodist) in his 1990 book *U.S. Lifestyles and Mainline Churches.*[29] His starting assumption is that there are "three broad but sharply different lifestyles. . . . I call them the cultural left, the cultural middle, and the cultural right."[30] Sample's paradigm differs from Berger's in that it has a separately defined middle as well as a left and right. His emphasis is on lifestyle rather than class. Berger is sometimes labeled a neoconservative; Sample's basic instincts are liberal. But the approaches are compatible to the extent that both emphasize the culture as the starting point in understanding what goes on in the churches.

Sample also experienced the move into the symbolic-knowledge side of the middle-class split described by Berger. He put it colorfully:

> The longer I pursued higher education, the more I noticed that I was picking up the rules and learning how to obfuscate my vocabulary so that my training "showed." . . . Deeply stained into my consciousness was a new way of life, and I feared that my real roots would creep up out of the ground at any moment and send my pseudo tree of culture crashing into the verdant garden of the academic world. . . . Please understand, there was a great deal I needed to be alienated from—my racism, my classism, my sexism, my love of violence, my militaristic patriotism, my narrow loyalties, and on and on. Yet I also felt, even then, that I was being alienated from some things that were of life-giving value and had an authentic human clarity, the loss of which represented some ineffable loss of soul. . . . My parents could see it but could not quite name it, although I remember my father once saying, "Well, son, you just keep on and you're going to get so far out in front of us we're gonna mistake you for the enemy and shoot ya!"[31]

A former ecumenical council president (who earlier stated her views on the struggle for power) expressed a similar view: "I worry that some of this evangelical-liberal split is a white, male, U.S.A. split rather than a conservative theological split. I think where I am liberal is on the international issues, that it's not just what is best for the United States, or white people, or men. I see lots of strength around the world, and to have that international viewpoint is part of what our ecumenism is about."

Writing in the *Christian Century,* John M. Gessell, a liberal Episcopalian, analyzed in cultural terms the conservative attempt to organize a separate Episcopal Synod of America (ESA) within his denomination. The roots of this movement are secular, he says.

> The ESA's understanding of authority is formed by secular values of self-reference, personalism and privatism. It fosters sectarianism and private judgment in place of the doctrine, discipline and worship of the Episcopal Church. It wishes to stay in the church by picking and choosing the aspects of the church it can affirm. It has set up a private center of authority against the public authority of the Episcopal Church.[32]

Thus a wide range of social and other factors are seen as affecting—if not determining—positions taken within the church. Generally in our interviews the liberal leaders were more likely to emphasize the importance of social influences than were evangelicals. The latter were more likely to emphasize biblical and theological issues as being central. "The most dangerous polarization," said a college president who is also a leading evangelical, "is between those who can affirm the historic creeds of the church and those who cannot, . . . between those who stand within the circle of orthodoxy and those who are increasingly 'post-Christian' in that sense." The issues, she said, are the creeds, the authority of Scripture, Christology, the uniqueness of Christ, the unity of Jesus with the Father, and the reality of the Holy Spirit in people's lives—"every doctrine of systematic theology, from revelation right through to eschatology." In connection with the present project she warned her interviewer about the danger of relying too heavily on sociological analysis, which, she said, is a tendency in our church. "There is such a thing as genuine theological differences," she said, "and they have consequences."

Other evangelicals gave similar analyses, sometimes in terms of spirituality versus a political agenda, frequently in terms of biblical authority. Some evangelicals, however, while describing their own position primarily in theological or biblical terms, saw cultural influences as having a significant impact on the liberals they opposed. A United Methodist evangelical leader, one of the founders of the Good News Movement in that denomination, was quite outspoken in this regard: "The liberal branch of the church is captive to a secular ideology. . . . Most of the boards are dominated by leftist ideology. The only people I see left in the world that seem to believe in Marxism-Leninism are at 475 Riverside Drive" (an address for the headquarters of his own United Methodist Church as well as for the National Council of Churches).

None on either side ascribed polarization entirely to cultural factors. All saw it as in some sense theological, and most recognized that the church is inevitably influenced in some measure by its culture. In both camps, some were more likely to see social and cultural influences affecting the other side rather than their own.

Terminology: A Rose by Any Other Name

The sheer complexity of the multiple, overlapping divisions in the church creates problems of terminology. While Wuthnow used the terms *liberal* and *conservative*, Hunter used the terms *progressive* and *orthodox*. Among the church leaders we interviewed for this book, most used the terms *liberal* and *evangelical* to designate one another, although *conservative* is often used instead of or with *evangelical* by liberals, and evangelicals frequently use it when talking about themselves.

Some liberals prefer to be called *progressives* or *liberationists*, and many wish they could be called *evangelical liberals*, because they feel the term *evangelical* belongs to them too. *Evangelical* is clearly a religious term, while *conservative*, *liberal* and *progressive* each have strong political connotations that often do not apply to the person being described. There are politically liberal, even utopian, socialists, who call themselves evangelical. There are many politically conservative persons who are religiously liberal. One evangelical who participated in our research via modem commented, "My experience is that my liberal brothers find us a very difficult animal to pin down, because we are intensely concerned with social justice issues relating to poverty, homelessness, racism, women's issues and so on while being just as hard set against changing our attitudes toward basic moral issues."

A pastor of a Reformed Church in America congregation observed, "In the past you were either a liberal liberal or a conservative conservative. The conservatives all voted Republican and believed in the King James Bible. Liberals were liberal liberal. I believe what God wants is people who are conservative in their faith and liberal on social policies." He was voicing the widespread feeling that simple polarities are inadequate, and among those we interviewed many were reluctant to give themselves a label whose definition was both unclear and insufficient to their self-perception. Because there was no consensus on preferable terms, we chose to use *liberal* and *evangelical* throughout this book, though with some freedom, since we recognize the limitations of all terminologies.

Self-Identification. When conducting interviews, we asked our respondents if they would accept the label used by others to apply to them. (Half of our interviewees were perceived as liberal, half as evangelical.) Most accepted the perceived label, but usually added some modifier, such as "I am a moderate liberal" or "I am a moderate evangelical." Only one claimed "I am a conservative evangelical." Perhaps because the liberal label has a broader range of meanings, liberals were less comfortable with it than evangelicals with their label. Clearly, neither camp is monolithic. Within each group can be found not only a spectrum of positions from moderate to cutting edge, but also internal controversies and disagreements. The case for a broad middle ground tending slightly toward one or the other position was reinforced by these responses.

One United Church of Christ seminary professor identified himself clearly as a liberal. But he reported that his sharpest conflicts were not with evangelicals but with the "liberationist-Marxist fringe" of liberalism.

In a few cases liberals related that they had earlier been clearly identified as such but had since become more moderate. For instance, the layman quoted twice above said, "I'm somewhere in the middle. I used to be a real dramatic liberal of the sixties and did all the things associated with that, involving civil rights and the Vietnam War. I integrated six schools in the community where I lived. In recent years I'm shifting. But I resist the term *conservative.*"

A few rejected labels altogether. But many of those who refused to label themselves agreed that they were probably identified by others as being in the suggested category. In almost every case, as the discussion proceeded, there was a tacit assumption if not an explicit statement that liberal-evangelical polarization is a real and serious problem for the church. The side with which the interviewee identified (perhaps unconsciously), and the side seen as the opposition, usually became quite clear.

Only three of the church leaders interviewed could not be categorized by us, the authors, as being predominantly in one camp or the other. Interestingly and perhaps encouragingly, two of these were representatives of the church press. Both expressed commitment to particular issues that might be identified with one side or the other. Both showed deep concern about the polarization and its effect on the church. But each analyzed and discussed the two sides of the polarization with a detachment that gave no evidence of personal identification with either. These two might be placed in the middle. One African-American pastor in New York City also seemed to combine both evangelical and liberal perspectives in a unique way.

This is not to say that there were not other leaders, both liberal and evangelical, who discussed the situation with relative impartiality, showing understanding and appreciation of those with whom they disagreed. With the three noted exceptions, however, all could (on the basis of their answers to interview questions) be classified, for purposes of this study, as primarily identified with either the liberal or the evangelical wing of the church. And in most cases that identification was, with some qualification, explicitly acknowledged.

A Willingness to Reach Toward the Center

Perhaps the most hopeful finding of this study was the paucity of extremists on either side. Both liberals and evangelicals tended to be wary of what they regarded as extremism on the *other* side, but nearly all professed a willingness from their own side to reach out in a quest for mutual understanding and respect. Obviously there are some radicals at both ends. An Episcopal leader labeled them "concrete-minded"—people "with little ability for inquiry, for reflection, for self-doubt." But the frequently expressed opinion that most extremists at either end of the spectrum have left the centrist denominations seems to be accurate. By and large, mainline Protestants are moderates.

If some of the participants in the Re-forming the Center series of consultations are correct, hope lies not only in being a moderate, but in the refusal of many Christians to align themselves with one polarity or another. A study by David Sikkink and Christian Smith, in which 128 people from a wide spectrum of Christian traditions were interviewed, revealed that interviewees did not construct their personal religious identities in terms of a liberal-evangelical (or conservative) divide. Most of them wanted to be considered "just Christian." Even denominational labels were seldom significant when they identified themselves, except as a confessional stance that avoided either polarity. But labels were useful to them to describe "what they are *not*." Many had a mix-and-match set of religious characteristics that came from a bewildering variety of sources. Few were able to articulate, unfortunately, a clear, positive master frame to describe what they *are*. They resisted being identified with a community, because it was a threat to their selfhood, their individuality. Some were uncomfortable with institutions and defined their faith in terms of an inward, subjective spiritual experience. Others found "respectability" through an institutional expression of their faith.[33] This is a mixed message for those who yearn for peace and strength within denominational structures.

The president of an aggressive faction, regarded by liberals in his communion as the heart of the opposition, made it clear that both he and his organization are basically committed to their denomination: "Our objectives, in our incorporation papers, say we will work within the church. If we were to think of leaving we would have to be dissolved. We have felt very strongly all along that there is no biblical support for leaving the denomination. . . . I don't know what God's plan for the church is, and he's not going to tell me. My only duty is to be obedient and be faithful."

Seeing the complicated, intertwined divisions in our Protestant denominations, a spokesman for the Re-forming the Center project concluded, "Such complexity is an invitation for each of us to explore new ways of living at peace with each other as Protestants and with our neighbors in general. Such a complex peace is not the boring peace of uniformity. Nor is it the quiet peace of conformity. Instead, it is the loud peace of the play ground and the town meeting. It is this complex peace, this peaceful pluralism, that has formed the ideal of America's peculiar form of Protestantism (and perhaps the form of all American religious faiths) since the founding of the Republic."[34]

A minister described the cost of not finding this peace, saying, "We are long past the time when we can afford the degree of unresolved and uncivil polarization we are now experiencing—for the sake of the kingdom. . . . We can witness to the world of our partnership in the gospel. Our fragmentation is the greatest thing keeping us from being a powerful force in our culture."

4

....

Biblical &
Theological Help
in Understanding
the Splits

*Both sides of the liberal-conservative division claim a biblical base. And that's a
terrific bind for us. . . . If we were Unitarian Universalists who would care? But
we're not. If we're not a people of the Word, we're not a people at all.*
A MIDDLE JUDICATORY EXECUTIVE

Concerned Christians must listen to and learn from observers who
use the tools of the social sciences to analyze the church's problems,
as we have done in the last chapter. Churches are human institutions,
made up of human beings. We are part of our culture.

But churches are not *solely* human institutions, and sociological analysis does not exhaust our sources of wisdom and understanding. We
believe the church was established by Jesus Christ. Our relationship to a
sovereign God is our most distinctive characteristic. In seeking to understand and deal with our polarization, therefore, we must look to our own
tools of analysis.

Within our own context we seek wisdom from the Holy Spirit, whom
we believe to be present in the church in a unique way. We use the spiritual
disciplines of prayer, worship and listening to the "still, small voice." We
also seek wisdom through the process of theological reflection and dis-

course, based on centuries of human deliberation within the church. But our most basic source is the one provided by the Lord of the church: the way God has spoken to us through Scripture. For all Christians the Bible is, in some sense, a unique resource and treasure.

Yet here we encounter a major problem. The bind identified by the church executive quoted above is real for Protestant Christians. In the sometimes bitter divisions that rend the church, *our attitude toward the Bible itself—and its authority over our lives—is a critical point of contention.* The church leaders we interviewed for this project, whether evangelical or liberal, made this clear.

"This is our most basic polarization," says a college president prominent in the evangelical camp, referring to the authority of Scripture. A denominational executive, a leader in the liberal camp, agrees. Speaking of a dialogue on abortion that she had organized for her denomination, she says, "I felt that the thing that divided us most basically—on this issue, and I believe on other issues as well—was our view of the Bible."

Yet if it is our view of Scripture that most basically divides us, it is also our common commitment to the Bible that offers our greatest hope. We Protestant Christians are inescapably a people of the Word. We may regard the Bible as the Word of God, as the heart of "the tradition" or as a witness to humankind's struggle to understand the nature and purpose of God. But to the extent that it is authoritative for us, Scripture itself points inexorably to the need—indeed the absolute necessity—for reconciliation among quarreling people who consider themselves disciples of Jesus Christ. "Is Christ divided?" Paul asked the squabbling Corinthians. This remains the question that a polarized church must ask itself when seeking to live out a gospel of love.

In this chapter we shall first examine the way in which the Bible itself is at the center of the liberal-evangelical controversy. Drawing on our interviews with church leaders, we will look at the divergent ways in which biblical authority and interpretation are viewed in today's church. We have already indicated our own positions in our faith statements in chapter one.

Second, we will turn to the Bible itself for help on this Scriptural problem. We will suggest a biblical perspective (on which both of us, as a liberal and an evangelical, are agreed) that makes no claim of ending the disagreements but rather helps us to live with our diversity.

Finally, we will look at the problem from a theological perspective. Once again, we will not offer a theological *solution* to the problem of biblical authority and interpretation, but rather a brief look at how our theological tradition enables us to manage it.

The Bible at the Center of the Controversy

It was painful for us to hear, in our numerous interviews with church leaders, how frequently the Bible was the focus of dispute instead of our common well of inspiration and faithful commitment to our Lord. Attitudes toward the Bible vary among Christians from an almost idolatrous worship of the written Word to its use as a reference work for support of one's already determined opinions, independently acquired. Few people are found at these extremes, but too many of us are ready to ascribe such an extreme misuse of Scripture to persons who hold views different from our own.

The basic divide. James Davison Hunter's distinction between orthodox and progressive tendencies, referred to in chapter three, is helpful in understanding the divide. The orthodox tendency, he says, accepts—indeed, insists on—the reality of revealed truth, given by a transcendent God. The progressive tendency "resymbolize[s] historic faiths according to the prevailing assumptions of contemporary life . . . in conversation with particular religious or cultural traditions."[1]

A West Coast pastor who calls himself a "global evangelical" spells out his perception of the basic difference between the two views: "The distinction would be between those who see the Bible as divinely initiated revelation and those who see the Bible as a reflection of humankind's quest after God through the years. I see this as a watershed." Biblical authority turns up as a boil that erupts from time to time within issues, this pastor says, and the painful splits of the past have caused mainline Christians to live with serious contradictions and ill-defined labels. Evangelical leaders interviewed for this study were far more precise in identifying the difference between the two kinds of biblical interpretation than were the liberals, who were generally less specific about their view of biblical authority. The college president quoted above, for instance, deplores the presence in the church of "those for whom Scripture has lost all authority except by way of remembrance—a mother lode of images that sometimes have the power to stir but do not carry truth in anything other than an evocative way."

"For evangelicals it is a more important issue than for liberals," the president of a student-focused evangelical organization says. He discussed the issue at some length. What we mean by *revelation* is one of the main issues of polarization. Where does truth come from? Liberals and evangelicals have different answers to that question, he says: "Conservatives start with what God has revealed to us. Liberals start by looking at our world."

Faithfulness on both sides. This evangelical leader, who holds a high view of Scripture, was still able to give a balanced appreciation of the way in which liberals and evangelicals are, in their own way, faithful to the biblical heritage. He stakes out his own position clearly: "I want to be a person who lives under the authority of Scripture." Liberals also make that statement, he went on to say. But for them, "the Bible is a witness to the struggle of humankind to understand the nature and purpose of God." The weak link for them, he suggests, is the issue of authority. They don't take authority seriously. But, he adds, the weak link for evangelicals is that they don't take the culture seriously. They don't realize that we always come to Scripture with cultural baggage: "We read Scripture through white, North American eyes."

This leader, who is also a biblical scholar, takes the text very seriously and is concerned that many conservatives take the text no more seriously than the liberals they condemn. While liberals may disregard the text, conservatives may "squeeze it into their own mold," he says. Both sides do damage. He recalls his classically liberal Old Testament mentor at Harvard, G. Ernest Wright, pounding his fist on the table in class and saying, "I won't go on with this discussion. You must realize that as a minister of the gospel and as a Christian, I stand *under* the authority of this book. Your discussion is pushing me to stand as an authority *over* it, and that I will not do!" Wright set limits on his own authority. Some liberals claim a hermeneutic that is higher than the authority of Scripture, whereas some conservatives don't take the whole counsel of God seriously, this evangelical leader suggests.

He goes on to express an appreciation of his denomination because it allows plenty of space on which to stand in regard to the Bible. There is, he says, "lots of room to navigate—within the boundaries of our confessions." He reads carefully the literature of evangelicals and liberals, keeps listening to both sides and sees limits, gaps and strengths in both perspectives. Reading both sides destroys unhealthy and inaccurate stereotypes, he says.

Appreciative testimony about biblical faithfulness from a liberal perspective came from a social activist identified with China's Amity Foundation. He has come to admire greatly the remarkable steadfastness of Chinese Christians, sustained throughout the tribulations of China's cultural revolution by a faithful devotion to Scripture. When so many Bibles had been confiscated and burned, others were sometimes painstakingly copied by hand.

One of the authors of this book visited China and met an elderly Christian scholar who had his entire library swept away and burned by the Red Guards. He related that while he sat weeping in his office, he prayed that God would allow him to have one Bible. When he raised his eyes, he discovered a Bible left on one shelf. He hurried home to tell his wife the good news that God had answered his request. Rejoicing with him, his wife paused and said, "But while you were praying for a Bible, why did you not pray for one for me?" Acknowledging the justice of her need, he spent years copying his Bible by hand, eventually acquiring other texts so that he produced an improved translation while making his wife her own Bible.

The Amity Foundation official referred to above was deeply impressed in China by the resilience of an evangelical faith nourished by the Bible. He now urges that other liberals let the Scriptures speak first through prayerful reading, then as literature, and finally, only after hearing the integrity of the whole, in historical-critical study that is also of great value. Because evangelicals take their Bible reading very personally, he urges liberal Christians who tend to read more analytically to take time to share personally their own response to Scripture so that liberal and evangelical can meet within the text in shared Bible study. He states this clearly in ecumenical terms:

> Learning from one another in the church is not a process of mutual edification for cultural uplift. Ecumenical learning is rather a means of seeing ourselves in the other, and the other in ourselves. We see each other working on different translations of the same text, and we need help in determining if we have it right. Such learning is never direct. What we learn is only suggestive, in the way that a poem or a parable suggests. This kind of learning reflects the all too human experience of knowing, forgetting and

having to relearn, a situation where our "answers" need to be continually tested and reformulated in practice. It should help us in the search for new ecumenical paradigms.[2]

A new consensus? The middle judicatory executive quoted at the beginning of this chapter calls for a new consensus on the authority and meaning of Scripture: "We need desperately to get our heads together on this." He recalls that in the years just prior to their reunion, the two former branches of his denomination had developed statements on Scripture. "They were headed in the right direction," he says, but the two reports were "absolutely unused."

From the evangelical side, a seminary professor also points to these same two documents.[3] Both papers affirmed the authority of Scripture. But they recognized differing understandings of that authority and widely different interpretations of the teaching of Scripture on particular issues. Neither paper resolved the issue to the full satisfaction of both sides. Each, however, represented a serious attempt to live constructively with differences.

In dealing with the issues of society today, progressives and orthodox alike are faced with the problem of selectivity in turning to the Bible for guidance. Not all passages seem in clear agreement, and people bring their own biases to Scripture as they "respond" to one passage more than another. The role of women in church and society, for instance, has spawned significant and diligent study of Scripture by persons with quite divergent views. New insight has been found, although sometimes it is a reinforcement of one's original position. Many issues, such as those that confront us because of modern technology, have no easy scriptural referent. This leads to a search in Scripture that ends up with different passages, biblical themes and outcomes for ethical decision making. Subjects like genetic engineering, using fetal tissue for research, euthanasia, environmental stewardship and human sexuality raise serious questions about the way in which the Bible is consulted for guidance. How we study the Bible is often more at issue than whether or not the Bible is authoritative.

Furthermore, many of the important issues being debated today not only have some scriptural support for differing viewpoints but also put important values in tension with one another. Justice and mercy, concern for the present generation and concern for future generations, the long-term health of the environment and immediate human need, maintenance of peace at the expense of justice or the carrying out of justice at the cost of peace are examples. On such issues liberals and evangelicals, recognizing the tension, may be closer together than it sometimes appears.

The interviews conducted for this study have confirmed that there are real differences between evangelicals and liberals on the authority and interpretation of Scripture. Evangelicals give more weight to authoritative revelation, and liberals give more weight to cultural context. What is revealed, however, is not a clear-cut contrast between two opposite extremes but a spectrum of views in which some evangelicals and some liberals would be quite close together. Indeed, there may be overlap. Some who are liberal on social-justice issues or particular political positions may ascribe a higher level of authority to Scripture than some on the other side of these particular issues.

There is considerable evidence that most Christians are strongly committed to the authority of Scripture. "Biblical Authority and Interpretation,"[4] a 1982 report to the General Assembly of the United Presbyterian Church in the U.S.A, cited a denominational survey on the nature of divine inspiration of the Bible. The questionnaire offered a choice of five positions, ranging from the Bible as "without error in all that it teaches in science and history as well as matters of theology" (labeled in religious terminology as a "high" view of scriptural inspiration) to the Bible as "merely a record of moral and religious experiences" (a "low" view). By far the largest group (48 percent) chose the middle position between the two extremes: "All of the Bible is both the inspired Word of God and at the same time a thoroughly human document."

Overall, however, the curve was weighted toward the "higher" view of divine inspiration (37 percent in two categories) rather than the "lower" view that leans toward a human document (15 percent in two categories). Altogether, 85 percent ascribed a relatively "high" degree of divine authority to the Bible. This impression is borne out by other data. A 1997 Gallup Poll[5] gave somewhat comparable figures for Americans as a whole. In the Gallup study, 30 percent of adults questioned believe "the Bible is the actual word of God and is to be taken literally, word for word." Fully 50 percent believe "the Bible is the inspired word of God, but not everything in it should be taken literally, word for word." Acceptable to 17 percent is the statement that "the Bible is an ancient book of fables, legends, history, and moral precepts recorded by men." The total in the two top categories, with a relatively "high" view of biblical inspiration, is 80 percent.

With some measure of consensus on this score, there is hope for continuing dialogue and discussion. As noted earlier, the mainline denominations in which the controversy is strongest have few extremists at either end. The entire mainline population is closer to the middle than are religious Americans in general. The issue of biblical authority is a critical one, requiring continuing attention, but we can still find a way of living together. In spite of substantial differences, Protestants are a people of the Word. In one way or another the Bible is the touchstone for all of us.

Biblical Models of Unity and Diversity

With this measure of agreement we turn to the Bible itself for help on the scriptural problem. We, the writers of this book, are convinced that for the overwhelming majority of ordinary people who make up the church the Bible is authoritative. It conveys in some sense the Word of God.

The question before us as we look to Scripture has to do with unity and diversity in the church. What are the uses and what are the limits of diversity? Because diversity and its resulting disagreements were commonplace in the New Testament church, scriptural material dealing with the problem is abundant. Raging controversies, doctrinal disputes, even differing backgrounds, callings and perspectives—all are reflected in the Scripture. And several methods of conflict resolution—formal conferences, informal discussions and apostolic mediation—are part of the biblical record. Several of Paul's letters (especially those written to the disputatious Corinthian Christians) were occasioned by and aimed at settling church quarrels.

A prominent layman reminded his interviewer of this biblical context. Agreeing, when questioned, that the present polarization is real and serious but refusing to regard it as unique, he points to disagreements in the New Testament church and in every period since. He is right. And our understanding of the problem is based directly on biblical models. When from our varying perspectives we turn to Scripture, we do not expect an end to our disagreements but instead a way of living constructively with them.

The body of Christ as a model of unity with diversity. Among the most prominent of the biblical images of the church is that of the body of

Christie.[6] The apostle Paul develops this image for the explicit purpose of dealing with the puzzling problem of unity and diversity. The one body—the church—is made up of many members with a variety of functions and with the spiritual gifts that enable them to perform their various functions. The two dimensions of that image always go together: the one body and the differing gifts. It is a "unity with diversity" theme.

Differing gifts lead members of the body to focus on different aspects of the work of the church. Members of one congregation, at an annual meeting to discuss budget priorities, expressed sharp disagreements. Some argued for increased emphasis and more professional staff to strengthen Sunday-school and youth programs. Some argued for a full-time minister of pastoral care and for increased emphasis on support groups to meet the needs of hurting people. Others argued for devoting a higher proportion of the church's resources to outreach ministries, at home and overseas. Within this latter group some advocated more emphasis on sending missionaries abroad, while others called for housing the homeless and feeding the hungry within the congregation's own metropolitan area.

They were reflecting not only differing perceptions of need but also different spiritual gifts. The New Testament's body of Christ metaphor says God created Christians with differences, has endowed them with different gifts and has designed things so that diversity within the church is natural and normal.

There are three major passages elaborating the body of Christ image: Romans 12:4-8, 1 Corinthians 12:4-31 and Ephesians 4:4-16. Each addresses the problem of the diversity of spiritual gifts, interests and emphases within the unity of the church. Each time the metaphor is the human body, which is one entity but is made up of various parts. There are eyes, ears and feet, each different and each with a different function: "we, who are many, are one body in Christ, and individually we are members one of another. We have gifts that differ according to the grace given to us." (Rom 12:5-6).

Scripture's most famous passage on unity comes at the beginning of the Ephesians passage on the body of Christ:

> There is one body and one Spirit, just as you were called to the one hope of your calling, one Lord, one faith, one baptism, one God and Father of all, who is above all and through all and in all. (Eph 4:4-6)

From this sublime celebration of unity comes the slogan of the World Council of Churches, and indeed, of the whole ecumenical movement: "One Lord, one faith, one baptism."

When this famous sentence is examined in its context in the letter to the Ephesians, it becomes clear that what Paul is really addressing is the serious *problem* of maintaining this kind of unity in the midst of disagreement. And the same is true of *each* of the body of Christ passages.

The dissension is evident throughout the passage. In Ephesians 4:14 Paul speaks of those who are "tossed to and fro and blown about by every wind of doctrine." In 4:18 he refers to those who are like Gentiles, darkened in their understanding, alienated because of ignorance. And at the end of the chapter, in verse 31, he speaks of the presence of bitterness, wrath, anger, wrangling and slander among those to whom he is writing.

On careful examination even the opening words of this body of Christ passage point to that quarrelsome context. One is likely to breeze through the introductory verses of Ephesians 4 without paying too much attention, on the way to those famous words on unity. But Paul begins, "I . . . beg you to lead a life worthy of the calling to which you have been called." Why does he beg? Clearly the unity was not then present.

When the setting for each of the other two major body of Christ passages is examined, it becomes equally clear that the context is one of disagreements within the church. The Romans 12 passage follows a chapter in which Paul discusses a serious controversy, frequently reflected in the New Testament, between Jewish and Gentile Christians.

At the end of this passage Paul offers a series of pithy bits of advice, most of them calling for peace among people who are clearly quarreling with each other: "Let love be genuine. . . . Be patient in suffering. . . . Bless those who persecute you. . . . Live in harmony with one another; do not be haughty. . . . Do not repay anyone evil for evil. . . . If it is possible, so far as it depends on you, live peaceably with all. . . . Never avenge yourselves. . . . Do not be overcome by evil, but overcome evil with good" (Rom 12:9-21).

Similarly the 1 Corinthians 12 passage, the longest and most fully elaborated of the three, follows a lengthy discussion of some specific disputes over eating meat previously offered to idols (10:14-33); the place of women in the church, about which some were "disposed to be contentious" (11:1-16); and the celebration of the Lord's Supper, about which "I hear that there are divisions among you" (11:17-34).

It is in this context of disagreements and divisions that the church is described as the body of Christ made up of many parts and organs, of which even the weaker and "less presentable" are indispensable. And God has so composed the body "that there may be no dissension within the body, but the members may have the same care for one another" (1 Cor 12:25).

Explicit guidance on living with diversity. Some explicit guidance on living with diversity in the church, typical of the Scriptural stance, comes at the beginning of the body of Christ passage in Ephesians. After begging his readers to "lead a life worthy of the calling to which you have been called" (4:1), Paul goes on in verses 2-3 to offer some practical advice on how to achieve the sublime unity of "one Lord, one faith, one baptism" (4:5), which is the ideal, but which his readers do not really have.

Christians lead a life worthy of their calling "with all humility and gentleness," Paul says (v. 2). Humility in the context of disagreements within the church means recognizing that those with whom we disagree might possibly be right and that we might be wrong. It does not prevent Christians from doing their best to arrive at the right conclusions about troublesome issues or from following their consciences once they have reached those conclusions. But it is a warning against arrogance.

Christians are to live such a life "with patience, bearing with one another in love" (v. 2). To patiently bear with someone else is to put up with some things one may not like. Love "bears all things," Paul writes in another famous passage, 1 Corinthians 13. Those who love one another can accept conscientious differences.

This bearing with one another in love is more likely to take place *within* a congregation, where love is experienced personally, than at a distance. It is easy to resent those at denominational headquarters or those in some stridently pro-life or pro-choice organization about which one reads in the papers, who promote an abortion stance different from one's own. But that "bearing with one another in love" is the biblical stance on which the whole church, at every level, is built.

In Ephesians 4:3 Paul makes unity an explicit goal for Christians. They live lives worthy of their calling "making every effort to maintain the unity of the Spirit in the bond of peace." What Paul is calling for here in the midst of a divisive situation is a *bias* for unity, a conscious effort to preserve it, an attempt to find spiritual unity even when it is hard to do so.

A vivid example of such a bias for unity was seen in 1990 at the consecration of the Episcopal Church's bishop for the armed forces. The bishop-elect was a former military chaplain. Near the beginning of the ceremony a number of certifications were read: he had been duly elected to the bishopric, approved by the appropriate authorities and found to be fully qualified. Then the presiding bishop asked if anyone present knew any reason why the consecration should not proceed. A woman representing the Episcopal Peace Fellowship came forward and read a statement objecting, on behalf of her organization, not to this particular candidate but to the ordination and consecration of any bishop to serve the armed forces. It was a strong protest from the pacifist perspective against the church's cooperation with the military. But as she concluded her statement she related that both she and the bishop-elect had participated the night before in a prayer vigil for peace. She promised that despite her objections she would remain in the cathedral and take part in the rest of the service. Her spirit made it an eloquent witness for peace—not only the antiwar peace her organization promoted, but the peace in Christ that demands unity in the church.

Paul thus offers practical guidance for those faced with diversity and dissension in the church: an attitude toward the self characterized by humility and gentleness that keeps us from confusing our own opinions with the voice of God, a patient and accepting attitude toward others that keeps on loving fellow-Christians even when we disagree with them and a specific intention to maintain unity that puts our oneness in the body of Christ ahead of our human differences.

These passages provide a model, widely acceptable to evangelicals and liberals alike, for living with our diversity. In spite of the compelling image of the body of Christ, however, serious threats to unity do occur, as at the present time. A second recurring biblical theme for such times and situations, therefore, is that of reconciliation.

Reconciliation. Throughout this book the term *reconciliation* is used frequently. We use it to describe both the process by which evangelicals and liberals within the church address their differences and the goal toward which they are working. Unless the word is carefully defined, it can be misleading.

We use the term in what we believe to be the biblical sense. In ordinary usage, to *reconcile* means to restore a broken or damaged relationship, often by resolving differences. There are times when it is used in the Bible in this commonsense way. (See, for instance, Mt 5:24—"first be reconciled to your brother or sister"—or 1 Sam 29:4.)

As a uniquely biblical concept, however, reconciliation refers to God's action in the sacrificial death of Jesus Christ that restores the relationship, broken by sin, of human beings to God. A typical passage describing this is Romans 5:8-11:

> God proves his love for us in that while we still were sinners Christ died for us. Much more surely, then, now that we have been justified by his blood, will we be saved through him from the wrath of God. For if while we were enemies, we were reconciled to God through the death of his Son, much more surely, having been reconciled, will we be saved by his life. But more than that, we even boast in God through our Lord Jesus Christ, through whom we have now received reconciliation.

Other similar passages on reconciliation are found in 2 Corinthians 5, Ephesians 2 and Colossians 1.

But though this reconciliation of sinners to God through Christ Jesus is basic, it does not end the process. For those who are reconciled to God must also be reconciled to each other.

> But now in Christ Jesus you who once were far off have been brought near by the blood of Christ. For he is our peace; in his flesh he has made both groups into one and has broken down the dividing wall, that is the hostility between us . . . that he might create in himself one new humanity in place of two, thus making peace, and might reconcile both groups to God in one body through the cross, thus putting to death that hostility through it. . . . For through him both of us have access in one Spirit to the Father. (Eph 2:13-18)

Here the reference is to the New Testament division between Jews and Gentiles. This is also the case in a similar passage in Romans 11. But elsewhere the New Testament generalizes this interpersonal reconciliation that grows out of reconciliation with God. "In this is love, not that we loved God but that he loved us and sent his Son to be the atoning sacrifice for our sins. Beloved, since God loved us so much, we also ought to love one another" (1 Jn 4:10-11).

This biblical reconciliation takes place within the church, in the community of those who have been reconciled to God. It does not mean the elimination of differences and achievement of full agreement on all subjects. As we have been noting, the biblical model is one of unity with diversity. Nor does reconciliation mean suppressing or ignoring differences in order to act as if they did not exist. The biblical church recognizes and confronts diversity; it does not have to compromise principle by merely accepting some halfway point between two opposing positions.

Christian reconciliation is a spiritual process, a unity in a common Lord despite differences in interpreting that Lord's requirements. It is a bridging of what had been polarized that restores a loving relationship between people who may continue to disagree. It becomes possible "in Christ."

A look at two biblical themes does no more than sample the rich resources of Scripture for a polarized church. But these themes do provide a biblical perspective not for eliminating differences but for accepting them in love, for liberal and evangelical alike.

The Perspective of Theological Reflection

In using the church's own resources to develop an understanding of our polarization, we turn finally to theology. Much is said in this book about the processes by which opposing views can be understood and alienated people can be brought together. But for Christians theology is far more basic than process. Protestant Christians have a rich tradition of theological reflection on puzzling issues. The task is made more difficult, however, because the field of theology is itself fragmented in our times.

There was a time in American history when denominations shared a more common theological orientation. In the early days Americans' shared Reformed background and common experience of the Great Awakenings provided much theological unity across denominational lines. At times of sharp divisions (such as the fundamentalist-modernist controversies of the 1920s and 1930s), a shared reverence for the Bible and a common evangelical message still bound Protestant Christians together. As recently as the mid-twentieth century, neo-orthodoxy provided a generally accepted theological perspective for Protestants of many denominations. There were disagreements, as always throughout church history, but there were commonly accepted theological ground rules for confronting them. Karl Barth, Emil Brunner, Rudolph Bultmann, Dietrich Bonhoeffer, Paul Tillich—all at least dealt with the same issues.

Liberal theology. No longer is this the case. The late sixties brought a variety of liberation theologies: Third World, black, feminist (for instance, Gustavo Gutiérrez, James Cone, Rosemary Radford Ruether). In the nineties ecological theologies began to focus on planetary survival and even broader kinds of liberation, extending beyond humankind (for example, Larry Rasmussen). What all the newer approaches have in common is an insistence that every theology must be understood in a particular context.[7] The editors of the extraordinarily comprehensive research project that resulted in the Presbyterian Presence series call them "issue-oriented theologies." Contextualization of all theological inquiry and an acceptance of theological pluralism as normative have been major motifs on liberal seminary campuses.

This series, though Presbyterian, was offered as a case study for all mainline Protestantism. One volume deals with today's theological pluralism under the title *The Confessional Mosaic*.[8] The mosaic metaphor signals a theology fragmented into bits and pieces—"diverse forms and visions," as one of the editors, Milton J. Coalter, described it in a comment on this volume.[9] Similar themes are sounded in another volume of the series, *The Pluralistic Vision.*

"Expanding pluralism is without a doubt the central theme of Presbyterian theological and liturgical development in the twentieth century," says Coalter.[10] The same is true of liberal theology generally. In such a context we are faced with the double dilemma of dealing theologically with polarization in the church when theology itself offers little common ground from which to start.

These various theologies, although posing the dilemmas of pluralism, do fulfill important tasks. Some of them draw upon classic theologies and build on them. They attempt to correct the omissions and distortions of the past, particularly in relation to some group that has been ignored, dismissed or misused by theologians, who are human and fallible. By focusing upon the distortions and omissions and attempting a reconstruction that takes seriously what has been neglected or mishandled, it is quite humanly possible, of course, to do one's own distorting and dismissing. This is a time of lively theological ferment, however, and the "systematic" theologies of the future will eventually be enriched by these important new insights. Until we have some new synthesis that incorporates these partial theologies, however, contemporary liberal theology is not well equipped to overcome the strains caused by our diversities.

Theology in the evangelical wing. In such a period of theological pluralism, the evangelical wing of Protestantism has turned elsewhere for its theological undergirding. The second half of the twentieth century, in which evangelicalism has become a major force in American Christianity, has seen the rise of two major nondenominational evangelical seminaries, Fuller in California and Gordon-Conwell in Massachusetts.[11] These institutions have been attended by numerous ministerial candidates from mainline churches who have rejected the predominant liberalism of their own denominational seminaries and sought a more conservative alternative. Along with Wheaton College (another major evangelical fountainhead) and a rapidly growing evangelical scholarship and publishing enterprise, they have provided an alternative theological base for the conservatives of mainline churches.

The theology taught in these seminaries has followed the lines of classic conservative Protestantism. Augustine provides the base line; Calvin, Luther and other reformers are regarded as continuing the Augustinian tradition. The Calvinism nurtured by the Christian Reformed Church and the lively Calvin Studies Society has been an important contemporary source, as has the British evangelical movement. Louis Berkhof of Calvin Seminary and J. I. Packer, a British theologian teaching at Regent College in Vancouver and also currently a senior editor for *Christianity Today,* are major figures. The neo-orthodox greats of the midcentury period—Barth, Brunner and the Niebuhrs (Reinhold, H. Richard and Richard R.)—are studied, though with caution.

Apart from the theological undergirding provided by Fuller, Gordon-Conwell and other sources within the evangelical movement, some leaders and movements within mainline theology have also contributed to current evangelical theology. Donald G. Bloesch is a major contemporary theologian clearly in the evangelical camp. Methodist theologian Thomas C. Oden of Drew Theological Seminary has been instrumental in refocusing on the classic writings of the early church fathers. Presbyterian theologian John H. Leith, professor emeritus of Union Theological Seminary in Virginia, has been in the forefront of contemporary mainline Reformed studies.

In a sense, then, one of the elements in the contemporary "confessional mosaic" has been a thriving evangelical theology following classic conservative Protestant lines. But the theological worlds of the liberal and evangelical camps are quite distinct. The contextualized liberationist, black, feminist and ecological theologies receiving attention at most contemporary mainline seminaries have little in common with the Augustinianism and Calvinism of today's evangelicals. It should be noted, however, that classic and neo-orthodox theologies are regularly taught at mainline and ecumenical seminaries also.

The Reformed tradition. Both of the authors of this book come out of the Reformed tradition. Knowing that this tradition has been important for Protestant theology generally, we turn to it with some confidence that Christians of many traditions will find its insights helpful. As is true with appeals to Scripture itself, the Reformed theological tradition does not offer a solution to the problem of diversity. It does, however, offer a way of addressing it. Three aspects of the Reformed tradition and of classic Protestantism in general are especially relevant to a polarized church.

The first of these is the centrality of Scripture as God's primary way of communicating with humankind. A classic Reformed statement is found in the Westminster Confession: "The whole counsel of God, concerning all things necessary for his own glory, man's salvation, faith, and life, is either expressly set down in Scripture or by good and necessary consequence may be deduced from Scripture."[12]

Second is the process described in the final clause of that quotation: the deducing from Scripture "by good and necessary consequence." This is the basis of the important role human enterprise takes in theological reflection— and the source of our differences. It is no accident that preeminent among early works of Protestant theology was John Calvin's *Institutes of the Christian Religion.* Nor is it accidental that the Reformed tradition has been a major source of Protestant theology in the centuries since.

A third aspect of the Reformed tradition that illuminates our differences lies in its radical distinction between sovereign God and sinful humanity. Says a major contemporary theologian, "Calvin's theology and Reformed theology in general is significantly shaped by a radical distinction between the Creator and the creature, between the self-existent being of God and the dependent being of the creature. This distinction is another way of stating the doctrine of the sovereignty of God."[13]

Theology is an enterprise of fallible human beings. Like all our scriptural interpretation, it is subject to error. Only God is God, with final knowledge and final truth. Liberal and evangelical alike, sharing the Reformed theological tradition, are reminded that no matter how earnest our intentions or careful our exegesis, we may be wrong.

The Nature, Purpose and Mission of the Church

In this context let us examine a down-to-earth issue. From a theological perspective, one of the major areas of controversy in today's church has to do with the nature, purpose and mission of the church. A number of the church leaders we interviewed, both liberal and evangelical, saw internal differences regarding this issue as central in today's polarization. Shorthand phrases most frequently used to describe the divergent views of the purpose of the church were *evangelism* and *social justice*. This perception fits with the first of the three crises identified by sociologist Jeffrey Hadden (cited in chapter three), which had to do with the meaning and purpose of the church. Today's clergy, Hadden says, are redefining that purpose in terms of social justice.

An evangelical pastor describes the difference in terms of the way the two sides see the problem the church is called to address. Liberals, he says, see the world's suffering as the problem. The liberal church's response is to reorganize economics and politics to meet the needs of that suffering world. The nature of the church, for them, is to give hope, to be a helping hand to the suffering world. For evangelicals sin is the problem, and the hurting of the world is a manifestation of that problem. They also respond by addressing the hurt but most basically by addressing the sin. The nature of the church, for evangelicals, is to proclaim the good news that in Jesus Christ sin is taken care of.

From an even more conservative perspective the president of a confrontational group within a mainline denomination calls for a return to "the unique mission of the church" that no nonchurch organization has, which is based on the Bible. He says we must eliminate the political agenda:

We have no business with that kind of political agenda. I'm not saying we shouldn't speak to the political arena. But to be involved in politics—for instance, the Washington office and the office at the United Nations and all the things we do and say involving international policies—we're spending money and time that should be going into other activities.

The liberal middle judicatory executive, however, sees political involvement from a different perspective:

We used to say conservatives didn't want to make social pronouncements. But about the first thing the Presbyterian Church in America did when it created itself was to take a stand on prayer in public schools. So it was never that they didn't believe the church ought to speak to the state. It was always that they didn't agree with what we were saying.

The evangelical pastor of an ethnic-Japanese, West Coast congregation claims evangelism—understood as the proclamation of the good news of salvation in Jesus Christ—as the central purpose of the church. "Many of the denominational staff people are practically universalists," he says. "They don't believe people are lost in sin. They don't have a theology of evangelism, a theology of mission. We believe people are lost in sin without Jesus Christ and he is the only way."

An opposing view was expressed by the liberal director of a denominational women's ministry unit:

I think what we are all called to do is to bring some form of critical analysis to the structures of society that are unjust. I want the church to be able to speak to issues of justice in society, and to be faithful. . . . There are people who say we're here to save souls, but for them saving souls means getting more members in the church, period. You do that the best way you can or any way at all, and that means you don't deal with these issues. . . . If bringing the homeless person in and saying, "Stay here, and we'll work together on this system that keeps you homeless"—if that were part of what we mean by saving souls, I would agree, because that would mean binding up the wounds at the same time. I guess spiritualizing it to the point that we don't see the needs of the lives around us is what I find difficult.[14]

Yet there are points of contact. Although there were clear differences in what the evangelical pastor and the liberal administrator saw as the nature and basic purpose of the church—one emphasizing traditionally defined evangelism and the other social justice—neither was willing to totally exclude the concern of the other. The denominational leader sought a definition of saving souls that *included* binding up wounds, while the evangelical pastor spoke later of compassionate ministries in which his own congregation was involved.

Yet even in this overlap of views there lurk differences in the definition of social justice and evangelism. The social-justice programs in which many evangelical congregations are deeply involved and to which they frequently point are likely to be focused on compassionate outreach to meet human needs: the homeless, the hungry, the battered and victimized, the handicapped and oppressed. Liberals are likely to support such compassionate ministries yet regard them as Band-Aids, and they may feel that real social justice can come only through changing the structures of society.

Similarly, evangelicals are likely to understand evangelism in terms of the proclamation of the gospel, through overseas mission and local witnessing and in conjunction with new church development. Liberals are likely to seek a more inclusive definition, in which the quest for social justice is a vital part of evangelism.

Compromise definitions can be and have been worked out by joint committees and approved by governing bodies. There remains, however, an underlying conviction by many evangelicals that the proclamation of good news is at the heart of the nature and purpose of the church. Many liberals have a comparable underlying conviction that the church exists to bring about a more just society.

Perhaps Peter L. Berger's *The Heretical Imperative*[15] is illuminating in understanding the ease with which liberals take the humanitarian concern for social justice seriously but the uneasiness some of them have with evangelism. Some liberals have taken Berger's "inductive option," which makes *one's own experience* the ground of religious affirmation, albeit within a particular range of traditions. "The substitution of hypothesis for proclamation is profoundly uncongenial to the religious temperament," he says.[16] Many people who have struggled through their own experience to a faith stance that may not entirely assuage their hunger for certainty are likely to be uncomfortable trying to persuade others. They prefer to be nonauthoritarian, encouraging others to engage in their own struggle. This contrasts starkly with an evangelical who would "bear witness" not to vague spiritual principles or to the ideal of openness but to Christ himself. As an evangelical pastor put it in our Ecunet computer exchange, "He [Christ] is not just another religious option; he is the way through which we all must pass."

Yet a simplistic polarization—between evangelicals for whom evangelism is the purpose of the church and liberals for whom that purpose is social justice—is rejected by many on both sides. In an upcoming chapter we will note many encouraging signs of progress on what some regard as the false dichotomy between evangelism and social justice. Such efforts require wrestling with these differing definitions, however, or even serious attempts to reconcile views will ultimately fail.

Peggy Shriver attended a denominational consultation designed to unite evangelicals and liberals around both purposes of the church. A participant whom she interviewed commented that "the consultation was fatally flawed by a decision not to define evangelism and justice." This failure was obvious to Shriver in two parallel examples.

The first was of a southern congregation that took its responsibilities for dealing with issues of social justice in the state capital seriously. It also had a program for feeding hungry people at the church, including a Sunday lunch. The pastor expressed discomfort at seeing the congregation bowed in prayer in the sanctuary, while outside the stained glass windows a long queue of the homeless was lining up for a free meal. The homeless would be welcome, but only if they were comfortable attending a service with a high liturgy.

The other example was of an integrated congregation in a northern city where members of the congregation not only served meals to the homeless but sat and asked them about their lives and followed up with visits to the place where they could be reached. "We figure that people who can't feed themselves have some spiritual problems too," observes the pastor of this church. Some of the people met through this ministry become members of the congregation.

Here were two efforts to do both social justice and evangelism, but the difference in way these churches prioritized these goals produced significantly different results. (Another issue to be explored is how religious

institutions receiving federal or state funds to supply food to the homeless
are restricted by the government.) An important discussion about these
ministries could have taken place had a way been found in this carefully
designed denominational consultation to juxtapose them.

To the extent that both liberals and evangelicals are committed to social
justice and to evangelism, the dichotomy between the two understandings of the purpose of the church is a false one. Yet significant
differences remain, particularly in primary emphasis, and the underlying
concept of the purpose of the church remains a polarizing issue.

An Essential Starting Point

Whatever its specifics, a theology that accepts and affirms diversity as well
as unity is an essential starting point for the project represented by this book
and for understanding the nature and mission of the church. The vast
majority of those in the pews and, indeed, the majority of ideologically
committed church leaders believe we are called as Christians to work for
reconciliation, for conditions of peace and mutual love within the church.

Few interpret this biblical call to peacemaking in the pews as outlaw-
ing diversity. But permissible diversity requires an overarching unity.
Diversity of opinion—including disagreements on fairly basic matters of
faith and conviction—was characteristic of the New Testament church
and has been so for the church of every succeeding age. But the Christian
is expected to live with diversity in a spirit of Christian love and mutual
upbuilding. On this nearly all Protestants are agreed. Of the church
leaders interviewed by the authors as part of this project, all but one affirm
their basic conviction that there are authentic Christians on both sides of
the theological divide and that the appropriate course for the church in
the face of such polarization is to seek ways of reducing the tension and
living together in Christian love.

The one interviewee who does not share this outlook, a pastor of a
congregation, sees the purity of the faith as the highest priority and
convincing the other side of its error as the most appropriate course of
action. This is a legitimate Christian stance, affirmed historically by those
at the sectarian end of Ernst Troeltsch's classic church-sect typology. In
church history it has led to the exodus from the mainstream of those who
have formed smaller and less pluralistic denominations. Clearly others have

remained in the original denomination without theologically accepting its pluralism.

Many more Christians whom we interviewed, including some on both sides of the theological divide, are uncomfortable with either the extent or the apparent absence of limits on present-day diversity. Some evangelicals feel, as one interviewee puts it, that the most dangerous polarization is between those who can affirm the historic creeds of the church, the authority of Scripture and the uniqueness of Christ and those who cannot. This church leader has serious questions as to whether there can be real community with those for whom these creeds and doctrines no longer carry meaning. Some liberals feel that fundamentalists at the extreme of the conservative spectrum are interested only in winning the argument and that by their own attitudes they exclude themselves from any meaningful mutual understanding.

With the one exception noted above, however, all those we interviewed affirmed their commitment to the kind of unity with diversity taught in Scripture and in classic Protestant theology.

A seminary president bases an eloquent defense of this kind of openness to diversity on a central doctrine of the Reformed tradition:

> If we take Reformed theology seriously and really listen to our own doctrine that only God is sovereign, then we must recognize that my position and your position are not sovereign. . . . I think that's basic to the Reformed tradition. It means we have to be open to each other's corrective, however unlikely we think that corrective may be. . . . We are fallible human beings. None of us possesses absolute truth. We have always affirmed that we are more likely to find truth in community than in isolation. Community means listening to each other as well as sharing with each other—sharing with a sense of humility rather than arrogance, listening with openness rather than defensiveness. All that springs from our theology. And that's what the church needs to recapture.

This is a position both authors of this study, representing in some measure liberal and evangelical perspectives, strongly support.

Part 2

. . . .

How the
Tie Unravels

5

....

Snarls & Snags
The "Single Issues"

All of us have to take our vows for the peace and unity of the church very seriously.
We can't let ourselves be used for destructive purposes,
no matter which vision of the church we hold.
A MINISTER AND COLLEGE PRESIDENT

Where do we go from here? We have examined the sharp cleavages that split today's churches. We have looked at their cultural context and the ways in which observers see the polarization. We have examined this in the church's own terms, from a biblical and confessional perspective. In the closing section of the last chapter we affirmed a biblical and theological stance that honors both unity and diversity.

Are our divisions an inevitable reflection of a divided culture, with which we will have to live until the culture itself is healed? Are our respective views of the nature and purpose of the church reconcilable? Are there aspects of the rift that cannot be bridged?

These were questions we asked leaders from all parts of the church, north, south, east and west as well as from a variety of denominations and from both liberal and evangelical camps. Most were convinced that
□ though our internal divisions are related to the cultural divide, the

church has a special obligation—perhaps an obligation *to* our society and *for* our society—to seek to transcend cultural influences

☐ though there are different views of the nature and purpose of the church, there is much commonality

☐ though there are limits to permissible compromise and accommodation, we can live together in the church without violating those limits

Most important, we acknowledge that the Bible is authoritative for all of us. Scripture offers no prospect of a church without differences. But God is sovereign; we are not. We are commanded by God to overcome our hostilities and to live together in love.

The primary objective of the interviews and "listening sessions" conducted for this research project was to discover practical and workable ways of overcoming polarization. What success stories could church leaders and others tell us? What attitudes and behaviors have reduced polarization, pointed toward reconciliation and permitted us to live with our differences in love? What actions have been effective in specific instances and specific ways?

We discovered that there are indeed many success stories. But there have also been failures. Clearly there are snarls and snags that threaten "the tie that binds." In some situations differences have been widened and the polarization made worse. If we are to identify positive paths toward reconciliation, we must also examine the obstacles. What are the dangers to be avoided?

As we listened to the stories of church people and as we questioned church leaders, we began to identify harmful *attitudes*. Certain attitudes— toward oneself and one's own group as well as toward "the opposition"— hinder reconciliation. We also began to identify particular kinds of *actions*, behaviors that make things worse instead of better. We discovered, however, that apart from attitudes and the actions of one's adversaries there appear to be certain *issues*, specific areas of disagreement, that are *in themselves* polarizing. To these we turn first.

The Single Issues

"It is the social issues that divide us," said a pastor who has served as head of her denomination's national governing body as she reflected on the state of the church. "Polarization becomes worse over issues of reproductive rights (abortion) and lifestyle issues such as homosexuality." Seeking to draw a distinction between cultural and religious motivations, she went on to suggest that this problem arises when people follow their own "opinions" rather than the gospel.

A liberal pastor of a congregation in New York state offers a similar analysis: "I think there are three or four key issues that do separate us. And no matter how hard we analyze and seek to reflect on those and seek to understand one another, we are just a great distance apart on issues like choice and abortion, issues around sexual morality—particularly affirming homosexual lifestyles, but all sexuality issues." Not only are these issues ones on which constituencies within the church are most likely to clash, they are also issues on which they are likely to find no "give" on the part of the opposition. Some leaders call them "social issues." Others, noting the focused passion of activists, call them "single issues." In the political arena they are sometimes known as "hot-button issues."

The term *social issues* can refer to a broad range of problems far beyond these hot buttons at the center of the cultural and religious conflict in our times. For this reason we shall in this discussion use the term *single issues*. In the chapters ahead we will examine in a more general way the attitudes that stand in the way of reconciliation. We shall also look at specific kinds of actions that can become obstacles. But first, in the remainder of this chapter we shall look at those issues that are in themselves polarizing— the single issues.

A Denominational Case Study: Sexuality, Abortion and the Ordination of Homosexuals

The most conspicuous and public struggles over the single issues have taken place throughout the 1990s within the Presbyterian Church. In 1991 the attention of American Presbyterians was riveted on a report on human sexuality, provocatively entitled "Keeping Body and Soul Together." It became the religious news story of the year for much of the American press. The report had been prepared over a five-year period by the Task Force on Human Sexuality for presentation to the denomination's General Assembly, which met in Baltimore that year. It was one of the most controversial reports ever addressed by the denomination. Opposition to it reached massive proportions in the months preceding the General

Assembly meeting. Even before it was publicly released, denunciations based on unofficial or bootleg copies were widely circulated. The task force was accused of holding up release until the last possible minute to keep opponents from having time to organize. But if this was the strategy, it failed. Evangelicals, middle-of-the-roaders and moderate liberals as well mobilized in large numbers to defeat it.

In some ways the most emotion-laden issue addressed by the human-sexuality report was homosexuality. Ordination of self-affirming homosexuals (with the subordinate issue of whether homosexual practice is, in Christian terms, sinful) had for some years been a major agenda item for all mainline American denominations. The Presbyterian Church had officially regarded homosexual practice as sinful and rejected such ordinations. (A 1989 survey indicated that more than three quarters of all Presbyterians, both clergy and laypersons, believe homosexual relations are wrong.) The 1991 sexuality report would have condoned homosexuality and suggested removing barriers to ordination.

Beyond the homosexuality issue on which much attention focused, however, was a broader affirmation of various kinds of sexuality. Under certain conditions of mutuality and "justice-love," the report opened the door to premarital and extramarital sex. The traditional Christian ethic of sexuality and marriage was challenged.

The report called forth a larger number of "overtures" (communications proposing action) from middle judicatories to the General Assembly than any previous issue in the denomination's history. There were also numerous communications from local church governing bodies and other official groups asking that the report be rejected. And rejection was, indeed, the outcome, though it came with a call for continued study by the whole church of the issues that had been raised.

In early 1992 Presbyterian attention shifted to a report by the Special Committee on Problem Pregnancies and Abortion, which had been prepared for that year's General Assembly.

These two reports and the responses they evoked from the church were not parallel. The report on human sexuality reflected a position at one end of the Presbyterian spectrum—probably an extreme end. There had been numerous charges that the composition of the task force was "stacked." After the first year of its deliberations two conservative members had resigned, saying that the outcome seemed predetermined and their own position was not being heard. At the next General Assembly, additional representatives of the evangelical wing of the church had been added in an attempt to make the task force more representative. They were, however, unable to impact the process except through a minority report. The task force's majority report clearly represented a position at the far liberal end of the spectrum.

Speaking four months before the report was considered by the General Assembly, the editor of an independent church journal described what was happening with a high degree of accuracy:

> I think there is a liberal group in the church, associated with the forthcoming sexuality report and the sentiments it expresses, that has set itself up for a dreadful disappointment. This special committee to study human sexuality, which in my opinion is unrepresentative and is bent on promoting an agenda which the latest polls indicate an overwhelming majority in the church is simply not prepared to accept, has decided to "go for broke" on this report—no compromise. They're going to present a paper and recommendations that really go all the way in overturning the centuries-old traditions of the church in the area of sexuality—including homosexuality. I think the response is going to be so overwhelmingly negative that the most advanced liberal group in the church is going to feel like it has suffered a major defeat. The vast middle of the church is going to rise up and say no to this report.

His prediction turned out to be quite right.

At the General Assembly great care was given to the design and process of the standing committee that handled this report as its exclusive business. A process similar to the peace process used by President Jimmy Carter and his Middle East partners in reaching the Camp David accords was instituted, and the subject matter was almost as volatile as that addressed by these world leaders. Despite the document's shortcomings as a consensus-building paper, it became the instigator of serious dialogue on these issues for many Christians. But it was clearly rejected.

The Special Committee on Problem Pregnancies and Abortion, in preparing its report for the 1992 General Assembly, tried to take a different course. From the beginning it sought to prepare a report that all of its members could support, making room for the whole range of views on abortion representing the pluralism of the church. It appeared for a long time that this strategy would work. The resulting report did not try to lock the church into a rigid position, either pro-life or pro-choice, but instead allowed individual consciences to make their own determinations. It emphasized that the denomination "does not advocate abortion but instead acknowledges circumstances in a sinful world that may make abortion the least objectionable of difficult options."

Some pro-life committee members adhered to the original intention and signed the majority report. In the end, however, three members came to the conclusion that it was too permissive. They prepared a minority report taking a straight pro-life position.

In presenting the majority report to the General Assembly the committee chairperson said the special committee represented "the broadest spectrum of theological positions within the church":

> Because we were so divided by our convictions, our meetings were often punctuated by expressions of frustration, shock, disappointment . . . even anger . . . At one point, I had the idea that we would become so fragmented that we might bring in 14 reports and certainly at least three . . . The fact that 11 members of the special committee could reach agreement on a report at all is a miracle.[1]

Agreement was reached, he added, "because we believe the report represents a healthy balance of differing perspectives. In simple terms, friends, this report is where most Presbyterians really are on the question of abortion today." With some amendments the majority report was adopted.

Because there was no attempt to maneuver the General Assembly into adopting for the whole denomination a narrowly unrepresentative position, the abortion report did not occasion the turmoil brought on by the sexuality report a year earlier. This was one of the few instances we discovered of dealing with one of the single issues at the denominational level in a way that sought accommodation rather than victory. The report wisely affirmed the disagreement within the denomination on the issue.

In 1993 the sexuality issue once again occupied center stage for the denomination, this time focusing on the ordination of homosexuals. The presenting incident was a call from a church in Rochester, New York, inviting a self-affirming practicing lesbian minister to become its senior pastor. The denomination had in 1978 and 1979 officially barred the ordination of unrepentant practicing homosexuals. Its "definitive guidance" on the issue had been reaffirmed in the 1991 rejection of the human-sexuality report. However there was some question as to whether a homosexual minister ordained before the 1978 ruling could be affirmed in a call to a pastorate. The denomination's Permanent Judicial Commission, its final authority on constitutional interpretation, ruled in November of 1992 that the answer was negative and set aside the call.

In the aftermath of this case a movement aimed at reversing this ruling developed. It sought to change the denomination's Book of Order to strengthen the power of presbyteries to ordain ministers and the power of local church sessions to ordain elders or deacons on their own authority. (In the Presbyterian Church lay elders and deacons are ordained.) Other judicatories, however, sent overtures to the General Assembly asking that the previous stand forbidding such ordinations be reaffirmed. The General Assembly once again reaffirmed its "definitive guidance" prohibiting such ordinations. At the same time, however, it called for a three-year study of the issue, under conditions in which homosexuals could present their viewpoint in a nonthreatening context.

During the three-year study period one General Assembly replaced the "definitive guidance" with a stronger "authoritative interpretation" of the church's constitution, forbidding the ordination of self-affirming practicing homosexuals. At the end of the three years the 1996 General Assembly, in response to numerous overtures from both sides, once again revisited the question. This time the Assembly adopted an amendment to the denomination's Book of Order that became known as Amendment B:

> Those who are called to office in the church are to lead a life in obedience to Scripture and in conformity to the historic confessional standards of the church. Among these standards is the requirement to live either in fidelity within the covenant of marriage between a man and a woman or chastity in singleness. Persons refusing to repent of any self-acknowledged practice which the confessions call sin shall not be ordained and/or installed as deacons, elders or ministers of the Word and Sacrament.

Changes in the Book of Order adopted by a General Assembly must be affirmed by a majority of the denomination's presbyteries in the year following. This change was affirmed, and the "fidelity and chastity" amendment became part of the church's constitution. In an unprecedented reaction, however, a number of individual ministers and elders, and some congregations, announced their intention of refusing to obey the new constitutional provision.

The 1997 General Assembly adopted a new amendment (known as Amendment A) to replace Amendment B. This new amendment required those called to office in the church "to demonstrate fidelity and integrity in marriage or singleness, and in all relationships of life." If affirmed by the presbyteries, this would have had the effect of softening the previous year's action, allowing elasticity of interpretation. This attempt was defeated by the presbyteries in 1998, and the "fidelity and chastity" standard remained the official position of the denomination.

The Homosexual Ordination Issue in Other Denominations
Throughout the last decade of the twentieth century the ordination question has been fought out within nearly all pluralistic denominations. The United Church of Christ, having a long liberal tradition as well as a congregational polity that allows local decision making, has been the most open of the mainstream denominations. It has accepted homosexuals in the ministry for some years. Evangelicals within the denomination have been strongly opposed; the issue remains a controversial one, but the UCC is the one mainline denomination in which gay and lesbian ministers are officially recognized. In 1997 it appointed (in the Board for Homeland Mission) a national staff minister for lesbian and gay concerns. An effort at the 1997 General Synod to pass a resolution that would have encouraged "fidelity in marriage and chastity in singleness" for ordained ministers (wording similar to that passed by Presbyterians in 1996) was tabled. That left in place a flexible standard calling for "integrity and faithfulness" in marriage and in "other covenanted relationships."

In other mainstream denominations official policy still forbids such ordinations, but in most of them the struggle over this is ongoing and bitter. In the Episcopal Church the power of bishops over the ordination process has led to some such ordinations, tacitly accepted despite official denominational policy to the contrary. Statements by the church's bishops and action of a General Convention in the late 1970s had disapproved of the ordination of noncelibate homosexual persons. In 1996 a retired bishop was charged in an ecclesiastical trial with violating church doctrine for knowingly ordaining a sexually active gay man. The bishop was acquitted with a ruling that the action by the General Convention in the 1970s did not constitute church doctrine. The 1997 General Convention took no action on ordinations. It extended health-insurance benefits to domestic partners of members of the clergy and staff members (leaving it up to the diocese to define *domestic partners*) but refused to extend pension benefits to survivors of same-sex partnerships. The House of Deputies narrowly defeated (by a one-vote margin) a proposal to create a rite blessing same-sex unions.

Shortly after the 1997 General Convention a conservative Episcopal group (including four bishops), which calls itself the Episcopal Synod of America, held a convention. The delegates voted to form a separate province within the denomination. Leaders of the group denied that the proposed province constituted a schism, but they said it could pave the way for such a formal break in the future.

The United Methodist Church has been deeply divided on this issue for more than two decades. The official view of the church is that homosexuality is "incompatible with Christian teaching." The 1992 General Conference rejected a proposal to change that policy. In 1995 a minister serving in a prominent national staff position announced publicly that she was a lesbian, generating considerable controversy within the church. At the 1996 General Conference, a major effort to change the official policy was supported by the General Board of Church and Society and by nine annual conferences. It was once again defeated. During that General Conference, however, a group of fifteen bishops issued a statement dissenting from the denomination's position. In 1997 a group of pastors issued a "statement of conscience" disagreeing with the denominational ban on gay ordinations and same-sex unions. Several ministers have officiated at such unions amid controversy.

Early in 1998 a theological dialogue (the second of two) sponsored by the denomination's Commission on Christian Unity and Interreligious Concerns produced a paper called "In Search of Unity." It declared that issues related to homosexuality represent a fundamental challenge "so deep as to harbor the danger of explicit disunity or schism." Maxie Dunnam, president of Asbury Theological Seminary (and a member of the steering committee), said, "We're all weary of being preoccupied with the issue of homosexuality, but that is the issue the church is preoccupied with, and to ignore that is to ignore what is going on out there in the church."[2]

The Effect of These Struggles on the Church

In all pluralistic denominations in which the ordination of practicing homosexuals is a divisive issue, an adverse effect on denominational unity is evident. The future is uncertain. In some instances there may be outright schism. In others, there may be gradual schism through the erosion of members on the losing side as some sort of resolution is reached. In nearly all of them, the drawn-out struggle is likely to result in a continuation of the membership decline that has marked the past twenty years. The effect of this single issue on denominations is strongly negative. And behind it, of course, are the issues of biblical interpretation and of the nature and mission of the church and the whole range of polarizing issues we are examining in this book.

In the midst of the furor over the 1991 sexuality report, one of the few evangelicals serving at a senior level on the Presbyterian General Assembly expressed alarm at the way the church had been polarized over the single issues and at the bitterness engendered. He referred to the preliminary assumption we, the authors, voiced to him before our interview: that people on both sides of the polarization are authentic and devout Christians. "I'm meeting people on both sides that don't really affirm that," he remarked. On the single issues, he said, people were questioning the authenticity and faithfulness of their opponents. He felt that dissension over the single issues could seriously damage the church.

He is not alone in his observations. Among those interviewed for this book, the frequency with which denominational struggles over human sexuality, abortion and the ordination of homosexuals entered into the discussion indicated that these issues present a distinctive challenge to the churches at this particular time. We found similar concerns in all the inclusive denominations.

Other Single Issues

There are other single issues beyond sexuality and abortion. Certain gender-related questions are in this category. The ordination of women is no longer problematic for most mainstream Christians. The language of gender, however, is—particularly masculine imagery and terminology for God. It remains a major issue among evangelicals. One of the authors of this book conducted a purchaser's survey on language use in an ecumenical institutional hymnal and found that inclusive language referring to humans was strongly endorsed. References to God in stringently inclusive language received significantly lower approval.

A senior staffer comments on the atmosphere of obligatory p.c.—politically correct—terminology in his denominational headquarters. It permits no "Father" language and even calls into question the traditional baptismal formula, "in the name of the Father, the Son, and the Holy Spirit," he says.

"The writing-off is awesome," says another member of a denominational national staff. "Some conservatives write me off because I try to use inclusive language. And on the liberal side, one reference to God as 'he' can write you off."

Another single issue, more prominent in the recent past than today, has to do with war and peace. In the mid-1980s calls from mainline denominational agencies for "resistance" to national defense policy, through such means as nonpayment of taxes and other forms of radical activism, had been particularly divisive.[3] As with sexuality and abortion, national defense was an issue on which there was no meeting ground for divided Christians. During the 1991 Persian Gulf War the issue briefly held the church's attention, particularly that of the liberal wing of the church. In general, however, it has become a less urgent issue with the end of the cold war and the perceived reduction of nuclear threat.

Whether because of factors within the wider culture, factors within the churches themselves or both, homosexuality and abortion are the principle polarizing issues in today's pluralistic churches.

Contrast: Theological Issues

In sharp contrast to the battles over these single issues is the willingness of contemporary Christians to reach accommodations on theological issues. In one of our interviews a journalist pointed to the relatively smooth course followed by Presbyterians in reaching agreement on the Brief Statement of Faith in the 1980s. This short (eighty-line) statement summarizing all the major confessional affirmations of the church was adopted by the 1991 General Assembly. After preliminary approval by the preceding General Assembly it had been submitted to the denomination's 168 presbyteries, only two of which opposed it. Its final adoption came with hardly any debate.

Apparently it is not our beliefs in God, in Jesus Christ and in the Holy Spirit or our convictions about God's plan of salvation that divide us, says this strategically placed observer. It is our opinions on the social issues. Some have suggested that this contrast indicates stronger feelings about the single issues than about basic beliefs having to do with God and Jesus Christ. Perhaps we simply do not care as much about God as we do about abortion, they surmise. It is likely, however, that there are other factors at work.

One factor, undoubtedly, has to do with long-established church tradition. Differences over fine points of theology have been with us for centuries. Christians in pluralistic denominations have become accustomed to resolving them through church polity processes. Within this framework one of the buttresses of church government is the belief that the Holy Spirit can speak through duly constituted governing bodies who go about their task with faith and prayer. Long experience has accustomed Protestants to resolving theological issues through the polity processes. The protective proviso that God alone is the Lord of conscience and that Scripture alone is the highest written authority has been the safeguard that allowed such processes to work.

The single issues are in a different category. Private conscience does not always provide a court of last resort, since moral judgments regarding them are embedded in public law. The law, however, is open to change through both legislative and judicial processes. They are thus not only major issues in the churches today but are also major issues for the society at large.

In the United States both the abortion question and the acceptance of homosexuality have been kicked back and forth between recent presidential administrations and Congress. Political parties and election strategists have found it necessary to address them or to tiptoe around them. Constitutional issues relating to them have shown up at frequent intervals on the docket of the Supreme Court. The high level of controversy in American society at large is undoubtedly a major reason why these have been such intractable issues for the church. But there is a deeper reason too: Christians are unwilling to have their consciences bound on issues they consider biblically shaped or morally imperative by civil laws that they think can and should be changed. They insist on working to bring about such change.

In earlier chapters we have noted in more general terms the two-way relationship between churches and the culture that surrounds them. And in today's polarized society it is on these single issues that culture and religion impact each other most urgently. Many believe they are essentially religious issues. Certainly religious groups and persons with religiously formed consciences are prominent among American political and cultural activists. Television news clips of Operation Rescue protests routinely show a bussed-in church group being led in prayer by a pastor outside a blocked abortion clinic. The Religious Coalition for Abortion Rights is active on the other side of the protest.

It can be regarded as a religious battle that has moved beyond the churches and into the entire culture. Or perhaps it is best viewed as an entire culture fighting a war in which religious people are prominently manning the ramparts. Either way, to understand the polarization within the churches we must see its larger cultural context.

On the conservative side, Christians see a society increasingly devoid of moral values, a society that can be restored only by a return to the Judeo-Christian morality that earlier provided its base. On the liberal side, Christians see a pluralistic and multicultural society in which free choices among competing lifestyles and values are being threatened by conservatives intent on imposing their own values on all. The passion on both sides is engendered by the conviction that what is threatened is not just the way they worship—freedom of worship within their churches is still a given—but the whole society in which that freedom of worship has flourished. As we shall note in later chapters, the large number of persons who constitute a moderate middle are slow to respond to these issues, leaving much of the field to those ardently committed at either extreme.

This is at least part of the reason that within the church homosexuality and abortion, and to a lesser extent other single issues on which the whole culture divides, are *inherently divisive.* When they are addressed, the likely outcome is more polarization, not less. Since in our society they are currently political issues, a case is sometimes made that the place for Christians to engage in dialogue about them is the political arena.

Can the Single Issues Be Avoided in the Church?

To say that for this reason they should be avoided within the church is not a supportable position. The church does not flourish, nor does it faithfully serve its Lord, by wearing blinders. Precisely because these are essentially moral dilemmas, it is probable that the society's religious institutions and values will play a major part in ultimately resolving them.

We are, however, commanded not only to involve ourselves in the issues confronting society but also to maintain the peace and unity of the church, loving each other in spite of our diversity. We therefore may draw some conclusions about the way in which the church most faithfully grapples with these inherently divisive issues.

The stakes in a battle between competing moral visions that seek to define the whole society are perceived as extremely high. In both the church and the culture, those at both extremes rigidly hold their positions and are unwilling to give ground. In governing bodies at any level of church life, from local congregations to national assemblies, ballot-box victories can indeed be won by forcing votes. But long experience has shown that on these issues losers never go away thinking, "We were wrong and our opponents were right; we will therefore change our convictions regarding abortion" or homosexuality or whatever the issue.

In such a situation fights aimed at achieving parliamentary victory are counterproductive. Whether in a church convention establishing policy for a whole denomination, in regional governing bodies or even in councils or vestries of particular pluralistic congregations, forced decision-making on these controversial issues does not change people's minds and, on the contrary, is likely to be harmful.

Sometimes decisions must be made even when the issues are not resolved. When the National Council of the Churches of Christ in the U.S.A. was confronted with a request for admittance to membership by the Universal Fellowship of Metropolitan Community Churches (organized to welcome and made up predominantly of gays and lesbians), it faced an internal crisis of unity. A number of communions made it clear that they would leave the council if the UFMCC were admitted to membership. After much agony, prayer and negotiation, the council admitted that it simply *was not prepared to vote* on the issue. But in saying so it agreed to a series of consultations to educate its members. The dialogue committee that designed these instructive opportunities ended its report in 1992 with the hope of further conversations. The council, however, dismissed the committee and voted not to allow the UFMCC "observer" status, a minimal affiliation with no voting rights.

Resolution at the Denominational Level

We have not discovered an instance in which a pluralistic church has fully resolved its differences over abortion or homosexuality at the denominational level. Majority votes have established policy. But in all major pluralistic denominations that have dealt with these issues in churchwide conventions—Methodist, Lutheran, American Baptist, Disciples, Episcopal, Presbyterian—the defeated side has simply marshaled its forces to fight again another day. Such votes have not brought reconciliation.

Unfortunately, if no votes are taken there may come no teachable moment for hard truths. People often become engaged with an important complex issue only when a decision must be made. Recalling the civil-rights struggle of an earlier period, we are reminded that learning is frequently painful. It takes wise and prayerful leadership to know when the pain of decision-making is worth the risk of schism.

On single issues that are inherently polarizing in today's cultural context, the churches may need to employ a variety of ways of learning from Scripture, from one another, from Christians with different views and even from what God may be teaching us through the larger society. A policy paper may be the last, not the first, step toward achieving a nonpolarized, common mind. In denominational circles today there is a growing awareness that votes on the single issues will be most meaningful when a churchwide consensus has been formed. We will examine this trend in denominational decision making at greater length in chapter twelve.

Resolution at the Congregational Level

What about the people in the pews? A minister of the United Church of Christ comments on the tension among denominational leadership, by which he himself had been bruised. But "at the local congregational levels there have been a number of experiences of reconciliation," he says. In congregations all the classic ways in which the church addresses controversial issues—Biblical exposition and study, theological reflection, discussion, prophetic proclamation (but not political manipulation) by leaders, carefully designed educational processes—will, over a period of time, bring results.

But even within the congregational community, where personal relationships and face-to-face encounters make it possible to address the single issues directly, there are other productive ways of reducing the tensions these issues bring about. Church leaders interviewed for this study were asked whether the church is best served by discussing an issue or whether talking about it makes matters worse. Most leaders feel that it is essential to talk about our divisions. Few evangelicals, who often see biblical authority as the crucial issue, have reservations about addressing this concern directly. Liberals, however, are more likely to see the polarization in terms of the social issues (including these divisive single issues). Some have strong opinions about the way in which the issues should be talked about.

A number of leaders feel that movement toward reconciliation comes not by focusing on these single issues, which leads only to deadlock, but by addressing together those questions on which liberals and evangelicals can find some common ground. For the pastor of an American Baptist-related church in New York City, this means "framing the controversy in ways that will not make it permanent." He suggests working together on the problem of church growth and the crisis of membership. The fact that everybody has this problem "makes the conversation possible," he says.

The pastor of a church in upstate New York took the same approach. "The place to build community," he says, "is around those things that tend to unite us rather than those things that divide us." He too sees evangelism and membership recruitment as an area in which liberals and evangelicals can work together. "The national church development/evangelism unit has certainly drawn people from different backgrounds into that effort," he says.

The pastor of a New York City congregation also points to "compassionate actions in response to crisis situations" as an area in which liberals and evangelicals can work together. Leading evangelicals make similar suggestions. An evangelical college president identifies hunger and justice as issues on which joint efforts would mean "we wouldn't have so much energy to fight each other." A pastor of a West Coast congregation of the Reformed Church in America agrees: "Get them out where they can make a difference, working with the homeless, the hungry, the UN,

Congress—get them out where they're over their heads, and they'll quit being so fussy back in the church base."

Focusing on other matters is not by itself, of course, a satisfactory way of dealing with the single issues. There are occasions and situations in which they must be addressed directly. But the local congregation is the community in which these inherently divisive issues can be handled by studying the Bible, discussing, worshiping and working together in a climate of mutual love, not by pressing for political victories. In chapter ten we will look at a number of instances in which this has taken place.

A Variety of Patterns

As the church moves toward resolving these presently divisive issues, certain things will continue to happen. Some congregations in which people identify their positions on single issues as central to their faith will, by self-selection, become consensus congregations. Those who disagree will be encouraged, subtly or overtly, to leave for a more congenial church. Examples may be seen in pro-life congregations that participate on an institutional level in Operation Rescue demonstrations. At the other end of the spectrum are the More Light congregations, who elect self-affirming homosexuals to office in their own fellowships and seek the right to call them to their pastorates.

But most pluralistic congregations, ranging in orientation from moderately evangelical to moderately liberal, will see other dimensions of the faith as more central, will welcome (subtly as well as overtly) people on both sides of the single issues and will intentionally live with diversity. This middle ground is the region in which most Christians dwell. The single issues are obstacles in the way of reconciliation. But in today's society they are inevitably present. Inclusive congregations will study and discuss these polarizing issues with a goal of mutual understanding rather than make win-lose decisions.

Both kinds of congregations—those that have formed their own internal consensus and those that are open to all—will be important elements in moving toward the broad consensus that must eventually be formed by the churches in order to assist the society in defining itself morally.

6

. . . .

Dialogue
or Diatribe?

Attitudes That
Block Reconciliation

*There are liberals who are very intolerant. There are conservatives who
are very intolerant. There are liberals who look for conservatives
to misbehave themselves, and conservatives who look for liberals
to misbehave themselves. Those are hardest to deal with.
I don't have too many happy stories about either of those groups.*
A FORMER ECUMENICAL OFFICIAL

Our interviews with church leaders were full of indignant stories
about people in the other camp. People on both sides evidenced a
lack of trust. When a prominent liberal layman, active in denominational
leadership, was asked if he trusted the leaders of a conservative organization within the denomination he answered, "Oh, no! I don't trust any
of that crowd. Oh, I suppose there are some people I trust, but the
leadership is completely untrustworthy. They won't tell you the truth. . . .
They are liars and cheats and people of bad will."

From the opposite perspective, a spokesperson for that same conservative group said, "In dealing with the [denominational] leadership there
are always questions lurking in the back of our minds. 'Are they doing
this just to manipulate? Are they really being honest with us? Is there a
hidden agenda?'"

This spokesperson was asked, "Are there *any* of these leaders that you strongly disagree with but personally trust?"

"Up to this point, I don't know, I can't name any," he responded. "I have a very difficult time trusting the people in social justice and peace-making, and the women's unit and so forth."

Ill will was strongly apparent on both sides.

The Arrogance of Certitude

Some of the most troublesome obstacles to reconciliation are uncon-scious attitudes on the part of well-intentioned people. It is one of the anomalies of religious faith that certainty of conviction often breeds unintentional arrogance. No one wants a namby-pamby faith without deep belief. Even those most eager for openness to diversity within the church seldom suggest that what one believes doesn't matter or that one form of religion is as good as another. An authentic faith, deep and unshakable, is the Christian ideal. Yet paradoxically, those with the deepest certainty about their own beliefs are often the most intolerant of the "errors" of opposing views.

A woman serving as director of a denominational ministry unit de-scribes such arrogance:

> We get caught in a terrible self-righteousness, either as the church against the world, or as "my side" against "your side" or as "I'm more biblical" and "you're more sinful." The whole division is we-they. It's terrible in the church right now, even when I am "they"—as in "those women."

It is easier to identify arrogance in one's opponents than in oneself. The church leaders we interviewed, both liberals and evangelicals, recognized its presence in their own camp as well as that of the opposition.

In the liberal camp. "The liberal camp has given the impression of intellectual arrogance, elitism," says a liberal pastor. "At times we our-selves have done this, suggesting that 'if one were a good theologian one would see it this way.' You observe it in matters like the race issue, the Vietnamese war, even this recent [Persian Gulf] war."

The arrogance of liberal certitude is often identified in current jargon as *political correctness* or *p.c.* In addition to race and war, mentioned by this pastor, the focus of political correctness in church circles includes such things as inclusive language, acceptance of homosexuality and a pro-choice position on abortion—issues on which no variance from current liberal orthodoxy is acceptable.

Another denominational official spoke on this subject. He is himself a liberal by most criteria. He has, however, been a strong advocate of reaching out toward the evangelical wing of the church. He spoke of the strength of the "doctrine of political correctness" in denominational headquarters. He is, he said, personally opposed to the ordination of self-affirming homosexuals. "But you can't have such reservations in this place," he comments. "You are viewed immediately as homophobic."

He went on to speak of liberation theologies. He described himself as committed to a theology of liberation but with reservations in some areas. In p.c. terms, this is not acceptable. He reveals, "I have been criticized for saying the orthodox critique of liberation theologies is legitimate."

From a perspective outside denominational headquarters, a prominent theologian generally regarded as being in the conservative camp suggested that "political correctness is more fundamental in the church today than theology. Whether or not you believe God raised Jesus from the dead is an expendable matter. But whether or not you are 'correct' on the feminist issues or on the race issues (as their particular ideological group in the church understands them) is fundamental." And increasingly, he went on to add, "the seminaries have been corrupted this way."

A United Church of Christ seminary professor who is himself a liberal speaks feelingly of the arrogance and rigidity he had faced as part of a committee set up to prepare a denominational statement on economics.[1] He regards the committee as dominated by persons on the far left who held a Marxist, liberationist economic outlook. He explains,

> The staff and committee leadership had really "lopsided" the study in particular directions, and those of us in the middle felt that we were left out. In fact, we were disinvited from some committee meetings, and committee meetings were rescheduled at times. . . . Whether this can be resolved over time I don't know. World events, which have tended to undercut the attractiveness of the Marxist-socialist option, have laid some of it to rest. That was a very painful part of the church experience for me.[2]

An evangelical college president reported a similar experience with the Presbyterian General Assembly Task Force on Human Sexuality. She, along with one other evangelical task-force member, resigned from it after one year. "There was a very clear sense of what the agenda was and where it was going," she says.

In this instance, says the educator, "the language of openness" became a tool of a closed process. "When the language of openness becomes co-opted into a narrow kind of rigid adherence to a preset position," she comments, "the language itself becomes an occasion for suspicion." She goes on to describe that there was not a genuine listening and openness of process, yet the language of openness would be used on those who were more traditional, as a way to bludgeon them into adopting positions contrary to what they believed.

> That language of openness can be so intolerant. It's one of the ironies, I think. "How can you refuse dialogue?" they say. But in fact the other partner in the dialogue has already determined where they are. You are the one who needs to listen and learn, because of course you're homophobic if you have any kind of problem with the position they have adopted coming in. . . . So when I hear someone talking about openness and dialogue and all those things, my antennae go up and say, "Danger! danger!"

A similar charge of illiberalism on the part of liberals is made by a conservative Episcopal layman. "Some of the most close-minded people you run into are liberals," he says. "'Liberality of mind' I find to be often lacking. They will entertain every view but an opposing view, a conservative view, an evangelical view. They caricature those views."

On the conservative side. This same person acknowledges, however, that similar close-mindedness and caricaturing of the opposition takes place among evangelicals. The denominational official who was quoted above regarding the political correctness in church headquarters suggests that intolerance is equally strong at the conservative end of the church. "It doesn't feel to liberals like any move is being made from the other side," he says. "Folk in this building feel besieged."

A liberal pastor from Chicago told of an experience dealing with churches that had refused membership to self-affirming homosexuals on the basis of conviction that homosexuality is contrary to the word of God.

> Ideological purity is a tough, tough thing to deal with. If the people with whom you are speaking are absolutely certain they know God's truth, there is no way to have conversation. . . . The one thing they have in mind is to convince you of the wrongness of your ways and ideas and the rightness of

their ways. And that doesn't make for dialogue.

This pastor cites abortion as another such issue, noting that this attitudinal "fundamentalism" is seen on both sides of the issue: "There is no way to have any resolution until one side obliterates the other side."

A leading spokesperson for an evangelical organization expresses the tension felt by conservatives like herself in this way:

> One of the continuing critical challenges for me—and I don't handle it very well—is how one lifts up what one understands to be the scriptural teaching about who we are and how we ought to live and yet does not reject the person that is caught up in that way of living. I got a letter from a gay person who said, "If they reject what I'm doing, they reject me." I guess either we have to live with some people feeling rejected or else we have to be so inclusive that we're not the church of Jesus Christ any more. That's something I wrestle with.

An evangelical leader serving with a parachurch student ministry says he rejects the "wooden literalism" sometimes identified with conservative biblical interpretation. We have quoted him earlier (in chapter four) as insisting that biblical authority is the starting point and that it requires "taking the text seriously."

He tells a story that epitomizes the dilemma of the evangelicals' seeking to take the biblical text seriously while at the same time allowing for differences in interpretation. As the liberal UCC seminary professor quoted above found his strongest opposition at the extreme Marxist end of liberalism, so this evangelical parachurch leader found himself embroiled in a struggle with the biblical-literalist extreme of Christian conservatism.

He visited Yale University in 1990 to give a series of public lectures. While there, he also conducted a seminar for the staff of the local chapter of his student ministry together with a few representatives of the university chaplain's office and a few parents. The seminar subject was ministering pastorally to homosexuals on the campus and in the fellowship. The almost universal attitude on the Yale campus, a bastion of political correctness, was full acceptance of homosexuality as a legitimate alternative lifestyle. Since a campus pro-gay rally one week earlier had gotten out of hand and the university had broken it up, the administration was being labeled as homophobic. The whole subject was receiving press attention, and one reporter came to the seminar.

The reporter seemed disappointed that he heard no "gay bashing." However, his newspaper account of the seminar was regarded as moderate and accurate until the last paragraph.

> In the last paragraph he took two things I had said—and in both cases he quoted me correctly—but he took these two things out of context and put them together in the same paragraph. And what it sounded like was exactly the opposite of what I had said. Well, that got picked up from the *New Haven Register* by the Religious News Service, . . . which took his last paragraph, made it their first paragraph and put a headline over it that said, "Evangelical leader supports gay relationships." They sent it out over the wire service to 200 newspapers across the country. Well, all of a sudden I was in the middle of this huge thing where everything is polarized. It became a national controversy. . . . We had very angry conservative people who withdrew support . . . even from campus workers. And on the other side I was getting these accolades from homosexual groups. *Christianity Today* had called me right away and asked, "What is all this?" I told them I was misquoted and what I really said, and they said, "Oh, there's no story there." They didn't print anything until it had become sort of a national event. But a very conservative Christian publication in North Carolina picked it up and really went after me. . . . This thing went on month after month. It kept appearing in denominational magazines and newspapers, and it kept getting changed further. It was a real mess.

At the heart of the misunderstanding was the parachurch leader's statement, accurately quoted, that "there is some ambiguity in the biblical texts." He had stated that if you look simply at the seven biblical statements about homosexuality in their immediate context, the meaning is not totally clear: "In the wider context of a biblical view of sexuality," he said, "we have a pretty good biblical understanding. But if you look at the seven verses alone, in their immediate context, you can make a case for a lot of different views on homosexuality."

"Those were fighting words," he reflects. "'There can't be any ambiguity in the biblical text!' As far as a lot of people are concerned it is absolutely clear. So there is a kind of wooden literalism that sets in. There are deep-seated convictions and enormous fears."

In this instance it is a moderate evangelical—a biblical scholar who insists on scriptural authority and on taking the text seriously—who encountered that arrogance of certitude about Scripture. Extremist conservatives convinced that "this is what God says" were unwilling to allow for differences of biblical interpretation.

Such unconscious attitudes on both sides, whether the political correctness of liberals on social issues or the certainty of conservatives about what God says through Scripture, can be obstacles to reconciliation within the church. And the irony is that conviction, whether about social concerns or the teaching of Scripture, is an essential part of religious belief.

It would be a mistake, however, to conclude that deeply held belief in itself breeds the kind of arrogance, an arrogance that rejects differences, encountered by those quoted above. There is hopeful evidence that the opposite is true. The Gallup Organization explored the proposition that the more deeply religious people are, the more likely they are to be bigoted and close-minded. It developed a twelve-item scale to measure the segment of the population that is "highly spiritually committed." It reported that "while representing only 13 percent of the population, these persons are a 'breed apart' from the rest of society. We find that these people, who have what might be described as a 'transforming faith,' are more tolerant of others, more inclined to perform charitable acts, more concerned about the betterment of society, and far happier. (These findings, in my view, are among the most exciting and significant we have recorded in more than a half-century of polling.)" Another Gallup study showed that 83 percent of Americans say that their religious beliefs require them to respect people of other religions.[3] There is at least some evidence, then, that religious commitment at its best leads to greater acceptance of differences rather than to intolerant arrogance.

The pastor of a famous church in New York City, speaking out of his background in the charismatic movement about the way the intensity of the experience of the Holy Spirit in such circles puts others off, calls for "turning down the volume of assurance." It is not the level of personal conviction, but the attitude conveyed to others that is at fault.

Hope lies in the fact that there are both liberals and evangelicals with clear enough vision to recognize such arrogance within their own ranks as well as in the opposition. We found that kind of clear vision to be quite common among the church leaders we interviewed.

Language That Divides

A further note about words is in order. We are distanced from each other by vocabulary, asserts the evangelical pastor of a large church in the Southwest. He finds more political language than theological, gospel language coming from liberal leadership. Such language is not compelling. In a candid conversation between large-church pastors and denominational staff, the pastors pointed out that the language used in materials produced by the evangelism and global missions units was not like that used in local churches. This pastor cites a five-year theme, "Come to the Living Lord," chosen because it was language with which people in the pew could identify, that grew out of these discussions.

In a similar vein, a female evangelical minister speaks with feeling about the liberal boycott of masculine language. "We cannot use language of kingdom or kingship, Lord or lordship, because these convey a patriarchal, sexist imagery which must be purged. I distinguish between expansionist language for God, which employs the full range of biblical metaphors," she continues, "and exclusionary language, which forbids any Father language, Lordship or kingship." Even the Lord's Prayer cannot be used in this new thinking, she says. She feels that a line must be drawn: "We cannot give up the creeds, the councils, what Jesus taught us to pray."

Sometimes conservative use of "Jesus language" or explicitly theological language is denigrated by some liberals who find it embarrassing, claims this pastor. Their attitude is to devalue evangelical language, whereas evangelicals dismiss the political and social action language of liberals. Perhaps, because we lack common definitions and common language, we don't know how to argue theologically, and instead we argue ideologically, she says. Sometimes evangelicals take offense when they hear liberal "code language" and so note omissions of religious language. Liberals may hear phony piety in some evangelicals' words. Thus both groups end up devaluing each other, and dialogue becomes difficult; diatribe replaces decency.

We need "honest talk about honest talk," says a New York pastor who also is sensitive to the language issue. It is the actual language used as well as the way an issue or controversy is framed that can make a difference to the receptivity of both liberals and evangelicals. A conference around "the crisis of church membership" drew a spectrum of participants, he points out, whereas calling it a "church growth" conference would have brought mostly evangelicals.

Labeling and Stereotypes

If arrogance is an attitude about one's own position that places roadblocks in the way of reconciliation, stereotyping is a similarly damaging attitude about the opposition.

We have noted earlier the angry reaction on the part of conservatives (and even in some cases moderate liberals who have questions on this issue) who oppose ordination of self-affirming homosexuals to being labeled "homophobic." A comparable anger comes from liberals who are tarred by the implication that they "don't believe in the Bible."

A denominational staff member who is an evangelical speaks feelingly of his own experiences with labeling:

> In some "evangelical" [his quotes, denoted with raised fingers] circles, I find the pattern of labeling liberal positions as "liberation theology" right now a means of dismissing others as something less than authentic and devout Christians. At the same time in some "liberal" circles I find the pattern of labeling evangelicals as "fundamentalists" the same basis of dismissal.

He tells of a discussion with a group of conservatives about the working definition of evangelism developed by his office—a thoroughly traditional definition couched in terms conservatives would generally accept, calling people to repentance and a personal faith in Jesus Christ as Lord and Savior. A member of the group responded, "Yeah, but you really believe that Jesus Christ is liberator."

"By labeling me," says this church official, "he implied that I'm no longer authentic; I've sold out to the enemy apparently, because I came on the denominational staff.

"On the other side," he continues, "I've had conversations with some key liberals who likewise label me as a borderline fundamentalist, and having put that label on me think they no longer have to deal with me." This is one of the commonest forms of how liberals stereotype the opposition—applying the label "fundamentalist" to all conservatives. (The most derisive term is "fundies," which cropped up from time to time in our interviews.)

The senior pastor of a large church in California told of his experience with such labeling. He is an evangelical who has been called to a church in a largely liberal presbytery:

> The presbytery Committee on Ministry voted 15 to 0 against me, because of my label. The church was determined to get me and finally got the presbytery to back off. And after having been viewed with great suspicion in the presbytery for my first three or four years, I ended up being elected moderator of presbytery and seen as someone who had made a very positive contribution to the mission of the church—even from some people who would radically disagree with me theologically.

Evangelicals are equally adept at stereotyping liberals, and their labels are just as deeply resented. Says the executive of a judicatory in the Southwest, "I think one of the bad things the present opposition does is characterize people. In the six years I was on the general council, so far as I could tell, everyone on the council was 'bad.' Even the so-called official plants [evangelicals elected to the council to balance a perceived liberal tilt—the derisive term 'official plant' is, of course, in itself a form of stereotyping or labeling] got tainted. There were people who distrusted them, from the conservative side, because they were a part of the general council.

"One of the dimensions of the estrangement," the judicatory executive explains, "makes you perceive the people in the other camp as a monolithic group." He tells of conducting a series of conferences of evangelical ministers and denominational leaders in which "one of the things [the evangelical ministers] discovered is that the liberal leadership group is far from monolithic. There is a whole range of opinions. And that, I think, has been a salutary experience for them."

Labeling, as the evangelical denominational official quoted above said, is a way of dismissing. One does not have to deal with those who can be categorized as "weirdos." In the stories of both the California pastor and the judicatory official, it was the experience of dealing with the other side face to face that did away with stereotypes.

7

....

The Goal
Is to Win

Hostility,
Power Struggles
& Manipulation

*They came in and did some sarcastic skits, used some language which was
"unladylike," and the result was not increased sensitivity, but hostility and anger.
I'm not for being "nice" all the time or not dealing with anger.
But this action fueled polarization. If I'm a man sitting in the audience,
and the skit is ridiculing me, and making me feel foolish, stupid or hostile,
when I see myself as really kind of a well-meaning guy that tries hard—
if you make me look like an idiot, the reaction isn't "Oh, thank you for helping me
see the light." The reaction is, "I don't ever want to come to a workshop
led by the women's task force again!"*
A WOMAN COLLEGE PRESIDENT, DESCRIBING A TRAINING EVENT
DESIGNED TO "SENSITIZE MEN" ON WOMEN'S ISSUES,
WHICH BACKFIRED

W e looked in the last chapter at attitudes: the arrogance of conviction about one's own position and the stereotyping of one's
opponent's position. Negative attitudes can lead to hostile actions. The
church leaders we interviewed had numerous stories of such hostility.

Some of the stories are highly personal. A liberal pastor tells of a
hospital visit with his father, who was critically ill. His father's pastor,
who knew of the son's liberal positions, was there. When the son arrived
he said, "I must be going because my phone has been ringing off the hook
this morning with people angry about this Ministers' Manifesto."

The son relates his response: "I have never been so angry at a colleague in my life. He knew I had signed the manifesto. Here my father was critically ill—and in that setting, to bring up an issue that was so explosive, and so divisive between me and my father! If in that pastoral setting we could have embraced one another, it would have opened up the possibility of discussion and some kind of meeting of minds later on. But he eliminated the possibility altogether. He could never gain my trust and confidence again after that."

At a similarly personal level an evangelical pastor relates an incident growing out of an article he wrote for a seminary publication at a time when he was serving on a denominational committee. According to him, a leading liberal angered by the article said to him, "You will never get on a national agency again, and I will make sure that there are certain churches that will never come your way." This minister goes on to say that the first part of the prediction came true; and the second was verified when a church that had initially exhibited great interest in calling him as pastor later cooled their enthusiasm. One of his friends was told, "Oh, we didn't want to pursue it with him because he has a reputation of not being a team player."

Some of the hostility reported in our interviews was more generalized. An evangelical layperson described her dismay at the attitude she encountered when she was first appointed to a denominational council. She described herself at that time as "a babe in the woods—a nice little mother who had always volunteered to teach Sunday school, . . . one of the least offensive evangelicals you could find."

She went on to say, "I really was not aware of the depth of hostility and determination on the part of the 'sixties' leadership to destroy both evangelism and the global-mission understanding of the proclamation of the gospel. One of the liberals went on the global mission unit along with me, and every time he got up to try to make a point for global mission and world evangelization he was hooted down by his own former colleagues: 'What happened to you? You don't even believe we ought to be doing this!'" Similarly, liberals in the same denomination felt that a social-mission report faced an atmosphere of hostility from evangelicals when it was presented.

A Texas synod executive talked of an instance when anger took an organized form. In 1991 the 8,000-member Highland Park Presbyterian

Church (Dallas) split, with a majority voting to remain in the Presbyterian Church (U.S.A.) but a substantial minority leaving to form a new congregation affiliated with the Presbyterian Church in America. The pastor of the church, widely recognized as a leader among the denomination's evangelicals, had strongly supported remaining in the PCUSA and had tried to lead the congregation in that direction. In the period before the vote, the synod executive relates, some of the angry right-wing members "mounted a telephone campaign with a different person calling the pastor's house every hour" to urge him to change his stand.

Our interviews produced stories of bitterness and anger on both sides of the divide, people "standing off throwing rocks at one another, rather than engaging in 'Christian contention,'" as the synod executive puts it. Whether because of the arrogance of certitude, stereotyping of opponents or some other attitude, when anger and hostility take over there is little room for movement toward reconciliation.

A Disciples of Christ Case Study: GMP Election

A case study of the kind of power struggle that reflects such attitudes can be found in the defeat of Michael Kinnamon's nomination to a six-year term as the denomination's general minister and president (GMP) at the 1991 General Assembly of the Christian Church (Disciples of Christ). In a complex electoral process, Kinnamon, dean of Lexington Theological Seminary in Kentucky, had been proposed as a candidate by a search committee, selected as nominee by the denomination's forty-member Administrative Committee and approved by the General Board for submission to the General Assembly as the single nominee for the position. A two-thirds vote was required for election. Kinnamon received 65.2 percent of the vote, just short of the percent required.

Several reasons for opposition to his election were given, including his relative youth (he was forty-one years old) and lack of pastoral experience. The Disciples of Christ live with the same liberal-conservative division other pluralistic denominations have, with a particularly wide clergy-lay gap. Surveys at the time showed that their laypeople are more conservative and clergy more liberal than, for example, their Presbyterian counterparts. Kinnamon's nomination was clearly the work of the denomination's liberal clergy establishment. But the central issue became Kinnamon's commitment to "the full participation of gay and lesbian persons in the life of the church and its ministry."

Organized opposition by the conservative wing of the church began early in the nominating process. The elders of one Indiana congregation sent a letter opposing the nomination to all four thousand Disciples churches. In the highly politicized environment in the two months following his nomination by the General Board, Kinnamon spoke at forty local meetings in fifteen of the denomination's thirty-six regions, often in places where opposition ran highest.

Following the election at the General Assembly, there were widespread rumors of voting abuses. Kinnamon's opponents were accused of having bussed in to the Tulsa, Oklahoma, meeting as many as three hundred people for the sole purpose of voting against him. They reportedly registered, voted and left. It was also alleged that some people voted twice, moving from one part of the hall to another. Much discussion of these allegations appeared in the letters section of the *Disciple* magazine, the church's official publication. Formal charges were never filed, but the allegations were taken seriously enough to be considered by the denomination's Administrative Committee. No action was taken, though a promise was made to monitor more closely future voting.

Kinnamon's post-Assembly comments were remarkably free of rancor or recrimination. "I came to believe that it is only through the actual experience of disagreeing in love that some degree of trust might be restored," he said. He tried to interpret the event as a learning experience for the church, about itself, its divisions and their underlying causes. Regarding his own experience, he said,

> I learned again about the healing power of dialogue when undertaken with an appreciation for the integrity of the other. And I learned just how essential it is for the church to recover its commitment to seek God's guidance, acting not as a collection of special interests, but as a community of faith. The church is called to embody an alternative way of living and thus to contribute to the world's salvation in ways that we may not fully understand. The world does not need models of politicized fragmentation. It has plenty of those. What it needs is the transforming proclamation of God's love that binds us into communities of active love, even with those with whom we disagree.[1]

Despite the charity and hopefulness of Kinnamon's remarks, however, the story of the election itself was one of those "models of politicized fragmentation." It reflected the kind of power struggle that is all too often characteristic of polarization at the denominational level.

Another Case Study: *The Presbyterian Layman*

Within the Presbyterian church there are two symbolic focal points of polarization. Conservative anger tends to focus on "the Presbyterian Center"—shorthand for the predominantly liberal denominational "leadership" or "bureaucracy" (the term used depends on whether they are viewed positively or negatively) that constitutes the General Assembly staff in Louisville.

Liberal anger is focused even more strongly on *The Presbyterian Layman*, the publication of the Presbyterian Lay Committee. Some of the harshest words heard in the interviews with Presbyterians conducted for this book were aimed at the *Layman*. While most of these comments came from liberals, some milder criticism came from moderate evangelicals as well. Hostility between the liberal leadership of the Presbyterian Church and the *Layman* offers a case history of opposition gone awry.

The Presbyterian Lay Committee (PLC) had its origins in the late sixties. Its purpose was to oppose the adoption of the contemporary confessional document that became known as the Confession of 1967. From the beginning the organization was explicitly identified with the laity of the church, and it was well financed by wealthy backers. The PLC never sought to become a mass organization with a large membership roll. It had no "members" as such; its organizational structure consisted of a board of directors and a small professional staff. Its strategy was informational, and its major activity from the beginning was the publication of its bimonthly paper.

Though the fight against the Confession of 1967 was lost, the *Layman* became the voice and rallying point for those on the conservative end of the church's spectrum. There are other, generally more moderate evangelical parachurch groups within mainline Presbyterianism. Moderation, however, is not what the PLC perceives as its role.

The Presbyterian Layman does not depend on subscriptions. It is mailed free to as many Presbyterians as possible. And it is this distribution strategy that has brought the highest level of conflict between the PLC and the denomination's ruling establishment. When the *Layman* has been able to obtain a copy of a congregational directory (usually from a sympathetic layperson), the entire membership roll has been added to its mailing list.

This practice brought cries of outrage from liberal pastors who did not want it circulated within their congregations. And, indeed, from their perspective, they were right. The *Layman* was generally the only source of news and information about the larger denomination that went directly into the homes of ordinary church members. And while the accuracy of its reporting was a matter of dispute, its orientation was avowedly conservative and its opposition to the liberal policies and programs of the denominational staff was explicit. In numerous cases, denominational actions or policies that would otherwise have gone unnoticed were brought to the attention of conservative church members by the *Layman* and became points of controversy within previously peaceful congregations.

The *Layman*'s unauthorized use of congregational directories for its mailing lists became a cause célèbre with denominational leadership. The 1987 General Assembly directed the PLC to cease the practice. It refused, claiming that directories were not confidential and were in the public domain. It offered to delete from its mailing list the name of any person who so requested, and it published forms in its pages to make such requests convenient. But it continued to acquire Presbyterian names and addresses by whatever means it could.

Anger over address lists was added to long-standing charges of slanted reporting and unfair distortions. A synod executive labels the publication "as pure an example of anarchy and nihilism as I have seen." He accuses it of distorting by "quoting half a verse." A presbytery executive describes it as "vitriolic," noting that "there is nothing on the liberal side like this." One pastor labels it as distorted and unfair. Another pastor accuses it of misrepresentation. And a church journalist says, "There is positive hatred between the Presbyterian Center and *The Presbyterian Layman*."

Even a leader of moderate evangelicals is disturbed by the divisiveness seen in the *Layman*. She cites the case of the First Presbyterian Church, Houston, Texas, which in 1991 considered leaving the denomination and narrowly voted to remain in. Earlier, she says, its membership, while conservative, had been largely unaware of the polarization in the denomination. But once the *Layman* began to be mailed to the entire membership, the sometimes one-sided reporting led to growing concern, the eventual polarization of the congregation and the attempt to take it out of the denomination.

Another moderate, who at times defended the Lay Committee by noting that its constituency was unfairly excluded by denominational officials, nevertheless deplores the negativism of its publication:

> There's a kind of deviousness associated with the *Layman*, a willingness to accept any rumor as true. If there's *anything* wrong with what you're looking at, that'll be the *Layman*'s headline. They're always looking for the bad things, the failures. There's never any effort to give any credit to the national leadership: "It's all bad, it's a mess, get rid of it." And that's not fair to those people.

By 1989 feelings had become so strong that the General Assembly established a Special Committee to Consult with the Presbyterian Lay Committee. This group conducted extensive conversations with PLC officials and held a series of public hearings throughout the denomination. It was apparently surprised at the level of support for the *Layman* it encountered. Those who attended its open hearings were overwhelmingly pro-*Layman;* all but one of twenty speakers at its Chicago hearing voiced strong support. The committee also received thousands of pro-*Layman* letters, apparently generated by the publication itself. To obtain a more balanced picture, it commissioned for its own use a "scientific survey" to determine attitudes within the denomination.[2]

Feelings were exacerbated by an incident that occurred while the committee was pursuing its investigations. The editor of the *Layman*, en route by air to a consultation with the Special Committee, inadvertently left on the airplane a copy of a "briefing paper" prepared for members of his PLC board that made blunt and derogatory personal comments about individual members of the committee. By remarkable coincidence the next person to occupy his vacated seat on the plane was an informed Presbyterian who found the paper, recognized its significance and mailed it to the chair of the Special Committee.

The editor, who took full responsibility for the briefing paper, later apologized in person to the committee members. In mitigation, he related experiences leading to the conclusion that "in my personal engagement with leaders of our national church I have sustained wounds which have made me wary." He claimed he was a victim of "coercion within the ranks of Presbyterian officialdom" and was "blackballed as a troublemaker." He spoke of an elite group, "masters of manipulation," that "rewarded its friends and ruthlessly punished those whom it perceived to be its enemies."[3]

In its report to the General Assembly the Special Committee sought to play a reconciling role. It affirmed the objectives of the PLC but said the journalistic style and editorial policies of its publication are "a significant hindrance to this desired reconciliation." It also affirmed the need for dissenting voices in the church but said the *Layman* "has not always been the type of fair voice of dissent" needed. The Special Committee found the *Layman*'s use of church mailing lists "divisive." Conceding that the use might be legal, it asked if the conduct is "healing in nature." It recommended that the issue be resolved between the Lay Committee and each affected congregation.

The committee asked the PLC to add to its five published objectives a sixth: "To endeavor in all that we do to promote the peace and unity of the Presbyterian Church." (This action has not been taken.) It also asked the General Assembly to seek more theological diversity on boards and committees, to establish "interactive channels" for communication and to establish an Advisory Committee on the Health of the Church to hold open hearings each year through which Presbyterians can bring their concerns more directly to the General Assembly. (In approving the report the General Assembly did not adopt this latter recommendation, on the advice of the General Assembly Council.)[4] While some communication may have occurred in the process of the study itself and while some modest steps may have been taken as a result, it is probably fair to say that none of the committee's recommendations has been implemented in a substantive way.

The fight over the *Layman* is probably an example of a degree of polarization that cannot readily be overcome. This is not simply a matter of anger that has led to hostile actions on both sides. Reconciliation—with a wing of the church that it regards as being close to if not actually apostate—is not the goal of the Presbyterian Lay Committee. Sowing discontent among Presbyterians with the present direction of the denomination appears to be a conscious strategy. It calls itself an "advocacy group," and it sees its duty as to vigorously advocate theological and cultural positions that are far from those of the denomination's liberal leadership and perhaps more conservative than those of the majority of evangelicals within the church. Says a journalist, "They're in the business to promote a cause. They're in the business to create a revolution if they can."

Revolutionaries are not usually reconcilers. However, once their goal is reached, the organization asserts, it is prepared to disappear. "It was formed to go out of business," claims its president. Once reform and renewal occur, he says, the PLC will not be needed.

Meanwhile, however, the battle lines are fixed. For if reconciliation is not the goal of the Lay Committee, neither is it the goal of the present denominational leadership. One reason for continued strife is that the PLC has been highly effective in what it has been trying to do. Its "informational strategy" has worked. A prominent liberal layman active in denominational affairs considers the organization "a model of what a serious antagonist is." They won't give up. Their goals are clear. "They want the whole enchilada," he says. They know the stakes. And they have enormous resources.

Much of the anger on the side of the liberal establishment has been associated with the *Layman*'s publication of stories the denominational leadership would have preferred to keep from public knowledge. As one journalist says, "They're going for stories that others are not willing to get out." There have been ongoing battles over meetings not open to the press or public and records not made available, he continues. The establishment will not be able to live comfortably with the *Layman* until it is willing to be far more open and public about its mistakes and shortcomings as well as its successes and virtues. But the Lay Committee on its side must also be willing to make changes. Says this observer and writer, "I think in the church it's not 'All's fair in love and war.' I think the *Layman* should try to be less negative, more positive, but at the same time keep doing what people appreciate."

The Presbyterian Church has suffered severely from the anger and actions resulting from extreme polarization created over the *Layman*. Healing would require significant changes on both sides.

Power Struggles and Manipulation
Among the many ways of looking at the polarization in today's church,

one way is to see it as a power struggle, as we noted in chapter three. The two sides in power struggles are inherently irreconcilable. Their objective is not to bring people and ideas together but to win control. It may be that most disagreements include some elements of a power struggle, but to the extent that this win-or-lose element dominates, the conflict becomes far harder to resolve.

In the last chapter we noted the arrogance and rigidity encountered by a seminary professor in connection with his preparation of an economic policy paper for the United Church of Christ. It led to a bitter power struggle, as he describes here.

> There is something about what I believe to be the deep and pervasive effect of Marxist analysis. It's a fascinating thing to me: Marx has lost the world but won the minds of one set of human actors. Not because they're communists, or Stalinists or supported the Soviet Union or anything like that, but because the way in which they analyze the categories is in terms of a particular class analysis with realpolitik overtones, and that's the way they take up every question. They may be deeply religious at another level. But it is a particularly constricted form of power analysis, which ends up being, as I believe Marxism to have been, unprincipled. And that leads to the kind of toughness which becomes meanness in the way they set up committees, calculate who's going to be on what commissions and how they work that out.

This UCC leader perceived Marxist analysis as being used as a justification for manipulation in this case. Other members of that policy committee saw their work as having integrity, their membership as composed of persons with mutual respect. What was perceived by some as manipulation was perceived by others as selection of "the best people to undertake the task." It appears, however, that manipulation of political and organizational processes is widely practiced in church power struggles, whether recognized as manipulation or not. We have noted before the widespread impression among Presbyterians we interviewed that the committee which produced the 1991 human-sexuality report had been "stacked." The stated clerk of the General Assembly confirmed this: "That wasn't accidental," he said, referring to the composition of the committee. "And for two years I told the chairman it wouldn't work." Even a Methodist, observing from outside the denomination, had this impression.

But liberals have no monopoly on manipulation. An evangelical minister serving with a denominational evangelism unit says, "We stacked the evangelism task force, just as the other side did the sexuality task force. [laughter] I think it had more integrity, but I wasn't looking for liberals! We can all play the game on our own side."

The executive of another denominational ministry unit speaks of his largely unsuccessful attempts to appoint evangelicals to national staff positions. Asked if such evangelicals are sometimes perceived as "tokens," he replied, "Yes, and they're afraid of being manipulated. I would be too."

Beyond the appointment of staff, committees and task forces, there are other ways of manipulating outcomes. Says a female evangelical leader, "So often what we call dialogue is really an attempt to stack the deck. For instance, some abortion dialogues are not a genuine exploration of alternative points of view. Rather there is 'toleration' of an alternative, with a clear understanding that 'all the good guys know where we really ought to be.' And this only increases the polarization."

Another evangelical minister described a task force on the Middle East in which dominant members drafted an open letter—written in the name of the task force and distributed it on denominational letterhead—suggesting actions that were not in accord with conservative views. They did not ask conservative members of the task force, who did not share their point of view, to participate in the process.

Power struggles and manipulation are symptoms of a polarization that has become dysfunctional. In such a context, roadblocks become impassable barriers, and reconciliation between divergent points of view is no longer possible. Attitudes such as arrogance about one's own rightness (or righteousness) and the labeling and stereotyping of one's opponents lead to anger and hostility that make mutual understanding difficult. Active power struggles and manipulation multiply the difficulty.

"You can't manipulate the church into fidelity," says a denominational leader. "That will come only if the Spirit moves us. Only the Spirit is going to renew the faithful life."

Part 3

. . . .

Renewing
Our Bonds

8

· · · · · · · · · · · ·

Neighborly Ties

Dialogue

You may
read love letters aloud
and no one snickers,
put quotes around revealed truth
and sense no kinship with Servetus,
blurt a new thought rough as cinder
and see it polished to a gem,
watch a theory, neat as well-made beds,
be tousled and rumpled by lovers.

You may
admit a festering deep within
and let respectful questions probe the wound,
detonate some person's hidden fuse
and sweep debris together,
expose your awful emptiness
and be enriched,
ask huge questions that engulf old answers
and not despair.

For the search of two
is better than
the finding of one. [1]
PEGGY SHRIVER

A n ecumenical laity group, gathered together somewhat improbably in a country inn on a slope of the Great Smoky Mountains, was extremely diverse religiously—from agnostic to millennialist. Yet there was one common opinion among them: Let everyone find the church in which they feel comfortable and leave the rest alone. That senti-ment fits American individualism quite naturally, but it does not square with Christian faith. Jesus, in the last days before he was arrested, prayed for the church, saying, "I ask not only on behalf of these, but also on behalf of those who will believe in me through their word, that they may all be one. As you, Father, are in me and I am in you, may they also be in us, so that the world may believe that you have sent me" (Jn 17:20-21). Jesus desires that we become completely one so the world will know that God has sent Jesus to express God's love for all people even as God has loved him (Jn 17:23).

If we are to disturb our comfortable separation into like-minded enclaves within our congregations, our denomination and even among denominations, we must understand our reasons. A New York City pastor urges us to be clear about why we are "compelled to converse." If it is solely to "straighten each other out" or even to convert others to our way of thinking, our compulsion is going to be problematic. We must discover "the legitimation of our own vulnerability, in an honest exchange with God," he says, before we can have fruitful conversation with persons of differing persuasion. "Until we discover that we need each other, and how much we need each other and what it is that compels us to come together, we probably are not going to be as sensitive and as flexible as the reconciling possibility demands," he explains. We must honor Jesus' "last will and testament" that "we might be one." Our divisions are a constant embarrassment before the Lord. God has arranged that no one person or tradition can envision adequately the broad truth of the gospel, and we need each other for the broadening of the truth for our lives. It is God's design for answering the prayer of Jesus, claims this pastor.

Our interviews uncovered incident after incident in which the gospel desire to be "the church" overcame the pain and discomfort of confronting people with views that were strange or offensive to oneself. When people make the effort, for the sake of their witness to the world, to try to understand and respect each other, the resulting community can be deeply satisfying and powerful.

In part two of this book we looked at the unraveling of ties and the obstacles to reconciliation. We examined attitudes and actions that have sharpened differences and blocked the building of community. Now, in part three, we begin to look at the positive ways in which people have overcome divisions, engaged in dialogue and experienced community. Many of the most heartening stories we heard as we interviewed church leaders and listened to other voices were accounts of one-on-one neighborliness.

In the next chapter we will examine structured attempts to overcome polarization in organized settings, such as boards, committees and task groups. In chapter ten we will look at the special context for reaching out across divisions offered by the basic community of work and worship: the congregation. First, however, we will listen to those who have experienced renewed community in unstructured and sometimes unexpected ways, simply by reaching out in love to individual persons.

In local congregations the big polarities that separate us from one another are often symbolized in just one other person whom we know to hold certain views. If one could find a way toward mutual respect and communication with that person, one might begin to grasp some new understanding of a much larger segment of the church. Several people described such situations and how they responded—sometimes helpfully, sometimes with no effect. One pastor, who says his politics are more liberal than his theology, told us he found that he could maintain fruitful relationships with several friends who were conservative in politics or theology by concentrating upon their areas of agreement. One parishioner who was theologically quite conservative was very inspiring to him in his gospel-funded urban ministry program. Although they could not comfortably explore theology together, they could affirm their mutual concern for people in need in their Atlanta, Georgia, community. This pastor is friends with one well-known evangelical church leader, but they (unfortunately) maintain their friendship by not attending one another's denominational events designed to cater to either conservatives or liberals. Such polarized church structures sometimes interfere with important bridge building among individuals.

This same pastor described one experience that might well serve as a model for others to consider when they have a serious problem with a particular person. He and a university-related colleague, who was in his congregation and served on its governing body, had agreed on many theological and social issues until they came upon one issue in the church that seriously divided them. This division was so strong that his colleague stopped coming to church and they avoided one another. (Although this particular instance was not exactly a polarity of orthodox and progressive, it could as well have been.) Realizing that both he and his colleague believed in a reconciling faith, he telephoned his colleague and urged him in light of their mutual Christian faith to covenant to meet with him to discuss their differences over a period of six to eight sessions. They met on successive occasions, during which neither simply "gave in" to the other but through which each grew in respect for the other's legitimate point of view. Each also confessed to having overstepped bounds, but they acknowledged that the work they had in common was too important to let their differences interfere. The pastor says this direct, sustained approach has been effective in another situation too. He cautions that it is not easy—it is costly in time and emotional energy—and that one cannot do it casually. It is a form of love that will not let one another go or be written off. But for the sake of the work of the church, he and his now "restored" friend undertook a personal confrontation.

Another person who initiated reconciliation is a Methodist evangelical leader, who recalls the controversy that followed a speech he gave in 1975 at Lake Junaluska, a major United Methodist conference grounds, to a Good News conference on the crisis of theological education in the United Methodist Church. His speech was covered in the Methodist paper *The Reporter* in a way that highlighted his critical remarks apart from the context of his positive words. His remarks on there being no viable alternative to Wesleyan theology in any Methodist seminary so aroused Dr. Albert Outler, then of Perkins School of Theology at Southern Methodist University, that he prepared a heated letter to the editor of the *Reporter*. That editor read it to the Methodist leader on the telephone to ask if he cared to reply. "No, I'll pray on it," he said. He then decided to call Outler, who was less than persuaded by his explanation of his remarks. Three weeks later he drove to visit Outler, and in lengthy personal conversation they discovered that their basic concerns about theological education were quite similar. Out of that reconciling encounter came the Foundation for Theological Education, of which Outler was a founding trustee.

Sometimes not taking so direct an approach may be the loving thing to do, as the pastor of a suburban New York church narrates. One woman in his congregation, usually in agreement with many of his public, liberal positions, was deeply upset over his remarks about the Persian Gulf War, so much so that she walked out of church during his sermon. The pastor chose to discuss with the woman's husband what might be the best way of pursuing reconciliation. Her husband suggested the pastor let her take time for her feelings to cool. When her anger had subsided—after about six months—she returned to church services again. The pastor kept "in touch" with her through her husband, thus avoiding an emotional confrontation.

One of our Internet correspondents described an experience he had in seminary that allowed him to cross the liberal-evangelical boundaries effectively.

> I had a wonderful experience in CPE (clinical pastoral education) when one of the other participants among us UCC, Roman Catholic, Episcopalian and Methodist 'mainliners' turned out to be an Evangelical Friends minister. The EFA is a very Christ-centered Quaker meeting whose tenets of faith follow very closely many others' on the stereotypical spectrum: biblical inerrancy is preferred, specific personal conversion experience is important for membership, and winning sinners to the heart of Jesus is a valued part of their identity.
>
> After seeing a video of an ecumenical conference on AIDS, he was greatly troubled that homosexual lifestyles were not condemned in the conversation and that, in fact, one of the ministers on the tape chastised the congregation for being so late in responding to the AIDS crisis just because it got a foothold in the gay community first. When I say "troubled," I mean he was putting all of his history together with the powerful compassion demonstrated by priest after nun, minister after doctor [as they] related the power of God in this work. After sounding me out, he asked where was Paul's admonition for all these people. I screwed up my liberal courage and said, "Well, I have good days and bad days. And I write good things, and then I write superb things. I have chosen in prayer and in study to attend more closely to Paul when he writes 'nothing can separate us from the love of God' rather than his diatribe about sexual practice."
>
> Needless to say, he branded me with a scarlet L from that day forward and even joked about that. But! But because we were so different, we sought each other out to learn. I admire still his conservative heritage which says that our faith is important enough not to screw around with. Steve was willing to apply his ideals to his work better than I was, because my liberal self was saying things like, "Everybody does it differently; every way is probably OK." His friendship helped focus and define my personal spirituality in a way that I had not done before. We still did not always agree, but his words stuck with me about that: "I don't always understand you or how you can think the way you do, but I can see that you love the Lord."

The kind of working relationship Steve and I had is not always possible, but both of us were better for it. What a great model and a great lesson—that conservative and liberal are not opposites nor antagonistic.

Learning to Trust

Church executives devote much of their professional effort to the kind of institutional strategies for reducing polarization that we examine in the next chapter. They tell us, however, that one-on-one relationships have a major role in such strategies. For example, during her term as president of the National Council of the Churches of Christ in the U.S.A., one minister found herself frequently on the other side from certain key council constituents—including the Orthodox president-elect Leonid Kishkovsky and a leading Orthodox layman—when the NCC was confronted with some important issues. She and these Orthodox men were so different! Kishkovsky, with his Russian background, and she, with her southern American upbringing, often clashed; but they always came to one another with their disagreements, told the truth as they saw it to each other, didn't "cheat" behind each other's back and never considered one another "enemies." Sometimes Kishkovsky spoke for himself, but on occasion he officially represented an Orthodox posture, which he could not negotiate. Throughout their years of arguing and struggling over different points of view, she says she "never trusted anyone more" than she trusted Kishkovsky.

Declaring that taking time to get acquainted with a person with whom she differs is important, the former NCC president describes how she engages people who disagree with her. Sometimes after a difficult vote, when she has "won," she will talk with people in the losing position. She will tell them she isn't sorry she won but that *she understands what it feels like to lose* and that she does understand at least some of their views and reasons why they voted as they did. This conversation is healing. When we go to work on an issue in the church, she continues, we need to struggle within ourselves to see what is at stake, what is the heart of the matter, what is underneath it all. Then we need to explain that to those who stand on the other side and let them explain their position to us, she urges. We each need to say why something is important to us, even to those with whom we simply disagree. Then we have to work on how we handle an issue in which we know we can't agree. In the NCC, she says, we sometimes work on an issue for several years—like apartheid in South Africa, which resulted in a boycott of Shell Oil, or the Campbell Soup Company's labor practices, which ended in arbitration instead of a boycott. After years of studying and visiting a place some people will disagree that we should even take a position. She remembers becoming furious with an Orthodox layman who adamantly opposed a policy position on South Africa because one of the speakers in support of the position was critical of the United States. But later they sat down and talked slowly and carefully with one another, never coming to agreement, but also never "writing each other off for the rest of our lives."

She stresses the importance of telling the truth to one another and to ourselves. Sometimes we need self-examination to understand "where we are really coming from," and our convictions may have little to do with our religious faith. Or it may be that our problem is that our faith, whether liberal or conservative, is "split to smithereens" and so we are seeking solid ground, a better foundation.

From her extensive experience as a church leader, another southern woman advises, "If we are discussing something and we are going to vote on it and I am determined to do you in, then everything you say I will listen to in a certain way, listening for places I can swat you down. But if we are discussing something for which we are trying very hard to find a mutually acceptable compromise, I will listen for places [where] I can 'buy in.' These are two totally different ways of listening." She attributes these thoughts to author Parker Palmer.

Another church leader also urges us to build trust through mutual listening. Although the Assemblies of God bylaws prohibit ecumenical activity beyond the local level, an Assemblies of God professor who teaches at an evangelical seminary has been allowed to accept invitations from the National and World Councils of Churches. He has been active in both councils' Commission on Faith and Order and has attended both the 1989 Budapest World Faith and Order Commission and the WCC Canberra assembly. Through the many contacts he has made at these meetings, he has been convinced that there are many liberal and ecumenical Christians who want to hear what he has to say. He has learned how deeply pious and truly spiritual many of them are and how many are concerned for the gospel. It has been as important for him to hear them as it has been for them to hear him. "I appreciate . . . their genuine openness to realize what makes me, as a Pentecostal and evangelical, 'tick,' where my heart yearns, the concerns and critiques I bring to liberalism, which—on the whole—have been well accepted," he testifies. At the same time, he recalls, some liberals are close-minded with a new kind of fundamentalism that doesn't want to hear but only criticize. Likewise there are evangelicals who are exclusive, who prejudge instead of hearing what liberals have to say. His article on the Canberra assembly was rejected by the World Evangelical Fellowship for being "too nice" to the World Council and too self-critical.

Being a lone representative of a different faith perspective in large ecumenical meetings requires maturity, patience and a willingness to learn a new vocabulary. According to one evangelical scholar, the initiative, like the ecumenical invitations, should come from liberals because they claim to be ecumenical and to have an openness to other religious views and because they come from old, historic churches. They must be prepared, however, to be rebuffed repeatedly by evangelicals who are unwilling to be "wooed." But both groups need to reach out in ways consistent with who they are and really hear what one another has to say, despite the fears of what real listening might require of them, he suggests. Really hearing one another would mean the discovery that in some things the other is more Christian, that regarding some matters my group is wrong and that some relinquishment of power, some serious change in my tradition, will be needed. He explains,

> I am not for compromise, but I do believe that when we are confronted with truth change is inevitable, or ought to be, if it differs from our expression or understanding of that truth prior to the time we see the light on that subject. Honesty and integrity in self-perceptions, in self-critique, and the shattering of stereotypes and a willingness to change in light of new information is difficult for all of us.

Multicultural Understanding

An aspect of one-on-one neighborliness is trying to "get inside the skin" of the very culture in which the other lives. The former NCC president quoted above appreciates Tex Sample's efforts to interpret the cultural left, right and middle for one another in his book *U.S. Lifestyles and Mainline Churches*.[2] When approaching an adversary one on one, it may be helpful to steep oneself in the other's culture, which will increase one's self-awareness as well as one's awareness of the other. For example, one rather liberal United Church of Christ staff member suggests that the skills we use in trying to understand someone from another culture in another part of the world ought to be used in exploring the culture of evangelicalism if one is a liberal or in exploring the culture of liberalism if one is an evangelical. If James Davison Hunter, Tex Sample and Robert Wuthnow are correct in describing these different wings of the church as being culturally distinct from one another, then this advice, along with that from the former president of the National Council of Churches, makes sense. An American Christian would not attack a Korean Christian for exhibiting Korean cultural characteristics, so why should one trample a Christian neighbor whose religious culture differs from one's own? Yet when the gospel challenges the cultural behavior of any group, we need to be attentive.

Such a challenge to live by the gospel is important, one local pastor reminds us, when we are examining our behavior during racial tension. He remembers that at the height of the civil-rights movement his congregation in Georgia heard there was to be a "kneel-in" by African-Americans at various local churches. The church officers discussed what they would do if a group came to their all-white congregation to worship. They agreed to seat anyone who came to worship, because as one elder put it, "You can't turn anyone away from worship with a Bible in their hand."

But the struggle for racial openness continues today, as an African-American female pastor testifies. During her year as moderator of the Presbyterian Church (U.S.A.), she was dropped off by her host (who went on to park the car) at the front of a church at which she was to preach. The usher who greeted her at the door noted her skin color and told her that the Baptist church was down the street. She told him, to his great embarrassment, "I am a Presbyterian. I am your moderator, and I am here to preach this morning."

A pastor from New York was given a unique way of learning about himself and his relationship to the evangelical culture. He had begun his religious life in a very conservative Methodist tradition, and as he continued his religious development and went to seminary, he looked unfavorably upon his early upbringing. In his middle judicatory he found himself responding negatively to candidates from Gordon-Conwell Theological Seminary, so much so that he was urged to accept an invitation to spend a study week at Gordon-Conwell. He did spend a week there, visiting classes, working in the library, talking to people and worshiping. He found more basic Reformed theology than he had anticipated. Although he had questions about some interpretations, he found that they were seriously wrestling with the classical tradition. He had been helped to mature in his reexamination of his religious roots. This allowed him to listen with more openness to candidates from Gordon-Conwell in future judicatory meetings and to be more alert to the needs of evangelicals in his own congregation.

During his years as a pastor in the Northwest, one church leader active in his region didn't "bounce around from committee assignment to committee assignment" but instead stayed with one committee and got to know and enjoy the people on his committee, which he feels made him a more effective leader in his judicatory. He came to care about people radically different from himself, including one pastor, Ted, who was significantly more on the liberal scale (whereas he was more conservative) and with whom he seldom agreed theologically. He and Ted came thoroughly to enjoy one another, to understand each other, to trust each other, to be friends. He trusted Ted so much that when he became a university administrator he referred some students to Ted's church, because he could trust what they would receive from Ted personally.

Ideas from Conflict Management

The literature of conflict management and resolution offers help in the art of learning to listen empathetically. Such material is useful to anyone who wishes to take the initiative in dialogue with persons from whom she or he is alienated in the church. Consider these excerpts from "Skillful Negotiation Communications" by Richard A. Salem of Conflict Management Initiatives.[3]

> I try not to think of the other party as my opponent, but as a partner working out a shared problem. I invest in building an effective partnership by *communicating my acceptance* of the other party. . . . "Accepting" another party does not mean I necessarily like or agree with the person across the table. It means I am treating that person with respect and dignity. . . .

After "small talk," I encourage the serious discussion to begin with the identification and exploration of the issues and our feelings about them, rather than a statement of our demands. In this way, we learn more about what is really important to each of us and why. We begin by talking rather than fighting. We get a better idea of what we will have to sacrifice in order to obtain what we need.

No matter how unacceptable or outlandish the other party's statements or positions seem to me, I try to avoid reacting impulsively or going on the attack. To the extent possible, I suspend judgment and hear out the party. I try to remain in a *discussion* which explores our differences rather than engaging in a *debate* in which we try to prove who is right and who is wrong.

I try to listen attentively and empathetically, thereby letting the other party know that I understand and care about what is being said and how the speaker feels about it. . . . If I do not understand or agree with what is being said, I ask open-ended questions to elicit additional information. . . . I try not to interrupt or state my views until I am sure the other person is finished. I will reflect back what I hear by paraphrasing or summarizing so we both can be sure I got it right. . . .

I find that when I listen in this way, the other party is willing to both impart more information and, having been heard, is prepared to listen to me. . . . It becomes easier to jointly work on our differences and at times find solutions we didn't know were there.

Salem also warns against communicating rejection, either verbally or nonverbally. Interrupting, being inattentive, ordering, warning, lecturing, blaming, preaching, name calling, avoiding and cross-examining are all behaviors that tend to devalue and belittle the other party. By contrast, empathetic listening "acts like a mirror, reflecting what you think is being said and felt," Salem says. Maintaining eye contact, nodding, keeping a relaxed posture and touching are nonverbal encouragements that show you are listening.

These skills are not esoteric, but they are a codification of "loving your neighbor as yourself" in terms of respecting and taking seriously another person. Many Christians have learned to behave in these ways almost without self-conscious effort. Our interviews were seasoned with the names of persons who, in their varied positions of responsibility within the church, had acted with such empathy, integrity and Christian forbearance that they as individuals had achieved reconciliation or had averted further polarization among groups within the churches. Those mentioned were local pastors, active laypersons, church officers and middle judicatory leaders, national staff, seminary professors and presidents, renewal-group leaders, caring parishioners—the role of reconciler and empathetic community builder has many understudies. Although the distance between Christians is sometimes very wide and overwhelming, the power of a single individual to be a healer is most reassuring—and biblical.

Such individuals may relate one-on-one to another person, or they may function within a community or group to address its divisions. The skills required for either context are similar, although in a group things do become more complex, as we shall notice in the next chapter.

9

· · · · · · · · · · · ·

How Do You
Love a Group
As Yourself?

Never cease dialogue, or drive anyone away, or make a decision
that reduces the cohesiveness of the community. The task of leadership
in the church is community building.
A SENIOR DENOMINATIONAL OFFICIAL

Direct, one-on-one relating in response to the commandment to "love your neighbor" is the most basic action of the Christian life. But Jesus' disciples quickly found it necessary to develop institutional structures in order to deal with the complexities of community life. Similarly, as we saw in the last chapter, differences are most basically overcome by the largely spontaneous ways in which individual people reach out on a personal level. Institutional relationships, like personal ones, require neighborly love—with its trust, forgiveness, truth telling and empathy—although in a more complex expression than that found among individuals. In this chapter we address the problem of "loving" groups—the meetings, boards, committees and task forces that do the work of our organized churches.

Church structures and their various task-oriented groups are in regular need of upbuilding. Because these structures are composed of human members, we should expect some dissension and conflict, especially when the issue at stake matters deeply to people of faith. When expressions of faith begin to serve as a wedge rather than a glue, however, special problems arise. Some differences seem to reassert themselves in many guises over and over again, especially at the national and middle judicatory levels of our denominations.

Evangelism Versus Social Action?

In recent years, for example, churches have had what many now see as an artificial dichotomy between evangelism and social action—a subtle version of the "faith and works" argument. In chapter four we examined this perceived dichotomy in some detail in terms of the nature, purpose and mission of the church. If the observations of those we interviewed are accurate, this division in the church between evangelicals and liberal activists has been at least partly overcome, which has lessened the polarization. A Fuller Seminary professor notes that evangelicals are increasingly active in social justice, although their strategies tend to differ from those of liberals. A recent study, published in the *Yearbook of American and Canadian Churches 1992* and prepared by Carl S. Dudley and Thomas Van Eck, found that "an evangelical theology does not automatically restrict a congregation from engaging in community ministries, nor does a liberal theology inevitably lead to attitudes that support social ministries."[1] A much stronger predictor of a congregation's attitudes is its historical self-image and its location—usually in an urban setting.

There seems to be much accord on the importance of acting in direct, personal ministry out of compassionate faith on behalf of the weak, injured or neglected in the society, but there is less agreement on political expressions of that concern. A denominational consultation on evangelism and justice, described in chapter four, found harmony between evangelicals and liberals when they discussed programs that met human needs—shelters for the homeless, clinics and visitation of the sick, food pantries and other merciful efforts. But participants did not really enter the thicket of contention over a national health policy, or taxation policies or legislation to raise the minimum wage. However, the openness of both progressives and orthodox toward programs like Habitat for Humanity is significant evidence of reconciling leadership in the church. Some illustrations of collaborative, compassionate outreach may prove helpful.

A judicatory executive in Iowa was for a number of years pastor of a suburban church in Cincinnati that had had a "food-basket approach" to poverty. He began to institute "coffee clatches," informal gatherings of suburban women with poor inner-city women in which they came to know one another as individuals who share a common humanity. The summer-camp program that suburban children attended had a number of poor children added to its rolls, and a special camping environment was created. People began to have experiences that changed their perspectives. Sometimes theology itself did not change, but attitudes did.

An Episcopal leader of a prominent church on Wall Street tells of one incident that shows how a congregation and a member of the community can come to terms with each other in the area of social action. Street ministry—feeding the hungry, providing shelters for the homeless—has some appeal across the religious spectrum, but this Episcopal church angered a prestigious neighboring-restaurant owner, along with a number of other neighbors and members, when it opened a day center. At meetings people screamed and threatened to file a hundred-million-dollar lawsuit, and the restaurant owner's was one of the loudest voices of opposition. Although his wife, late one night, urged him to consider that people need to eat, it took the rector's visit and the efforts of many church people as well to finally get through to him. Representatives of this church took him on a tour of the center and on a trip to see other drop-in centers. They assured him that the center would be well policed, disciplined and controlled and would not affect his restaurant's clientele. They contacted him personally to ask, "Why are you upset? What do you fear will happen? What is your worst case scenario?" They enlisted city officials to support the center alongside him. They urged him to trust the track record and tradition of the church, whose other programs had been "class acts." When he finally changed his mind, it turned 180 degrees. He has become the number-one donor, serves on the advisory board of the center and is a frequent visitor. Daily he takes leftover restaurant food to the center, and he meets recipients on the street who cheerfully ask, "What's the soup today, Ed?" Ask him and his wife today about the church center, and they will reply, "We were just wrong! God opened our eyes!"

Testimony to the growing concern for social justice among evangelicals is offered by a church leader whose regional judicatory in the South is primarily evangelical. She sees several large evangelical churches being challenged to look at the total mission of the church—not only at evangelism and global mission, but also at such programs as Habitat for Humanity and hurricane-relief efforts. A few years ago Hurricane Hugo provided one "push" toward change in the South, but this leader attributes much change to effective, restoring leadership. Healing leaders are persons whose own agendas and desire for personal power are not their primary motivating factor; the lordship of Christ, the proclamation of the gospel and the witness of the church is what truly stirs them. Some of them are liberals who listen and heal, she said. She also spoke admiringly of a leader with much influence in the black churches who was willing to risk her own reputation and influence for the spiritual health of the church. Such healing leaders are people of honesty, humility and courage who are willing to listen and to give the benefit of the doubt. Such leaders at the national denominational level are trying with deliberate planning to re-include evangelism and global mission along with social mission. They are also deliberately including evangelicals, just as they have in the past been deliberate to include women and minorities.

Personal Gestures Toward Group Unity

Sometimes the words spoken by an empathetic person to a group whose members think they already know where that person stands—over against them—can be salutary in dealing with divisive issues. An ecumenically minded Lutheran was asked to speak at an Evangelical Lutheran Church in America conference set up to present a wide range of views on a number of key issues before the ELCA. As a faculty member at a leading ecumenical seminary, he had been typecast by many at the conference as a staunch liberal, deliberately put on the docket opposite a prominent neoconservative. During the conference's final session, he discussed in public reflection the dynamics of the conference and commented on the particularly difficult time white men (especially white male clergy) in the ELCA were having in today's society and some of the reasons for it. Many white clergymen had expected him to "beat up on them" because he is a liberal, and they expressed their appreciation for his unexpected understanding. "I felt we should lift up and join people's sufferings as a part of the gospel. 'There is some of us in all of us,'" he says.

A Pentecostal leader of much renown, David du Plessis, like the evangelical professor quoted earlier entered into conversations with persons representing a wide variety of opinions. For du Plessis this opportunity came when he participated in the NCC's Faith and Order Commission, which was staffed at that time by a Roman Catholic, Brother Jeffrey Gros. In another interview a professor at Andover-Newton identified a number of outstanding leaders—from evangelicals such as Richard Mouw of Fuller and Stephen Mott of Gordon-Conwell to liberals Roger Shinn and Charles West, and leading liberation theologian Gustavo Gutiérrez—whom he respects for their openness to dialogue, for taking a discussion to a deeper level and for hearing alternatives to their own initial position.

One pastor of a large congregation in California speaks admiringly of two seminary presidents in a classic illustration of people reaching out across religious boundaries—David Hubbard, president of Fuller, and Donald Shriver, president of Union Theological Seminary in New York, whom Hubbard invited to speak to the Fuller board. Taking a redeye flight across the continent (and missing novelist Toni Morrison's long-anticipated presentation at Union) for the Fuller address, Shriver gave a humorous yet serious after-dinner speech to Hubbard's board, many of them veterans of numerous battles against liberalism. Speaking about what they held in common and what differences they offered to each other, Shriver good-humoredly allowed these "veterans" a chance to sigh in relief. "Here were two good friends in the Association of Theological Schools presenting and being presented to the Fuller board with no agenda other than the desire to make such a public gesture. These were two human beings who did not trade away their institutional histories for one evening of collegiality, but they could affirm some things in common and calmly recognize their differences," summarizes the pastor.

When an invitation from another wing of the church comes in an unexpected gesture toward unity, the opportunity for conversation can be fruitful, even if only for a few people. A pastor in Canton, Ohio, told us this story:

> I (a mainline pastor), while serving a downtown congregation in a small
> Indiana town, was invited, along with every other minister in town, to a
> meeting sponsored by a group of Pentecostal ministers and laymen (Full

Gospel Businessmen). The topic was unity. They wanted to explore ways in which we might "come together in the name of Jesus Christ." Out of a possible group of thirty mainline pastors, about six showed up. The presenters were very kind, almost sweetly loving, but, alas, a little assuming. At the end of the meeting a date was set for the next "conversation." Out of the six mainline folks I was the only one at that next meeting. I met with a group of eight to twelve Pentecostal ministers and lay men and women weekly for more than three years.

I learned that their piety expressed itself largely through direct experiences with Jesus. They welcomed and rewarded personal revelations. "God told me" or "God has laid it on my heart" were common phrases used to speak of the will of God. One minister announced that Jesus came to worship at his church last Sunday morning. Everyone but me said "Praise God!" The dear man went on to say that Jesus came in the rear door, walked down the center aisle, stopped to tell him that his mission was pleasing God, then turned and left. I had two questions which I waited a month to ask. "What did Jesus look like? Why did he leave—isn't Jesus already there?" His response could have been written by Bultmann when this fine man spoke of the eyes of faith.

My relationship with the group went through several changes. They tried to validate me, in their eyes, by praying that I would speak in tongues. That didn't happen. I explained that I felt they saw me as an incomplete Christian because I did not display that "gift"; they denied it. Growth took place when a newcomer to the meeting boldly expressed his conviction that only ministers who could show the "evidence of speaking in tongues" were baptized in the Holy Spirit. The group immediately argued that one could be a minister even without "the baptism." I quietly said, "I am baptized with the Holy Spirit and I do not speak in tongues. Do you believe me?"

What is striking about this story is that the author committed himself to these people for *three years* and that he came to respect expressions of faith different from but no less powerful than those of his own religious community. That this trust and respect were mutual is evident in the support given him when a challenge was made by a newcomer. He did not bristle with indignation, either, when challenged but instead spoke with quiet confidence about his own convictions. The spirit with which he entered into this loving conversation was important, as was his peers' spirit in initiating it. Their approach might need some improvement, however, as this pastor gently suggests when he notes others failed to attend further meetings.

In another instance, two middle judicatory executives—one a liberal, the other an evangelical—incarnated as a team the unity they hoped to maintain for their denomination as it struggled with issues that were destroying that unity. Embodying that division in certain respects, they offered themselves to many congregations to discuss the issues as a team.

One of them observes that he finds helpful Milton Rokeach's "grid" that puts "what a person believes" along one plane and "how one holds that belief" on an intersecting plane: one can be conservative and open-minded, liberal and open-minded, conservative and close-minded or liberal and close-minded. One's hope for reconciliation and collaborating compromise comes with the open-minded conservatives, moderates and liberals, not with the close-minded of any group. With the belief that the denomination has a healthy share of open-minded Christians from across the spectrum of perspectives, the two executives proposed to churches and judicatories that they make presentations and lead discussions *together* on issues divisively confronting the church.

A national staff executive with the United Church of Canada relates his experience of committing, along with several others, to extensive dialogue over a two-year period with church leaders from another perspective than his own. He does not feel that much new insight or understanding emerged from that long encounter, largely because neither side had come to listen or had learned how to listen. The guidelines for empathetic listening suggested by Richard Salem might have been helpful with this group to avoid initially such simple problems as waiting for someone else to stop talking before taking a turn to speak. The agreement of liberals and evangelicals to commit themselves to dialogue for such an extended time was a precious opportunity—but it also required some very careful preparation. The barriers built up over many years and numerous antagonistic encounters did not simply disappear because they had agreed to meet.

Planning for Collaboration

Although a denominational conference on the difficult subject of abortion did not accomplish all that its designers had hoped, the event was prepared with great care. The conference used guidelines for small-group dialogue that were designed to foster carefully balanced discussions, a goal not entirely achieved because, in the view of the organizer, some participants did not report their position on abortion with full candor. A national staff member said that the purpose of the conference was not to change minds but to make positions clearer, better understood and respected and to encourage attendees to be open to considering alternatives. Using guidelines for speaking was helpful, even adding humor at times. Thinking carefully before speaking, limiting a speaker's time, being nonjudgmental and really hearing another's views, not preparing one's own thoughts while others were speaking—these are all helpful guidelines. (The staff member referred to an article in the *Utne Reader* that urged a return to the European "salon" model for the contemplative discussion of issues and that suggested something akin to the Native American practice of passing around a "talking stick" be tried. Only when handed the stick may one speak, and when hands are empty one must listen.)

One of our Ecunet correspondents offers a set of steps helpful for church groups gathered around issues that divide members into conservative and liberal camps. He suggests these five steps, which are informed by his own experience:

☐ *For the participants to affirm that they are Christians seeking the truth as Christians and that the Christian gospel stands in judgment above all political ideologies.* This is a vital step because of mistrust between the two worldviews. Prayer is highly recommended.

☐ *For all participants to be genuinely willing to reexamine their own views.* Without this, there is little point in dialogue.

☐ *For participants to begin discussions on a particular topic by critiquing their own positions and stating as candidly as possible any weaknesses.* This enhances trust and provides a starting place for dialogue.

☐ *For participants to conduct the dialogue with questions and not by assertions.* Violating this rule is always a mistake. Questions make the other person think. Assertions make the other person become defensive.

☐ *For participants, as Christians, to periodically reaffirm their search for truth.* Such affirmations help to neutralize the tension between the two worldviews and enable a dialogue to take place that is governed by gospel criteria.

Another suggestion in standard conflict-resolution literature is to *state what the other person is saying to the other person's satisfaction before proceeding to make one's own statement.* This, in a rather formal discussion procedure, becomes one of the guidelines for dialogue.

When a group consistently faces internal conflict in attempting to do its work, a radically different approach may be useful. The co-chairs of the Presbyterian Committee on Reunion, over its long and ultimately effective life, recall the despair and frustration they shared as they assessed the lack of progress over several nettlesome issues that were necessary to grasp and overcome if reunion were to be achieved among Presbyterians in the North and South. They entered a 1980 meeting in Memphis with a feeling that it would be their last committee gathering unless a breakthrough occurred and that the committee would have to be put "on hold" until some more propitious time.

Both the northern and southern branches of Presbyterianism, severed from one another during the Civil War, had much to learn about each other in the committee. During his fourteen-year journey on the committee, one northerner says, he had to confront and divest himself of prejudices against southerners and southern culture that he had not known he held. Some on the committee had the gift of humor, which helped during some painful discoveries. Gradually they also discovered the richness within their differences, the quality and character that each brought to the table. Caricatures were lessened, fears decreased, institutional prejudices overcome.

In spite of all that growth the committee had reached a near impasse when it came time to prepare a draft. The General Assembly, however, had recently named several conservatives to the committee, which meant confronting some differences "in the flesh." (One woman member protested having to enfold "fundies" within the committee and was reminded gently by others that women themselves had faced similar rejections by men.) But the Memphis meeting was a turning point. With the presence of conservatives, discussion *about* them became discussion *with* them, and a new dynamic occurred. Some more silent members came forward to provide helpful language and a healing spirit of compromise. To the amazement of all (excepting the Holy Spirit), the Memphis meeting ended with a draft the committee felt it could submit, with its own unanimity and enthusiasm, to the churches for a vote.

This experience is matched by attempts to confront polarization at other levels of denominational life. One middle judicatory leader described the frustration among those on a candidate committee that had become so polarized between liberals and evangelicals, it was difficult to act upon candidates. This man, who was committee chair for a number of years, explains that the division came about over what kind of leaders they wanted as pastors and what kind of preparation they wanted these leaders to have. Some on the committee clearly did not want evangelically trained, intolerant persons with narrow theology and little denominational loyalty (as they would characterize them) in their judicatory. Such candidates, like those coming from seminaries such as Gordon-Conwell and Fuller or from parachurch organizations such as InterVarsity, were immediately suspect. Although liberals argued against admitting candidates from these nondenominational sources, they were not opposed to candidates coming from Harvard—so clearly the issue was not denominational loyalty or tradition but theological stance, observes the committee chair. Nor would liberals on the committee want to ordain such candidates to a parachurch responsibility in their judicatory. Others, like the chair, wanted candidates with a strong confessional viewpoint, an idea of religious and biblical heritage and a clear sense of pastoral direction. Candidates were caught in the middle of the committee's strife.

The candidate committee held several retreats in which they tried to understand each other's formative spiritual experiences. They asked questions like "What are we afraid of—for the church, for the candidate, for ourselves?" "What are we afraid we will lose or that someone else will gain?" "What can we affirm and appreciate in one another?" Together they exposed fears, saw many of them as irrational and became less polarized among themselves. Although issues continued to separate them, they found ways of working with them. They did some studies to track their fears and to discover if they were true or not. They explored the clues and marks of a good pastor and then listed them and discussed how they were independent of polarizations. The chair also tried very carefully to assign tasks within the committee that fitted the unique gifts of each member, so that their contributions could be more fully appreciated.

Similarly, in chairing a placement committee, this same leader found that affirmative action for women and minorities was a key polarizing issue. Processes and procedures were very carefully designed to protect people, and these helped with the evangelical-liberal tensions within the committee. Each subgroup on the committee had its list of concerns that differed from the other. Rights of the congregation (conservative) were in tension with rights of the middle judicatories and denomination (liberal), but these procedures and processes helped resolve the differences.

In general, this thoughtful leader suggests that small groups must discover areas of commonality and define them, distinguish the substantial fears from irrational fears and develop personal relationships. This may require a willingness to stay with one committee for a long time in order to be effective, to develop trust with one another and to care about people quite different from oneself.

Building Trust Relationships in Groups

Time. Building relationships of trust, working through differences that have layer upon layer of fears and stereotypes to uncover and coming to some areas of agreement and common ground all take time. Many church meetings and special events suffer from the reality that "time is money," and that time *costs* money when people are brought together from many distant points to work together on complex issues. Meals, hotel rooms, meeting space, staff time, and the donated work time of many remarkably generous church laity are expensive. Taking time to explore personal life stories, sharing worship and prayer, stopping an agenda to deal with a snarl of opposing views or even following some rather intricate procedures and processes may seem too expensive to many participants. They seem to "waste the church's money."

But one Methodist pastor remembers an Oxford conference on faith and economics that achieved its goals precisely because time was taken to search for common ground, to talk "beyond the language" to hear what was really meant, to listen to the Scriptures speak and to include opposition voices without dismissing them or labeling it a conflict prematurely. The truly wasted money is that money spent to arrive willy-nilly at a particular position, leaving behind bloodied, unconverted, angry participants. Eventually time and money must be spent to clean up the wreckage.

Although more time might not have helped the United Church of

Christ avert all the problems it faced as it prepared its own "Christian Faith: Economic Life and Justice" pronouncement, more time might have helped the UCC avoid some of the conflict. The UCC's procedures were critically examined by Professor W. Widick Schroeder in his book *Flawed Process and Sectarian Substance*. This book analyzes the gradual shift in committee participants as the work progressed and some of those who held more centrist positions gave way to (or were excluded from, depending upon the perceptions of members of the committee) a socialist-leaning minority who wrote the final draft.

Participant Professor Roger Shinn, reviewing Schroeder's book in the *Christian Century*,[2] acknowledges the barriers of time and money that did not permit many meetings, thus leading to superficiality and an attempt to contrive a formula to conceal differences. The pressure to achieve a consensus and a document that could be brought before the whole UCC church was tremendous, he asserts. One consequence was that the UCC Pension Board prepared its own statement on "The Market System and American Democratic Polity," which differed significantly from the committee's work. Another consequence was an alienation from the pronouncement committee of some who felt their participation had been "dropped" by those who pursued consensus through a more clear-cut ideology. (This sentiment is held by the UCC professor we quoted earlier.) The pressure to reach closure on complex theological and economic issues in a short time played a role in the production of a statement that, though adopted by the UCC General Synod, left some, including Schroeder, calling it a "flawed process."

One woman executive of a southern middle judicatory also suggests that taking time to talk is valuable. Many in her judicatory know already where their colleagues stand on issues, yet they learned from each other regarding the inclusive-language issue by taking time to speak back and forth. How we learn to treat one another when we differ is important. "Such talking prepares [us] for tough times," she says.

"Taking time" was the subject of a lively, colorful exchange within Ecunet. During this conversation one pastor wrote,

> I've been trying to decide why liberals and conservatives live together so well here at (my church) in Rock Island. (Just watch, tomorrow will come the big explosion!) At least a partial reason is that people know there is

room—more than that, intentional welcome—for diverse points of view. A person need not sally out with all guns blazing in order to be heard. Debate can occur at leisure.

John and Herb can sit in the pew in front of Bessie, who has serious doubts about welcoming gays into the congregation, without anyone being in a rush to change anyone's mind or feelings. John and Herb can talk to Bessie knowing her as a lovely, if a bit lonely and sometimes superficial, lady. Bessie has to do her thinking about gay couples knowing that she enjoys Herb and John. Lou, a big-business Republican, and Mary Ann, a socialist-leaning Democrat, have a safe and comfortable territory [in which] to learn from each other.

If we did not have *time* to appreciate one another and discover how much we agree on, we'd be fighting all the time. And that time is, I suspect, a mental creation. Since debate is never closed, we need not be in a rush to tear into each other.

To the extent I'm responsible for that climate I can thank some colleagues who helped me move on from early attack-dog intellectual training to seeing the congregation as a "safe place." The fact that all these colleagues are female may be only a coincidence.

To these comments a computer conversationalist in Austin, Texas, replied, "Some of that old 'attack-dog intellectual' bit is still there, but the bark has softer edges now. Time sorta does that to all of us, doesn't it? That, and getting knocked around a bit, sorta like how stonewashing new blue jeans softens the fabric and mellows the color."

Sometimes it is not so much the amount of time taken as the timing itself, as a local pastor observed as he waited until his upset parishioner had healed emotionally before further confronting her as her pastor. One layperson speaks of the value of having an "armistice"—an acceptable period of doing and being and handling hostility, allowing time for feelings to cool off. Often the most important time of reconciliation occurs after a very divisive decision has been made. Those who felt defeated by a vote may also be feeling rebuffed and judged as being in the wrong. They may be defensive, angry, disappointed, hurt and ready to stalk out. A former ecumenical-council official's efforts to seek out persons with whom she has been in disagreement apply here: she recommends you reaffirm relationship with someone whose views have been rejected, assure the persons defeated that you understand at least some aspects of their position and explain what valuable truth you felt you had to uphold, for these are ways of saying that we do not vote one another out of the body of Christ. A religious journalist who has sat through many a church meeting suggests that "we don't make enough effort to try to reach each individual when that person is hurting and disagreeing with the majority. We forget to care."

When an opponent is down, care and concern shown by someone who has been on the opposite side is especially treasured. A prominent Methodist who was in many ways a forceful opponent of leaders of the National Council of Churches, befriended Bishop James Armstrong when Armstrong felt compelled to resign from the presidency of the National Council of Churches as his life collapsed in some disgrace. This evangelical Methodist leader, along with a second Methodist bishop, raised funds to assist Armstrong until his life circumstances improved. This leader also remained a steadfast friend of the second bishop until that bishop's death from AIDS.

Space. Related to the importance of taking the necessary time to allow relationships and decisions to ripen is the importance of a "safe space," as a Rock Island pastor observes in his congregation's life together. Local congregations that are not under duress to produce a document, fulfill a mandated agenda or make a necessary decision on behalf of some structure of the church are places where Christians can quietly love and learn their way into a deeper understanding of one another and perhaps increase their common ground. When the human-sexuality report was becoming a national story in secular newspapers, many local Presbyterian congregations were using the report as an occasion to explore relationships and issues they had been avoiding (as Bessie and Herb and John are doing in the anecdote above). They probed with cautious fingers the tender, inflamed subject of sexuality, some of them inviting gays and lesbians to speak for the first time in that capacity within their congregations. The report made such painful discussion timely, and the congregation itself provided the safety and comfort in which to speak, usually with no intention of coming to some common statement or declaration.

Space was an important factor in a seminary's yearning for greater community among its faculty, students and administration in the midst of increasingly diverse views. The seminary's efforts under the leadership of its president brought to light, through dialogue and a follow-up survey, the need for simple, casual gathering places on campus. By keeping the dining room open all day, scheduling some social gatherings after chapel and searching for more "spaces" in which to encourage communication, a new opportunity for bridging differences and establishing community flourished.

Fairness. One of the cardinal concerns expressed by groups with many differing viewpoints is that of fairness. What may be seen by one group as wise promotion of its views or strategic political maneuvering for a "good" outcome is perceived by others as taking unfair advantage in selecting a speaker sympathetic to one position, "stacking the deck" with like-minded people on a committee or even using worship to present the "only acceptable" Christian view. A "healing leader," as described above by a judicatory official we interviewed, is one who avoids any taint of unfairness by seeking to be sure that no group feels manipulated by the agenda, overwhelmed by numbers of opposing views or cornered into praying for something with which they disagree.

The quest for fairness sometimes means seeking a "balanced" viewpoint represented in a particular committee or event. A denominational official found that the effort to achieve a balanced representation of views on the abortion issue had hazards too, as judicatories felt pressured or bypassed when the delegates they had named were determined to be too heavily weighted toward pro-choice and the delegation's composition had to be adjusted. Sometimes it is exceedingly difficult to provide the desired balance—whether a balance of particular religious perspectives or positions on issues, a balanced racial or gender mix or a balance of some other factors (for example, geography, church structures, age groups and so on). A trusting "benefit of the doubt" may be necessary when a careful search for balance has still not been achieved.

That somewhat beleaguered national staffer (who tried to ensure balanced discussions at a denominational conference) provides a helpful image when she urges us to "walk in one another's shoes." When we plan an agenda, prepare even a small meeting, choose a subcommittee or select a speaker, we can be healing leaders if we practice empathy for those who represent a view different from our own. What "makes sense" to one group may simply "make enemies" of another!

Testimony About Helpful Church Structure
Incidents related in this chapter have come from congregational, middle

judicatory and denominational levels of church life. It may be noted, however, that all of them involve face-to-face groups in which persons can directly encounter other persons. In denominational meetings and structures where face-to-face exchange is not possible, the story is less positive. Many of our interviews uncovered appreciation of things the churches are doing to work on tensions, perceived unfairness and divisiveness within the church family, at denominational and ecumenical levels. An open-meetings policy can play a significant role in assuring church members that work done on their behalf is not done secretly, and it helps to dispel false rumors and probably curbs rhetoric that could be hurtful or unproductive. When a reporter with a different viewpoint from yours is present, you might think a little more carefully about how your actions and speeches might be "read" by others who share that reporter's perspective. One editor of a dissident magazine testifies to the value of an open-meeting policy and claims he, in turn, is striving for greater accuracy and less stridency.

Liberals have predominated in the central offices of the mainline denominations and ecumenical agencies since the build-up of bureaucracies after World War II. Although from time to time efforts are made to broaden representation of theological and social-political views, the attempts are met with some skepticism. Anticipating "tokenism," some evangelicals dismiss the effort as not serious, some who are asked to serve refuse, and others suspect a new evangelical staff or committee participant has "sold out." Sometimes after a few meetings the minority-view persons cease to attend, perhaps having come to the conclusion that the outcome is stacked against them. Liberals, from their perspective, may feel that evangelicals are not responding to their efforts to be more inclusive, and their zeal wanes. Simply "naming" them to a committee is just the beginning, not the end, of attempts to confront polarization.

Evangelicals who have agreed to serve on staffs or committees dominated by liberals have a double obligation: They need to assert with clarity and freedom the evangelicalism they represent. But when they experience trust and respect from liberals they encounter, they also need to report this to their fellow evangelicals. One such staff person in a denominational headquarters has tried to convey the encouraging, collaborative experience he has had with liberal staff, but he regrets that many evangelicals do not quite believe him. The testimony from those evangelically oriented national staff who are serving in denominations that struggle to accommodate diverse theological perspectives is not all positive, however. Liberals are seen to be more "liberal" and open on the diversities of race and ethnicity, gender and sexual orientation than on theology, some contend.

Liberal leaders who make an effort to bring evangelicals to these staff positions, often with modest results, may find that their sincere appreciation of the evangelicals' gifts is received guardedly on both sides—a legacy from past hostility and suspicion. Liberal administrators, asserts one of them, must therefore be willing to be misunderstood or to be suspect in order to move beyond mere power struggle. We must "take in trust the risk of trust," he urges. It is a risk partly because doctrinal issues far more complex than the social justice-evangelical dichotomy await the church. The significance of Jesus in a religiously plural world is perhaps the most critical theological issue of the future, declare two national staff members—one liberal, the other evangelical.

Some liberals are very harsh in their attitudes toward evangelicals, especially those evangelicals they do not know, preferring to keep them out of positions of power and influence. Arrogance is a temptation for every position. In fact, the refusal of some evangelicals to take an active role in the affairs of the larger church and their willingness to live in large churches in isolation from the denomination may also be acts of arrogance.

Polity differences may require new ways of addressing the imbalances that have afflicted denominational structures over the past fifty years, but the strategies employed within those differing configurations are not necessarily dissimilar. The efforts of liberals to include more women and minorities in their structures, though not fully comparable, may offer some parallels. Arguments that "I don't know any qualified women or Hispanics or African-Americans" have gradually given way to patient search and referral. Long-standing evangelical networks and parachurch groups (both denominational and ecumenical), as well as large evangelical congregations, have developed leadership in depth. The question of identifying "qualified evangelicals," therefore, may hinge on what is meant by *qualified*. Questions such as "Will they fit in?" "Can they be trusted?" and "Will they try to block the agenda?" may reflect a subtle determination to maintain control. Liberals must extend to evangelicals the freedom to be themselves.

As we noted in an earlier chapter, the mainline denominations have spawned a number of organizations that are outside the official structures of the parent denomination and that represent particular theological perspectives within it. These groups not only provide a "home within a home" for those with certain theological-political-social viewpoints who are uncomfortable with the denomination's public stance, they are also intended as pressure groups for change and renewal of the denomination. In some instances, though they may seem abrasive critics, these very groups keep the denomination from fracturing, and some actively seek reconciliation.[3]

Less known, perhaps, have been the efforts of the National Council of Churches in recent years purposely to reach out to and establish better communication with the National Association of Evangelicals and also with the Roman Catholic Church. Visits by NCC staff from New York to Wheaton, Illinois, for conversations with NAE staff have not produced sudden fraternity or a merger, but they have lessened tensions, opened up opportunities for further conversation and overcome some misinformation. A special NCC committee headed by Lutheran Bishop Herbert Chilstrom was set up to converse with evangelicals and Roman Catholics. The purpose was not to draw them into the NCC—a new ecumenical embodiment would be required to bring them together—but to recognize that without them the ecumenical council is not whole. Taking "soundings" on possible future steps, the committee was attempting to be accountable to Jesus Christ through serious and continuing conversations. In a similar positive spirit Billy Graham and NCC General Secretary Joan Brown Campbell have held several meetings, including public radio interviews.

Religious educational institutions also struggle with these divisions, especially in seminaries. One southern seminary president, sensing that the tensions within the community needed more aggressive attention, arranged with the faculty to cancel morning classes and instead to hold a community forum at which such questions as "What are you most afraid to say in this school?" were discussed in a packed assembly. Again, Jimmy

Carter's Middle East peace-process model was employed. People divided into groups of three, each taking a turn to answer a posed question, to relate back someone else's answer and to take notes on another's answer. Then group members named one of their three to a larger nine-member group, which repeated the procedure. Finally, three from each large group were named to a "fishbowl," to which the rest of the group listened. Out of this elaborate process a set of concerns was compiled, a survey was later taken to determine the most important concerns, and the results were reported to the community and the administration for action.

One of the top three concerns, which voiced the situation underlying most of the other issues, was that this seminary was begun in another, more homogeneous era, and today it is functioning with a system that is no longer adequate for the new kind of diversity that already exists. Have institutional values changed to represent the new reality of an increasingly pluralistic student body and world community? This question had implications for curriculum, for faculty selection, for worship styles, for language use and for ordinary communication channels. Efforts to respond to this basic challenge throughout the institution's life are continuing.

A seminary long noted for its great diversity of thought and its rigor in holding its community intact is Union Theological Seminary in New York City, whose welcome to "all sorts and conditions" of people and ideas is legendary. One of its African-American faculty members remarked upon the progress of that institution as evidenced in its gospel chorus, which, although founded by blacks, is now fifty percent white—at the invitation of the black singers. Usually whites incorporate blacks into their programs and projects, implicitly defining them according to white values that they assume to be superior, he says. At Union blacks have challenged "white hegemony," and their persistent critique of and struggle against "white culture" has begun to transform the atmosphere, with some pain on all sides. African-Americans have increased the evangelical breadth at Union, although some white evangelicals still struggle for recognition.

Another example of taking a step beyond the "caucus mentality" that tends to dominate institutions coping with pluralism, notes this same faculty member, occurred at a biennial United Church of Christ Synod, which was held in Norfolk, Virginia. African-Americans used to hold their own separate worship service, but in Norfolk the service belonged to the whole synod; everyone was invited to the service as part of the "official program," and many whites attended.

One evangelical black on a national denominational staff speaks of a global evangelism task force as the best example he knows of people with diverse views who prayed and negotiated to produce a paper that then "sailed through" the national governing body. "If only we could multiply these experiences!" he exclaims. He and other African-Americans look to the liberals to deal with their needs, but theologically many of them are more comfortable with evangelicals. And when needed, evangelicals can be reached on issues of racism through scripture. They respond to the scriptural, theological dimension of issues, even though they may be reluctant to receive the interpretation. He suggests that liberals count too much on socioeconomic presentations and not enough on theology and the Bible in the church. He has demonstrated in seminary continuing-education classes for pastors and laity that racial polarity can be addressed effectively through theology and Scripture. One businessman elder came to his class just to please him, but afterward he told the teacher with tears in his eyes that God wanted him there to deal with his racism.

Other church leaders at various levels of the denominations testify to the importance of finding ways for more face-to-face truthful conversations between people with different perspectives. One middle judicatory executive urges that each group place "sensors"—responsible spokespersons from the "other side"—into meetings, not to act as full participants but to listen and provide accurate feedback on what is said, thus monitoring the stories by journalists who tend to thrive on controversy. This would be "intentional penetration" of one another's camp, to use culture-war lingo.

This executive visits and speaks frequently in "tall steeple" churches, which tend to feel either alienated from the denominational structures or simply self-sufficient. When people in these large congregations say they don't want to offend anyone, he counters, "'You're talking about a gospel I don't know anything about!' How can we have salutary healing in the church if we don't offend anyone? We can be mere salespeople (a 'sellable Jesus') or we can reflect the integrity of the gospel." He believes God's will emerges out of Christian contention that is more than just throwing rocks.

Bringing people face to face depends again on church polity to a degree, but the concepts are transferable. Gathering as much noncontroversial material as possible into one action, a "consent agenda," has allowed more time for serious discussion of hotly debated matters at middle and national judicatory levels for one church. Allowing middle judicatory spokespersons direct access to national committees on business they have proposed is another approach. Holding conferences with a serious effort to expand their spiritual dimension along with their social action has proved effective and healing, especially when a careful balance of participants is pursued. Inviting national staff into local congregations for two-way discussion has lowered some barriers and "heat" and has helped participants break down preconceived ideas of "monolithic" differences.

Above all, says one leader, we need to recognize the importance of telling the truth, especially the "truth" told by those in power positions in our denominations. "Truth is the ultimate solution to the illegitimate exercise of power. Truth does come out, but the system must be zealous to correct its mistakes. The church is forgiving of error—but not of untruth, because it destroys trust," he says. In his view the "lust for power and control" is a disease that afflicts all factions within our churches.

To that wisdom should be added the word of a pastor of a large Chicago congregation: he urges that we be affectionate toward people with whom we have serious differences, without moderating the passion of our own position. The differences will not go away immediately because we use kind words, but our words have more long-term effect than a bullhorn or "hard words with a hard edge." This liberal pastor, who has served on a commission dealing with a congregation's refusal to allow homosexuals membership in their church, deplores the loss of the art of compromise by persons who assert ideological purity on either side of such questions, but he stresses the importance of empathy, respect and affection— and of speaking the truth with love.

Roman Catholics Are Struggling Too
Although in the interest of focusing these discussions we have concen-

trated primarily on the divisions in Protestant churches, we can benefit from insights brought by our Christian colleagues in the Roman Catholic Church. Catholicism in the United States is struggling with many of the divisions and polarities that Protestantism faces, only in some slightly different expressions. Listen to this description[4] prepared by the National Pastoral Life Center for the new Catholic Common Ground Project:

> It is widely admitted that the Catholic Church in the United States has entered a time of peril. Many of its leaders, both clerical and lay, feel under siege and increasingly polarized. Many of the faithful, particularly its young people, feel disenfranchised, confused about their beliefs, and increasingly adrift. Many of its institutions feel uncertain of their identity and increasingly fearful about their future. . . .
>
> But even as conditions have changed, party lines have hardened. A mood of suspicion and acrimony hangs over many of those most active in the church's life; at moments it even seems to have infiltrated the ranks of the bishops. . . . Candid discussion is inhibited. Across the whole spectrum of views within the church, proposals are subject to ideological litmus tests. Ideas, journals and leaders are pressed to align themselves with preexisting camps and are viewed warily when they depart from these expectations.

The Catholic Common Ground Project has been established to address these concerns through conferences, papers, deliberations and other meetings that bring conflicting views into dialogue. Some working principles for these engagements contain wisdom from which Protestants also can benefit:

> ☐ We should recognize that no single group or viewpoint in the church has a complete monopoly on the truth. . . . Solutions to the church's problems will almost inevitably emerge from a variety of sources.
>
> ☐ We should not envision ourselves or any one part of the church as a saving remnant. . . .
>
> ☐ We should test all proposals for their pastoral realism and potential impact on living individuals as well as for their theological truth. . . .
>
> ☐ We should presume that those with whom we differ are acting in good faith. They deserve civility, charity and a good-faith effort to understand their concerns. We should not substitute labels, abstraction or blanketing terms—"radical feminism," "the hierarchy," "the Vatican"—for living, complicated realities.
>
> ☐ We should put the best possible construction on differing positions,

addressing their strongest points rather than seizing upon the most vulnerable aspects in order to discredit them. We should detect the valid insights and legitimate worries that may underlie even questionable arguments.

☐ We should be cautious in ascribing motives. We should not impugn another's love of the church or loyalty to it. We should not rush to interpret disagreements as conflicts of starkly opposing principles rather than as differences in degree or in prudential pastoral judgments about the relevant facts.

☐ We should bring the church to engage the realities of contemporary culture, not by simple defiance or by naive acquiescence, but acknowledging . . . our culture's valid achievements and real dangers.

Many of these working principles voice views similar to those of Protestants we have quoted, but some have a direct clarity and freshness of expression that add new depth to our mutual efforts to strengthen and heal our churches.

10

. . . .

Confronting
Controversy in
Community
Congregations

*I have hope, not advice. I have hope that for all parts of the church
our understanding of the Christian faith is one which leads us to identify
with persons in their joy and in their suffering. Such sensibility for other people
in the society makes other sorts of agendas take secondary place. Lines that divide
are usually overcome whenever we get close enough to people
in their joys and sorrows and participate with them there. . . .
Jesus' capacity to suffer and rejoice with people drew people around him.*
A LIBERAL SEMINARY PROFESSOR

Local churches are safe places for exploring in human depth many
issues that tear our society apart—not only religious differences but
racism, poverty, lawlessness, hunger, women's sense of exclusion and
even the alienation of groups such as the elderly, the youth or the disabled.
Polarizations occur around many of these issues, though often they do
not break neatly into liberal-conservative categories either religiously or
politically. Where in the society can such matters be discussed with
assurance that the issue "cannot separate us from the love of Christ" or
from one another if not in our congregations?

Although much of what has been said in the previous chapter applies
directly to local congregations confronting internal strife, some of our
interviewees' stories may provide hope and insight to congregations "at

risk" and thus merit special attention. We will look at pastors and congregations who pursued cohesion as they dealt with and acted on issues that tended to pull them apart.

With Liberty and Justice for All

In one overwhelmingly Republican, "country club" congregation, moderate leadership wanted to work on resolving the nuclear-weapons issue during the era of the "nuclear freeze" discussions. One pastor describes how she, through a carefully designed and fair process, led this California congregation into this truly explosive dialogue without its tearing them apart. When the church session met on retreat and the subject was broached, one member was so angry that he called the others communists. But within two years, through a series of adult-education courses, workshops and task forces on both sides of the issue, the session of that congregation adopted the denomination's peacemaking emphasis with only two dissenting votes.

How did the leadership accomplish this? They didn't try to "sell" a particular viewpoint but acknowledged that Christians could sincerely hold various positions. They brought in strong spokespersons, not "straw men," to speak for differing views. For example, they listened respectfully to Christians working in the defense industry, and in these discussions stereotypes were shattered. The leadership had a serious commitment to fairness and accorded dignity to all by creating a "space" for listening. One high-ranking military man said it was the first time he had been given a fair shot in the church! Too often we begin "dialogue" with a certain outcome already in mind. One feels compromised when an opposing view is presented and the listeners, congratulating themselves on being very tolerant, remain certain who the "good guys" are. This pastor says that too often there is "party-line righteousness" on both right and left, on both conservative and liberal sides, and not a true open exploration of the issues. We need to look at the various ways people really learn—but this only happens when the process is not already charted or "loaded" but open-ended. When people are backed into a corner, they don't change!

Learning How We Learn

That moderate pastor is an evangelical. A liberal denominational executive, who is also a woman, agrees that we need to examine how people are actually "educated" into a new understanding of an issue. She stresses the importance of committing oneself to listen and learn about difficult issues in a community. When a congregation thoroughly studies an issue and comes to some position, she says, the person who may still disagree with the majority is, however, committed to the community and may participate in whatever aspects or strategies his or her own conscience may allow. If the educational process has been a good and fair one, both sides will respect one another, understand their personal differences and continue to grow. Damage occurs when pastors are so threatened by controversy that they do not allow their congregations to take on difficult issues. Seminaries should offer their students conflict-resolution training, this administrator believes.

She describes a congregation that studied the conditions in Central America, invited persons who had traveled there to come and speak, listened to college professors who had fled from Central America and explored the meaning of *refugee*. After a long educational process the session voted to become a sanctuary church. She describes also the decision of Riverside Church in New York City to become a sanctuary congregation after an eight-month study process. Some lawyers in the congregational meeting seriously questioned the idea, and their concerns were not cut off. Eventually some of the lawyers began to help the refugees, once they came to know them face to face.

Personally experiencing other worlds is one of the most effective means of learning, this denominational staffer declares. She urges congregations to send some of their members to other lands so they can experience and "feel into" other cultures and discover how their own culture is perceived elsewhere. We may not change our own positions on issues, but we will become more understanding and respectful of differing views. One problem with the national governing assembly process in many of our denominations, she observes, is that it is so legislative and "paper oriented"; people go to lobby and to win, not to cooperate and learn. Local congregations are in a much better position for actually learning if they will shed their individual self-righteousness and let God be present to them in their *community*. But, she cautions, when God enters your midst, you may be called beyond dialogue and into active obedience.

This same church executive—who found herself under house arrest in Central America during a time of great tension and confrontation that gave rise to the "sanctuary" movement in the United States—recalls with amazement the simple faith of Roman Catholic Central American refugees who trusted her, an American Christian, enough to say, "Walk with us so we won't be killed." They believed in the goodness of God and the goodness of other Christians, even "enemy" American Christians. They trusted her word with their lives, and this was a faith-giving experience for her. In our local congregations, she implies, we entrust ourselves to one another in community. We learn to walk in truth and love together, whether evangelical or progressive in our religion, whether conservative or liberal in political ideology.

Sometimes a sense of fairness and openness is achieved in less demanding ways than those described above by this administrator and the California pastor. Another senior pastor tells how his Albany congregation was involved in many tough issues, some of them involving heated national politics. He used a "concerns microphone" in the sanctuary during announcement time for persons who needed an opportunity to speak or to "vent" an opposing view. When someone announced that the "local committee to impeach the President" would be meeting, many people were upset. At least eleven of them came to the microphone to protest such a meeting in their church—but none of them left the church in anger. When he preached a sermon on Watergate, a parishioner started to walk out, suddenly remembered the open mike, used it and stayed in the congregation.

Oddly enough, more people were inclined to leave that church over simple matters such as maintenance of the church building than over theological disagreements. One congregant left because he disapproved of replacing the carpeting after a big church fire because it cost too much and he felt the money could have been better spent on missions. One of the risks of having a representative form of government in our churches, says this pastor, is that we give some tasks and decisions over to officers and that they sometimes fail to do enough consulting and explaining. This failure may or may not be relevant when issues of faith perspective are forefront, but sometimes the issue at hand is a religious one clothed in nonreligious garb. Often people just feel that their views have been ignored, their point of view excluded from consideration.

Giving better officer and new-member training. Two of our interviewees, one a pastor and the other a layperson, suggest that more training of officers in their duties and more training of officers and new members in the faith, traditions and governance of their denomination are needed. People need to wrestle with what it means to be in church membership, in a "covenant community." In a religious consumer climate of personality cults, such as those around "televangelists," the layman says, people too readily simply "shop" for a pastor and a church and too casually "change channels." The best opportunities for helping people understand what they are getting into—what their commitment is intended to mean—is when they join the church or take a responsible office. (Remember, for example, the story of Ted and Carol Manning in chapter one.)

There is an unprecedented mobility of membership. People shift not only from one local congregation to another but from one denomination to another with no commitment or understanding of the historical story and culture of each denomination, says this active lay leader. His own congregation doesn't know the denominational standards of governance or any of the confessions, and it is difficult to get anyone to run for church office. Only when the denomination is embroiled in controversy, like that faced by the Episcopal Church over its prayer book or by the Methodists over the ordination of homosexuals, do members of the local church become concerned about their denomination. Perhaps teaching people what it means to be a Lutheran (or a Disciple or a Methodist or a Baptist) will cause some people to leave the congregation, but those who stay will know why they are there. He is very pleased that his new pastor hopes to teach the congregation about its denominational heritage.

Acknowledging that ideas weren't born yesterday. Communicants' classes and officer retreats are also places where a solid grounding in church history is helpful, especially when it is related to the wider church and puts a perspective upon the present, adds a judicatory executive. An ethicist from the United Church of Christ also urges reading more history: "They weren't so dumb then," he asserts, "and though they may not have done what you want on your issues, they worked well on some different ones." Things have developed very quickly recently, compared to the past, and our current popular model for social change takes momentum from the French Revolution, Marxism and the rapid decolonialization that followed World War II, he explains. These are dramatic public revolutionary acts of solidarity, but there are other channels for change, ones that nurture, form, upbuild. We could use more respect for the slow upbuilding and construction of social institutions, the ethicist suggests. We would do well to remember how long the church took to come to a common mind on such important matters as the doctrine of the Trinity, for example. Perhaps in our churches we come down too quickly on one side or the other of some complex issues.

To a sense of history, tradition and governance, a middle judicatory executive would add more grounding in the Bible. Neither liberals nor evangelicals are impressively biblically literate. Bible study provides a sound base when differences arise, and we must learn how to use the Bible well long before an issue of contention causes people to scurry through its pages, hunting for support for their position. Many new people in the church have little familiarity with Scripture, and it is the church's obligation to teach them about it.

Combining Inward and Outward Journeys

A progressive pastor and former moderator of his church's national governing body speaks warmly of two congregations that, like his own, combine strong spirituality and social witness. The Church of the Savior in Washington, D.C., emphasizes a shared deep commitment to one another in community and to God. A broad range of Christians are drawn to this rich mixture of community covenant, spiritual growth and active social concern. Another lively congregation, says the former moderator, is in his judicatory: St. Alban's, a theologically conservative congregation whose pastor was trained in the Salvation Army. Through his eloquent, humble leadership they have marched in Washington for justice in Central America, worked on drug and jobs issues, developed a strong youth group and have had to double their worship services.

This former moderator is wary of peaceful, noncontroversial churches. Destructive controversy tends to diminish in congregations as common purposes are discovered. The best force for unity in a church is working together where we can on controversial issues, he says, and recognizing that we fight about only what we think is important; peace can sometimes be dull and useless. He urges people not to lose heart, to do what they feel called to do, to respect the convictions of other people who differ from themselves and to leave it to God's providence to determine the outcome. He also likes to paraphrase community organizer Saul Alinsky, who said he never tried to destroy enemies, just to defeat them, because tomorrow he may need them as allies.

A participant in the Ecunet discussion continues this thought:

> What we all need to learn is that it is possible to fight *with* and *against* the same person or entity. Relationally, it is difficult for me to join hands with a person on Monday against racism and then on Tuesday ban that person's gay group from meeting in the church—and then on Wednesday invite that same person to church for an evangelism service. On Thursday I will join with that person to expose redlining, on Friday be told by that person I am not welcome at the Planned Parenthood meeting, and on Saturday be invited by that person to a prayer retreat. . . . But it is only possible when we serve a God who calls us to love our enemies.

One of Chicago's leading pastors says that exciting, vital churches today have the "two poles" of the church living in "respectful uneasiness." At his downtown church the old-time social activists, including some nonreligious altruists, participate in social programs (for example, tutoring programs that enable illiterate children to read), and gradually the love of Jesus becomes real to them. Then there are the persons who come with specific spiritual needs or who are evangelicals, and they learn to put their love into action. Both dynamics go on at once. Parishioners in various stages of their lives move back and forth between these emphases. "Burnout" occurs when people are "out of sync" with their own needs, he warns.

An Era of "Ideological Purity"

In this downtown congregation healthy dialogue has occurred over tension-producing issues, such as American involvement in Central America, about which persons tend to feel very strongly. Although its church board, after much debate, did not vote to become a sanctuary church, they did engage in a fast for Central America—a compromise position. Although some persons were still disappointed by this vote, their views were not fully rejected by the group. But for persons who are "ideological purists," compromise is unthinkable.

Something "mystical" began in the late 1960s, says the Chicago pastor, and continued on into the Reagan administration: political parties became strongly ideological, and there were few "liberal Republicans." He would resonate with much of James Davison Hunter's "culture war" analysis, in which the polar extremes of society have defined the debate on issues before the public citizen has had a change to define them.[1] Hunter shows clearly that the church has been drawn into the polarity of ideological purism to its detriment. When they don't get their way, ideological purists have nowhere to go—except out. The church is then drained of energy and vitality as it attempts to hold its factions together. There is a lot of church "door slamming" on the bellwether issues, and sometimes it is by liberals who are not exhibiting very "liberal" (free, open, generous in spirit) behavior.

Ideological purity is tough to deal with, the Chicago pastor continues. It disqualifies open dialogue and screams through bullhorns, so what occurs is obliteration, not the lofty arts of compromise. A purist seeks only to convince others and does not listen, which precludes real conversation. Although he respects ideologues, this pastor also acknowledges how difficult it is to get them to truly enter a conversation, and yet he keeps trying. He believes we must expose these purists to one another within the church's "beloved community"—in Bible classes, prayer circles and study groups.

One's preaching can be empathetic to differing views while still expressing a strong position that does not "excommunicate" others with its "hard truth," he claims. One can even be very passionate about a particular viewpoint without being an ideologue or insensitive to the weight of another view. For instance, before giving a sermon on a controversial subject like gun control, he stated that God doesn't love less those who disagree with God, nor would he, the pastor, love less those with whom he disagreed than those with whom he agreed. If people know you love them, you can preach firmly and clearly.

The evangelical pastor of a large church in Seattle understands also the dilemma of the push for purity in the church. But how long would a "purified" church stay pure? he wonders. While many liberals see little distinction between fundamentalists and some evangelicals, this Seattle pastor describes liberals as the "new fundamentalists"—joyless, intolerant, lacking in grace, supporters of a "terrible cause" without the fruits of the Spirit.

This pastor is opposed to the church's taking an official stand on controversial issues of conscience—like the Gulf War. His church survived its differences by praying for the president and supporting the troops, while regretting war itself, even though some saw in the war the coming of Armageddon and others were militant pacifists. There were study classes in the congregation that explored opposing views with mutual love and acceptance in community.

The congregation had both militant pro-choice and pro-life members. He refused to preach on either side and urged both sides to honor one another as sisters and brothers in Christ. Some left because of his silence on the abortion issue, but those who remained realized that Christ died for all, no matter what position they held.

He did, however, preach against sex outside of marriage even though the church had a huge ministry to homosexuals. Many in the congregation were homosexual, and they were loved and respected, but they were not allowed to be church leaders if they were not celibate. Some homosexuals in his congregation claimed that they did not have the "gift of celibacy." The pastor called their attention to other single (heterosexual) people in the congregation who refrained from sex because they were not married, as the Bible requires them to do.

A nurse from his congregation encountered intolerance from extreme liberals when they did not allow her to serve in an AIDS hospice because she would not condone gay intercourse. The "purists" in the hospice required acceptance of the gay lifestyle, and the pastor's attempts to mediate with the hospice board did not achieve anything. But the congregation continued its love and acceptance of homosexuals, and they continued to come to worship.

The most important thing to do in preaching, says this minister, is to go back to the basics of the faith, to learn to tell our story. Then we can be empowered by God to be launched into mission toward a loveless society, the real enemy. We are all lonely and in need of community, and although all our families are dysfunctional, the church is, or can be, the functional family in which we, stripped of our pretenses, are accepted and no longer lost.

Another evangelical minister, drawing on his experience as a pastor in California, urges pastors to choose carefully those times when he or she must express opinions from the pulpit with which other Christians may conscientiously disagree. There are many other times and places for making one's personal statement on highly controversial issues. This evangelical went to Nicaragua and came back saying things that many people didn't want to hear, but he chose to say them only when there was opportunity for dialogue. Some national church pronouncements suffer from a one-way, "Thus saith the Lord" tone, which may end in trouble instead of transformation.

A United Church of Christ seminary professor sees the local pastor acting as both a bottleneck and a funnel for such national pronouncements, denominational study materials and denominational tradition. Pastors decide what to address, distribute or throw away, so "the church's position" often depends upon the willingness of local pastors to interpret it. Depending on the pastor's intention, this may either harm or help communication between the denomination and the local congregation.

Realism of the Laity

The laity is really at the center of the church. Many of them are not caught up in the internecine struggles among "professional church leaders." They live with the concrete realities of these difficult issues, says a seasoned pastor of a large church, and they must survive in the dichotomy between what happens Sunday and how they live the rest of the week. Unfortunately, some professional church leaders do polarize laity. Yet many laity are less ideological than their leaders, see complexities more clearly and may even intimidate the pastor, he confesses. But we lose the dynamic center of the laity when ideological purity takes over, when we respond to sound-bite discourse. We must learn to see and appreciate the gray areas and to value relationships more than rigid principle. Unless we can do this, allowing some "loopholes," civil and reasonable discourse may not be possible. Somehow, he argues, we must claim the freedom to converse with those opposed to us. We have the responsibility to talk without trading in our beliefs. We must not trade in our own "purity" for peace and unity, but we must also recognize that our purity is not entirely "pure" and that we do not rely on our own purity or the leniency of our opposition but on our mutual center in Christ.

An Episcopal layman on the staff of a Washington think tank emphasizes this final theological point using somewhat different language: we become tolerant because we know that we sin and that we all are in need of God's grace, a concept of original sin and total depravity we need to rediscover. God's gracious mercy should teach us to be gracious, unflappable and secure in our faith while aware that our faith is grounded in God's forgiveness through Jesus Christ. When we recognize that our sins and those of our neighbors are forgiven in Christ, we can be secure and civil, not self-righteous or condescending. We need not call into question the motives of those with whom we disagree, but like the apostle Paul, we can try to see things from the other's point of view. In democratic politics we come together after a political campaign, and it ought to be that way all the time in the church, he believes. There is, however, a social psychology (see, for example, Eric Hoffer's *The True Believer*)[2] at work that leads some Christians to believe the authenticity of their Christian faith is proven when they make enemies! They can be found in any religious camp. But Christians who have appropriated the gospel, who know the "breadth and depth and height" of God's love, can be gentle and open-minded toward others.

But when we try to allow "our own religion" (our limited perspective) and not God to save us, we fall prey to the demonic, says a leading African-American Holiness pastor. He understands much of the polarization in our churches to be our attempt to use religion to increase our own status and well-being. Our religion becomes a substitute, or surrogate, for God. We become afraid, even (or perhaps especially) within the church, to disclose our partly formed convictions. We need to refine within the church itself the art of "sanctuary" for free expression without rejection. We should be able to come boldly before the throne of grace to present our doubts and fears. Sometimes liberals may need to acknowledge more of the tenets of their faith, while conservatives might need to acknowledge the doubts that accompany their faith. Standing before God, we need an honest, open exchange. We may need to sacrifice our "religion" so that we, conservative and liberal alike, can show we are compelled to converse with one another, not simply to convert one another, because we need to work together to do God's will. And in the local congregation we can find the time and space for this to happen.

11

. . . .

Moderates &
Constructive
Encounter

People must realize that we have no choice, that we cannot go on the way we are.
They must make sure that this denomination puts in decision-making
situations—memberships on committees and staff assignments—
people who are genuinely different, who take opposing views and who are looked upon
with trust by elements of the constituency that feel left out.
A SENIOR DENOMINATIONAL OFFICIAL

We have focused thus far in part three of this book on stories about moving toward reconciliation—in one-on-one situations, in face-to-face groups and in congregations. Drawing on experiences related in the first ten chapters, we now turn our attention to some of the factors that make reconciliation possible.

We begin by reflecting on the significance of a reality that has surfaced from time to time in this project: Most Protestants are essentially centrists. Their differences do not cover so wide a range as to make communication across the divide impossible. At times we have heard people from both sides resist labels such as "centrist" or "middle-of-the-road" because they may suggest compromise of principle. Healthy centrism is not a matter of making concessions on basic beliefs to reach a lukewarm compromise. However, a number of leaders on both sides described themselves as "moderate liberals" or "moderate evangelicals" in our interviews, which suggests that moderation is important to their self-definition. Most of these leaders were from mainline denominations. The term *mainline* carries the connotation that churches wearing this label have traditionally reflected the mainstream of American life, not the extremes.

Tendencies Toward Moderation

There is a Christian fundamentalist right wing in American society, which is largely beyond the bounds of the centrist tradition. In the 1920s and 30s, following the famous Scopes "monkey trial," most fundamentalists left the mainline churches for small conservative denominations, independent Bible colleges and churches on the far right of Protestantism. A major distinction between evangelicals and fundamentalists is in attitude rather than theology: many fundamentalists resist any association with Christians who (they believe) hold suspect theological positions.

Beginning in the 1940s, the term *evangelical* came into currency as a way for moderate conservatives to distinguish themselves from such fundamentalists. In mainline churches moderate evangelicals are far more numerous than fundamentalists. This is also the case in many denominations outside the mainline and in some independent congregations. A prominent leader of the evangelical wing of the United Methodist Church spoke in an interview of the series of challenges and debates in Methodism that led to the establishment of the Good News Movement, the flagship group for evangelical concerns in that denomination. The liberal leadership "had not been challenged before from within the mainline denominations," he told us. "They had been challenged by people like [Jerry] Falwell, but not by people who were part of the mainline denominations. We are in the mainstream. We are not fundamentalists or extreme right-wingers."

There would be some overlap on social issues between conservative mainliners and right-leaning denominations such as the Conservative Baptists or the Assemblies of God. But because mainline conservatives are moderate, they tend to stay closer to the center. Many of the extremists have departed from the mainline pews. Within Presbyterianism this trend has been especially striking. Two relatively new denominations, the Presbyterian Church in America and the Evangelical Presbyterian Church, are made up largely of those who have left the mainline group since the 1960s. A similar process among ultraconservative Episcopalians led to the formation of the Episcopal Synod of America. Many very conservative members left mainline Lutheran churches when the Evangelical Lutheran Church in America was formed through merger.

At the other end of the spectrum there is a nontheistic, humanist left in American society, also largely beyond the bounds of the mainstream Christian tradition. This is the secular "new class," led by elites in the media, academia and government who have no significant ties to traditional religious groups. The secular left has some influence on Christian liberals, particularly when they join together to work for specific goals. But the secular worldview is generally rejected by liberal Christians, who retain their belief in God.

As is the case on the right, there would be some overlap between liberal mainliners and denominations further to the left, such as the Unitarian Univeralists. But because mainstream liberals are generally moderate, they tend to avoid extremes. And just as those on the far right have left their old congregations for more congenial company in the small conservative denominations, so those who are at home in a nontheistic humanitarianism have largely drifted away from the mainline denominations into the secular culture.

Among the rest—the relatively moderate Christians who make up much of today's Protestant church—there remain sharp differences, as this entire book has demonstrated. But it is extremely important to recognize what analyses such as John Davison Hunter's *Culture Wars*[1] tend to obscure: *Protestants are clustered predominantly in the middle range of the religious and cultural spectra.* Their heritage of moderation as well as their natural inclinations impel them to try to get along with each other.

The prickly abortion issue has lost some of its sharpness in inclusive denominations because large numbers of moderates have come to recognize that their differences are not as great as they once appeared. Most Christians oppose most abortions. They reject abortion as a means of birth control and regard it as a last resort. But they are unwilling to have it ruled out as a possible choice in extraordinary circumstances, and they are reluctant to make final moral choices for others. Debate may still be dominated by those at the pro-life end of the spectrum who regard all abortions as murder and those at the pro-choice end who regard any limitation on abortion as infringement of the right to choose. But growing awareness on the part of the majority that they are somewhere in between these poles has begun to lower the level of conflict.

Centrists

An evangelical seminary professor described "centrists" as "those who attempt to be instructed by the historic creeds and confessions but also attempt to be tutored by the historical-critical method when they are concerned with the interpretation of Scripture." They "have antennae out to all sectors of the church." At a later point in the interview he elaborated on this perception:

> We fall into the pattern of talking about this major "gulf" or division. But there are tens of thousands of people who are straddling that gulf, who have a foot on both sides—or who hop over, back and forth. And they are not compromisers; they are being true to their perceptions of reality in the world and the church, by being at one moment here and the other moment there. They overlap the divisions. I think easily the majority of the church overlaps the divisions in this sense. This is demonstrated in our attitudes toward Scripture. [A survey] showed that some 86 percent of the people are in the middle.

The laity of the church in particular, says an evangelical pastor of a large California congregation, are largely in the center:

> They don't spend a lot of time thinking about the issues we professionals think and talk about and find ourselves polarized over. They may have something to teach us. They have to live with the realities of these issues [such as abortion] day in and day out, more than we theological types do. It probably is not a highly reflective center, this pastor went on to suggest. The laity occupies the middle ground for down-to-earth, practical reasons.

From a liberal perspective, a middle judicatory executive from Texas expresses a similar opinion. "There is a much larger middle than we give people credit for . . . a vast middle," he says. "I think the larger church just thinks [the polarization] is silly. They have enough sense to know Christians shouldn't treat one another that way. I think there are a lot of people who are flat-out tired of it. I wish they'd rise up some time and throw both camps out!"

Both views were confirmed by an editor for a religious news service, who herself is not clearly identified with either side. "There is a great big middle," she says, "and very small extremes." Lots of congregations are in the middle, she adds, "and they don't want to enter the fray."

Making Room for the Concerns of Both Sides

In such divided but basically centrist churches, the process of reconciliation begins by making room for the concerns of both sides. An evangelical minister pointed to this necessity in congregational life. The last chapter included his account of the presence of both militant pro-life and pro-choice people in a large church in Seattle. He continues his account here:

> We have to be big enough to say that there are two "rights" in that conflict. Every Christian is pro-life. Who wants abortions? But who doesn't want to honor the woman's rights? So you've got two things, and we have to maintain them both. In your group, keep pressing for what you think is right. Picket if you choose. Same thing over here. But the pulpit will not preach pro-life or pro-choice. Some people left my church because of that. But those who stayed learned to get along with each other. You've got to honor the fact that this person is someone for whom Jesus died. He lives. He has integrity. She is a smart person. She sees a different side from what you do. Try to change them—but don't call them less than a brother or sister in Christ. They may be wrong, but don't dishonor them.

One area in which the church has been reasonably successful in making room for the concerns of both sides is the evangelism-social action dichotomy. In chapter four we noted that the portrayal of the two as opposites, as mutually exclusive or even as reflecting the characteristic division in the liberal-evangelical polarization is likely to be a distortion. In the context of reconciliation in groups we returned in chapter nine to this tension and found that joint social action is often an effective strategy for transcending differences.

It is true that a concern for evangelism is at the heart of evangelicalism. Similarly social justice is a high priority for liberals. But neither side rejects the claims of the other, and a reconciling process makes room for both. An evangelical United Methodist, who is professor of Christian ethics at a major seminary, calls for a church that tries to be "theologically holistic." Historically there has been a polarity between evangelism and social witness, he says, but "we have to be intentional to avoid it." There must be a concern for evangelism on the part of liberals and for social justice on the part of evangelicals, he adds, and the two sides "must be able to deal with each other as brothers and sisters."

Genuinely making room for both concerns, however, includes permitting evangelicals to define evangelism and liberals to define social justice in ways that are fully meaningful to each side. Compromise definitions, worked out by committees but ignored by the two sides, paper over differences but do not help. "There must be relationships that let you disagree," says a female liberal leader. "It's not easy, but we have got to learn to do it."

The evangelical pastor of a church in California revealed that he would soon be nominated by his denomination's national judicatory for a position on the governing board of the National Council of Churches, which is generally regarded as a bulwark of liberalism. He said of the NCC nomination:

> I see no inconsistency. Some say, "Are you theologically schizophrenic?" I say, "No, I'm ecumenical." I'm a global Christian who has a sense that I am not prepared to trade in my own deep convictions theologically and spiritually to any conciliar movement. At the same time I am not prepared to straight-arm myself from any ministry that professes Jesus Christ as Savior and Lord, no matter how different the perception of what that means may be, in terms of use of Scripture or methodological or political approaches.

The nomination of such an evangelical to the board of the predominantly liberal NCC is the kind of action at the denominational level that gives recognition to the concerns of both sides. It moves toward the kind of equity called for in the quotation that began this chapter.

Thus far, in mainline denominations controlled at the national level by the liberal wing, such equity has not been common. And this has been a major complaint of evangelicals who decry the practice of putting occasional "token" conservatives in visible places while carefully maintaining liberal control. Said the president of a denominational evangelical organization, "Don't just 'do lunch' with a conservative, but put into practice an informal mandate to work for theological diversity at every level—every task force, committee, ministry unit—alongside racial and gender diversity."

Less intentionality is required at the congregational level, where diversity usually comes ready-made. There is, of course, a certain amount of self-selection in the makeup of congregations. Liberal congregations attract other liberals; evangelical congregations attract other evangelicals. Still, there are few congregations in pluralistic denominations that do not have some of each. And in the natural order of things we tend, in congregations, to make room for the concerns of both sides. It is at the congregational level that evangelicals and liberals are most likely to rub shoulders, come to know and respect each other while allowing for disagreement, and live as Christian brothers and sisters.

Helpful in this regard is a thoughtful discussion of "common ground" by James R. Kelly of Fordham University. This Roman Catholic scholar examines the work of sociological theory and develops a compassionate and cautious view of the search for common ground in our religious traditions.[2] Some of our obstinate certitude that others experience as arrogance may also be understood sociologically as an attempt to protect one's religious identity. A stable identity in a time of rapid change becomes exceedingly important, even to enable us to make adaptations. If we are pushed off balance, so that changes are experienced as identity loss, we become disoriented and resistant. But if change can be gradual and perceived as a faithful adaptation within one's basic identity, we can make adjustments. Such careful adjustments are then followed by a reinforcement of stability and equilibrium as these changes and tensions are assimilated. With renewed assurance we can attempt to explore common ground with those who oppose us.

Kelly has a precise meaning for the development of common ground that holds intact one's integrity of faith. He rightfully, in our view, calls for two stages. The first is dialogue between the differing views to the extent that both parties grasp each other's moral-emotional-faith perspective at least in part. This ensures they can also search together for points of agreement that respect their mutual integrity. Second, when these "noncompromising points of agreement" are discovered, both parties take action together on some concrete endeavor. "Common ground" is not capitulation of one side to the other (a requirement by some conservatives). Nor is it claiming to already stand on "inclusive" ground that the other party may enter as one view among many (a liberal temptation).

Perhaps this abstract description of common ground makes more sense with an illustration. Pro-choice and pro-life Christians may not be able to come together on abortion policy, but they may be able to respect concerns in one another's position: for example, the earnestly voiced support for a voiceless and vulnerable human-life-in-the-making or the compassionate concern for poor, tired mothers who cannot imagine feeding and clothing one more child. Perhaps they can find a point of agreement in working to improve conditions in which birthing one more child seems intolerable or in developing parent-training programs for very young mothers.

Building Consensus

After we have made room for the concerns of both sides in the present polarization, we must take the next step of searching for consensus. Denominational consensus is not likely to be reached until it reflects the consensus of the grassroots membership. Leaders are beginning to recognize that consensus must be built from the ground up. The natural starting place for this consensus building is the local congregation, where people who disagree must come to know each other, learn to trust each other and pray and worship together week after week.

Even in congregations, full consensus on the major single issues may not be possible. On abortion, for instance, there may be no meeting ground between those who would outlaw all abortions and those who would affirm a woman's right to choose in all circumstances. But in personal contacts within congregations, a consensus may be reached at a lesser level, affirming what can be agreed on even in the midst of disagreement.

In a two-thousand-member church the governing board found itself embroiled in an attempt to define a position on abortion for the congregation. The wife of one board member was professionally employed by a strongly pro-life agency that engaged in pro-adoption, anti-abortion counseling of pregnant women. Her husband introduced a resolution stating that the board rejected the position adopted by the national church (which had been moderately pro-choice) and that it regarded abortion as the murder of children and contrary to the law of God. He asked that his wife be invited to come to the next meeting to give a presentation on the subject.

In the ensuing debate it became clear that there were members of the board who strongly agreed with the resolution and others who strongly disagreed. There was general awareness that the congregation was similarly divided. As requested they invited the woman employed at the pro-life agency to make her presentation at the next meeting. But they also offered equal time for a presentation by another member with an outspoken pro-choice position. And they agreed to publicly announce the debate, inviting members of the congregation who so desired to attend.

It quickly became apparent to board members that no consensus on the abortion issue itself would be possible. But the outcome of the encounter was a resolution embodying a lesser consensus, recognizing the presence of both positions in the congregation and restating the biblical mandate for Christian sisters and brothers to disagree in love. Ultimately the husband who had initiated the original resolution and his wife found that they could not live with what they regarded as acceptance of sin. They left the congregation and joined a more conservative church. But no other members left, because the desirability of living together in mutual love and respect did represent a genuine congregational consensus. We shall have another look at the process of consensus building, from the leadership perspective, in the next chapter.

Dealing with the Absence of Consensus: Positive Confrontation

In a divided church, reaching consensus is not the only answer to living with differences. A liberal pastor of a large Chicago church, speaking of the often-noted attempts to bring the concerns for evangelism and social justice together, says,

> I kind of regret the fact that the church doesn't have *both* of these valid positions articulated with a little more strength. Something happens when you try to sweep them all together. Neither comes out with much heart and soul. . . . I sometimes feel that if we die it's going to be out of boredom, not conflict.

He is pointing to the need, at times, for what a middle judicatory executive called "positive confrontation." The two sides, he says, "need to be in opposition. They need to oppose one another, and it needs to be a creative opposition. Just talking to your own little cadre of people is not only boring; it's a heinous thing. It's not an individual privilege; it's a rejection of brothers and sisters." A senior denominational official agrees: "The nature of the change needed to overcome the problem requires confrontation."

The difficulty, of course, is that what one group regards as positive confrontation may come across to the opposing group, which is being confronted, as highly negative. Something like this seems to be the case with the discord between the Presbyterian Lay Committee, publisher of *The Presbyterian Layman,* and the central denominational bureaucracy in the case study described in chapter seven.

It is in local congregations that positive confrontation can be most fruitful. Here persons with deep convictions do not confront causes or movements or advocacy groups, all of which are impersonal forces, easily disliked and dismissed. Instead they confront other persons—brothers and sisters in Christ—who have differing but deeply held convictions. It is as they work, pray and worship with these brothers and sisters that confrontation is most likely to be positive. One layperson put it this way:

> I've seen it happen in congregations, where you literally pour cold water on them, and say, "Let's re-learn how to differ, in a fair and faithful way." You just re-engage that whole congregation and its leadership in the hard realities of this rather amazing organization, the church. I've found that, although there may not be full peace, purity and unity after that's done, there is an armistice.

Both Groups Are Needed

We discovered among those we interviewed a quite general recognition that both liberals and evangelicals are not just to be tolerated but are *needed* in the church. This is a major reason that we deal with our differences by making room for the concerns of both sides, by seeking and in some instances finding a consensus and, at times, by positive confrontation. As the judicatory executive quoted above puts it, "The two sides desperately need one another."

Referring to his earlier experience as a pastor, a denominational executive says he has discovered that congregational life "will be richer if we encourage different perspectives, if we encourage different voices to be heard." He draws an analogy from church history: the failure of the Protestant Reformation to engage the Anabaptist movement was a serious loss, he contends. And the church today still needs the Anabaptists, the evangelicals. "We can't be fully and wholly Christian without both," he reflects, "even though we may give greater weight to one tradition than the other."

Even the leader of the most extremist, conservative faction in one denomination concedes the church's need for its liberal wing "from the standpoint of checks and balances. We know that through history. We need a balance." In reference to his group's emphasis on evangelism and the opposition's focus on what he called "the political agenda" he says, "We need a balance. Here's where the liberal mind needs to be a check and balance for the conservative, and the conservative needs to be a check and balance for the liberal—but again, all based on Scripture," he adds.

In writing this book we were strengthened both by defining our own stance and also by expressing appreciation of the other's. This appreciation, we believe, is a characteristic of centrist Protestants. One of the most hopeful findings of this research has been the widespread recognition, on the part of evangelicals and liberals alike, of our mutual need for each other in the church of Jesus Christ.

What kind of leadership can move the church toward consensus wherever possible while making room for differences and for the positive confrontation that expresses those differences, all the while keeping an awareness that the two sides need each other? This is the question we will explore in the next chapter.

12

· · · · · · · · · · · · ·

The Leadership
Question

There are leadership difficulties in all national-level institutions. Leadership is not a given in our culture any longer. We appear to be living in a period in which personal authority wielded by strong, charismatic figures is in short supply.

The speaker is himself widely recognized as a leader in his denomination: a liberal pastor who was instrumental in bringing the two branches of his church into a successful reunion. He speaks of a cultural reality that clearly affects the church as well as the larger society.

The question of leadership is a major concern in a polarized church. In chapter three we quoted a seminary professor's analysis of a polarization of the grassroots church at the congregational level versus the central denominational bureaucracy. One of this professor's chief worries is a church leadership that is not accountable, especially in its bureaucracy and seminaries, and cannot lead because it doesn't know where the people are. Although in the past the church attracted outstanding people into ministry and today some great leaders can be found in large churches, the majority of people going through seminaries, he claims, are not highly able leaders. They no longer can "rouse the troops" the way earlier church leaders could rally people and win their confidence. Fewer and fewer quality laity are willing to "waste their time" by serving on church boards, he observes.

An evangelical college president also paints the church's leadership crisis in stark terms: "I don't think we have any leaders," she says. Yet her own widely recognized leadership is a striking achievement, since she, as a woman, has achieved this status in the evangelical wing of the church where leadership is generally perceived as being far more male-dominated than in liberal circles.

Over the past twenty-five years, national denominational and ecumenical staff have been cautioned to seek a low profile, to be primarily facilitators and enablers rather than bold, authoritative leaders. The concept of leadership, in this time of turmoil, is evolving. Ronald A. Heifitz, in his illuminating book *Leadership Without Easy Answers,*[1] urges a leadership style he calls "adaptive work." A leader mobilizes people to face and tackle tough problems together—by clarifying values, goals, tradeoffs, strategies and missions. This is a style that may be needed today.

Dilemmas of Leadership in a Polarized Church

If we want polarization to be lessened or overcome and differences to be addressed constructively, we will need to identify leaders. Whether in small groups, in congregations or in the larger denominational context, the quality and direction of leadership can in considerable measure determine if movement is toward greater polarization and perhaps eventual fracture or toward mutual acceptance and love. The fact that this project has focused on persons in leadership positions at every level of church life is, therefore, of more than casual significance. Is the leadership of today's denominations as polarized as the churches themselves?

In important ways the answer is no. A substantial majority of the leaders we interviewed are seeking to reduce the polarization. Most of them have, and recognize that they have, responsibilities to people on both sides of the internal division. Bishop Frank Tracy Griswold, elected to a nine-year term as presiding bishop of the sharply divided Episcopal Church in 1997 and perceived as a liberal, sought immediately to reach out to all factions. He quoted Brazilian Roman Catholic liberation theologian Dom Helder Camara, saying, "The bishop belongs to all."[2]

Leadership status is ordinarily identified by the position held. This is true not only of bishops, but of pastors of congregations, laypersons elected to congregational governing boards, those holding elected or executive office for church judicatories and those holding similar offices in institutions such as colleges, theological seminaries, the church press and parachurch organizations. For all of these, leadership responsibilities are inherent in the positions they hold. Generally, people in these positions in pluralistic denominations are officially obligated to serve people from the entire church, including both conservative and liberal camps. All governing bodies and nearly all congregations and educational institutions have both evangelicals and liberals in their constituencies. Only the parachurch groups (large numbers of which are evangelical) serve constituencies from one side alone. And even they recognize that they must relate to the diversity of the whole church. Most of the leaders we interviewed are consciously seeking to serve all people.

Further, nearly all see their task as one of reducing tension and promoting unity. Nearly all are seeking to lead their divided constituencies in the direction of mutual understanding and acceptance. An evangelical United Methodist minister illustrates this by describing a pastor who chairs a conference committee on candidates. The chairman's own liberal attitudes come across in the questions he asks of candidates, this minister reports, but he works at relating to evangelicals. He is aware of the importance of impartiality in the position he holds, and he therefore approaches it with an element of self-criticism. Constructive leadership is aware of personal bias and compensates by consciously seeking impartiality and reaching out in an effort to bridge differences.

Liberal and Evangelical Leaders

This widespread characteristic of good leadership points, however, to the other side of the leadership dilemma: nearly all church leaders *are* personally identified with one wing of the church or the other and are perceived accordingly by those they seek to lead. The design of this project assumed that to be the case. We set out to interview leaders of the liberal and evangelical factions in approximately equal numbers. What about leaders who transcend the divisions and who wear neither label? We found a few. We indicated earlier (in chapter three) that we were able to characterize all but three of the many leaders we interviewed as holding views identified primarily with either category. Some of our interviewees personally resisted categorization. A number of them insisted on modifying the liberal or evangelical label with an adjective such as *moderate*. One seminary president gave a sympathetic and balanced analysis of both liberals and evangelicals, but he took his own place in the spectrum for granted as he spoke of "my brothers and sisters at the opposite end." It is fair to say that most of the leaders of the church, as we perceived them, are trying to "straddle the gap." But it is also fair to say that they are doing so from positions within the two wings of the church. They are themselves primarily identified by others as either liberals or evangelicals.

The Pattern of Distribution

A pattern of distribution is also reasonably clear. Many of those recognized as liberal leaders serve in the administrative structures of their churches, at both denominational and middle judicatory levels. Most are clergy. Top-level positions in the program agencies are seldom occupied by clearly identified evangelicals. Other liberal leaders are pastors of prominent (though not usually the largest) congregations. Many are related to seminaries; mainline seminary faculties are predominantly liberal.

Evangelical leaders are found primarily in the unofficial "renewal" organizations of their denominations and in "tall steeple" pastorates; many of the largest congregations are evangelical in orientation. Evangelical educators are frequently (though not always) identified with seminaries and colleges that are not part of the official denominational systems.

Liberal leadership, then, is concentrated in the program agencies or bureaucracies and the seminaries. Evangelical leadership is found in the parachurch groups and the larger pastorates.

Is this pattern affected by the structural type of the denomination? In churches with an episcopate is polarization thereby transcended? Our observation would indicate that it is not. In the Episcopal and United Methodist Churches—the two mainline denominations with long-established episcopates—and in Lutheran churches with an episcopate, the pattern of polarization parallels that in nonepiscopal churches.

One reason may be that the bishops' functions tend to center around the placement and care of ministers. In organizational terms they are personnel administrators, and in the Christian context they are "pastors of pastors." Such functions can be carried out largely without regard to liberal or conservative theological or social leanings. Fairness to those of other views, rather than neutrality, is the desired quality; most bishops are known to their own constituencies as being personally liberal or evangelical. In the Episcopal, Methodist and Lutheran Churches the episcopacies are divided, as are the denominations themselves.

Beyond the bishopric, the strongholds of the liberal and evangelical wings are parallel to those in the nonepiscopal churches. The denominational bureaucracies are largely in the hands of liberals. The clergy are divided. The majority are liberal, but pastors of many of the largest congregations are evangelicals. A large number—perhaps a majority—of those in the pews are evangelicals, but their leadership is found to a considerable extent in the unofficial internal renewal groups, such as the Good News Movement in the United Methodist Church, the United Church Renewal Fellowship or the Disciples Renewal Movement.

Even in the Roman Catholic Church, the church with the strongest episcopacy, the ecclesiastical authority of the pope does not assure a united membership. The Catholic Church, like its Protestant counterparts, has its liberal and traditional wings. It has liberal and conservative bishops. The pope himself is regarded as a conservative. Despite very strong official church stands, polling data indicate that on the religiously grounded "single issues," such as abortion and homosexuality, American Catholics split in approximately the same proportions as Protestants.

Reconciling Leadership
In congregations. Many of the success stories we examined in chapters eight, nine and ten focused on person-to-person contacts, most often in congregations, between people of opposing views. Where Christians live out their lives of faith from day to day, the basic biblical behavioral

standards of love, of listening and caring and of learning to trust through personal contact are upheld. Leadership in such situations can be personal and pastoral.

One senior denominational executive with a reputation as one who favors reaching out to evangelicals has exercised leadership in this direction on the denominational staff. But when asked for an example of bridging differences, he first recalled his experiences as pastor of a church. He feels he was able to affirm people of both sides, to persuade them that "there are varieties of gifts, but the same Spirit" when he pastored. He feels that his efforts were "more or less successful," but he notes that such successes in bridging diversity are not as likely to be measured in numerical terms as may be the case in homogeneous congregations.

The liberal pastor quoted at the beginning of this chapter has a track record in bridging differences as cochair of the long-standing committee that brought about reunion in his denomination. He too turns to the congregational experience for his basic model. He speaks in terms of "neutralizing bullies."

> Congregations have to learn to neutralize their bullies. You don't neutralize bullies by destroying them, by winning all the votes in board or committee meetings where bullies are trying to dominate. What I think I've tried to do personally and pastorally is to befriend the bully and establish a relationship on grounds other than where the bully feels threatened, so that the person is not demeaned or diminished in those arenas where the struggles of different points of view and the power struggles take place. . . . We've tried to give voice to different points of view.

We, the authors, by listening to many hours of taped interviews, sought to analyze the numerous success stories in which differences had been bridged and polarization lessened. As we looked for common themes, we identified the simple Christian values of listening, accepting, forgiving, talking together, praying together, learning to trust, reaching out in love and "doing to others what we would have them do to us." These were the themes that recurred again and again:

☐ "In conversation you find we are less far apart than you think we are," said an evangelical leader of a student-oriented parachurch organization.

☐ A Methodist evangelical comes to a similar conclusion: "We talked long enough to get beyond the language which tends to put the other person into a camp because of prior experience."

☐ The object of such talking, says a liberal pastor, is "not to change the other, but to understand."

☐ One of the most conservative leaders we interviewed, who sees little hope for reconciliation, says, nevertheless, "If we quit talking to each other it's a bad thing."

☐ A West Coast evangelical pastor says, "As one who has strong convictions, I want to make sure I treat the other person as human. I am deeply wounded when I am not treated as human."

☐ "You keep trying; you keep exposing them to one another," says a midwestern liberal pastor. "One of the jobs of the church is to be the beloved community, and you do that in classes, in prayer circles, in preaching. . . . You speak out, but you preface what you're going to say with respect and affection. That's a style of being the church."

☐ A liberal middle judicatory executive speaks of an experience of working together with a conservative whose judgment she trusts more than that of some of her fellow liberals: "There was a kind of openness there to think new thoughts, to look at things in new ways. Gosh, what a great experience that was. It was not a conversation so much as shared experience, shared hopes, shared dreams."

☐ An African-American evangelical professor describes a group in which there was great diversity but "almost immediately we trusted one another."

☐ "My most important advice would be 'love all of us,'" says a synod executive, referring to liberals and conservatives alike.

Anecdotes of talking together, of listening with respect, of reaching out in openness, of acceptance and of learning to trust one another at a personal, human level could be multiplied. And what they represent is not simply techniques of conflict resolution. They are expressions of the most basic Christian message: love. As a church journalist puts it, "It's so simple it's scary; it's 'Love one another.' If we do that we will listen, and we will accept each other's viewpoints, and we will discuss them fairly, and we will face facts."

Reconciling leadership at the congregational level—where one-on-one relationships and face-to-face encounters between groups routinely take place—is pastoral in nature. ("Pastoral" does not necessarily mean "ministerial"; lay leaders as well as ministers behave pastorally.) Such leadership draws on the church's own resources of worship, proclamation, study and fellowship. It reflects the church's own values of love, trust, listening, understanding, caring and serving.

In organizational and institutional settings. We have also seen instances of reconciliation in organizational and institutional settings, and it usually happened in committees, task forces or other face-to-face groups. But we noted in chapters eight and nine an important distinction: the reconciliation that takes place between individual persons who reach out to each other, engage in conversation and learn to trust each other is frequently spontaneous, whereas reconciliation in institutional committees and organized groups is usually the outcome of structured events. Groups are likely to need to build trust intentionally, rather than learning to trust, which seems to happen fairly spontaneously only in one-on-one situations.

It would be a mistake, of course, to identify the relatively spontaneous reconciliation of personal encounters entirely with the congregational setting and the intentional behavior of organized groups entirely with the institutional setting of the larger church. Certainly organized groups with intentional agendas are a major element in congregational life. And one-on-one and informal group encounters are an element in the institutional life of the larger church. Yet in a rough sense, the congregation is the basic unit of the church and the setting in which Christians live alongside one another. And it is the pastoral leadership (lay as well as clergy) in congregations that is likely to lead persons into the Christian way of "loving one another."

In larger and more impersonal settings, leadership must necessarily be more intentional. Success stories we heard from groups at the institutional level of church life tended to be focused on skillful leaders whose explicit goal was reconciliation. A journalist notes the progress made by the Special Committee to Formulate a Brief Statement of Faith for the Presbyterian Church under the skillful leadership of its chairperson:

> The work of the special committee . . . shows that with proper leadership and with members who come to the table with a certain degree of confidence and hopefulness a good product can result. . . . That is absolutely a success story.

Another observer makes similar comments about how the skilled director of her denomination's Global Mission Ministry Unit put together the global mission enterprise after the 1983 reunion of the northern and southern branches of the church. In this case the competing interests, on the surface, were the separate overseas-mission establishments of the two formerly independent denominations. But the underlying dynamic reflected the long-standing concern in both churches with world evangelism—to "go into all the world" as we're told in the Great Commission—in tension with the concern for global social justice promoted by both denominational establishments.

A former denominational moderator recalls instances in which polarized committees worked their way to positive conclusions through patient, open leadership. In one sharply divided committee, she says, the hostility was tangible at the start. But the leadership, she emphasizes, was skillful.

> There was absolutely open information. Whatever anybody needed was there at hand, and you felt in the room the beginning of an ability to listen to each other and face the problem. I don't think anybody was being quiet just to be nice; it didn't feel like that kind of group. But the fact that they took all the time they needed, and all the space, and were given all the information—and this patient, quiet moderator. In my experience, this was a classic "working through," a case in which a polarized committee worked together and reached a decision. Now that didn't change the labels on any of the people, but it did bring a positive result.

She recalls another instance in which a committee experience did change some people.

> It was a committee dealing with a report on "Christian obedience in a nuclear age." I was not in the committee meetings, but there were some people who wanted the whole General Assembly to hear what had happened to them in the meeting. They claimed they were changed —not from one camp to another, but *they* were changed by the experience. And that, too, had to do with the *leadership*.

The Denominational Level
The kind of mutual understanding and reconciliation that takes place in congregations and within face-to-face committees or groups at higher institutional levels is seldom exhibited in denominations as a whole. Nor

is it often apparent in the large gatherings that govern them at either the middle judicatory or national level. It is in the formal meetings of district associations, annual conferences, presbyteries, general conventions and assemblies, and in connection with the bureaucracies that serve them, that divisions remain intractable.

In view of the fact that most members of mainline denominations are moderates, why is this the case? Most leaders, liberal or evangelical, label themselves "moderate." Most leaders call for unity and recognize responsibilities to people on both sides. Why, then, does the agenda appear to be set by the extremists in either camp?

The difference between congregational and denominational modes of dealing with divisions has become increasingly apparent in this study. There appears to be an inherent distinction. In direct and personal relationships within congregations—even quite large congregations—there is a tendency to seek to live together in peace and love. The congregational emphasis is relational. Effective leadership is aimed toward mutual understanding and the reconciliation of differences. The long-range movement is in the direction of consensus and harmony.

In the official and less personal denominational relationships and in gatherings of delegates doing denominational business, the dynamics are different. Here decisions are by majority vote, and the underlying mode of operation is political. The emphasis is on making the right choice and faithfully reflecting God's will as the delegate or leader understands it. The task is not relational, but propositional. So the goal is not accommodation, but winning. Even when preliminary worship brings spiritual unity and when elaborate efforts are made to encourage Christian relationship, the basic dynamics are unchanged. In the maneuvering that leads up to voting and during the voting itself, the goal is to win. In this context, those who state differences sharply and clearly are more likely to be heard than those who downplay differences. So the polarized extremes, rather than the reconciling middle, appear to be defining the agenda.

The difference in dynamics is not accidental: congregations worship and work together in love; denominations deal propositionally with larger issues. Like-minded denominations can deal with these large issues in an atmosphere of mutuality. But in inclusive denominations the emphasis is likely to be on the differences. Out of the most religious of motivations, people who see the will of God differently struggle to ensure that God's will (as they see it) prevails. Is there any way, then, in which polarization can be overcome at the denominational level?

Three Lessons About Reconciling Leadership

Three lessons about leadership can be drawn from these observations together with the success stories in earlier chapters. The first has to do with the style of leadership that is the church's own—pastoral leadership.

For much of the twentieth century the church has been caught up in society's industrial revolution and has sought competent managers for positions of institutional leadership. Much good has come from this movement. Whatever else they may be (and from the Christian perspective they are much more), churches are, at the human level, organizations made up of people. Researchers and scholars have learned a great deal about how human organizations function and how they can be made to operate more effectively. Management of human organizations has become an academic discipline as well as a professional specialty. Business, government, the military and the nonprofit sector have all adopted managerial insights and tools. Churches would be foolish indeed if they did not take advantage of this prolific field of knowledge and technology. But the church must never forget that though it is made up of people, these are the people of God. The church is the body of Christ.

The managerial style of leadership has been most wholeheartedly adopted at the denominational level of church life. A case can be made that the development of centralized budgets and denominational bureaucracies (largely a twentieth-century phenomenon) in all major Protestant churches has been a product of the managerial revolution.[3] Managerial practices and tools have limited usefulness in most Protestant congregations, the majority of which have fewer than two hundred members, but in larger churches they have been adopted at the congregational level. Large congregations nowadays tend to have far more elaborate staffs and organizational and committee structures than was the case in an earlier day. But because congregations exist for the worship, nurture and outreach activities of individual Christians, congregational leadership has remained primarily pastoral and liturgical. The original biblical models and the traditional ecclesiastical models still shape congregational ministry.

Management deals only with the human side of organizational behavior. Pastoral ministry, which is the church's own mode of leadership, focuses on the transcendent side—the relationship among the individual Christian, the Christian community and God. If this study has learned that the pastoral skills and one-on-one relationships of listening, caring, praying and serving together in Christian love are those most likely tools for overcoming polarization, the lesson for the larger church is fairly obvious. Managers are focused on process. Pastors are focused on Christian love. A more pastoral and less exclusively managerial style of leadership may be called for at all levels of church life. The human-organizational dimension of the church is not unimportant, but the transcendent dimension is its heart.

A second lesson is that in today's polarized church, denominational decision-making on divisive issues cannot take place in a bureaucratic vacuum. It must be done in conversation with the people of the church at the congregational level, where pastoral leadership is already present and where individual and small-group contact is the normal mode of interaction.

Win-lose battles in which the church must follow God's will as one's own side perceives it are all too common in polarized denominations. They will cease only in areas where some measure of denomination-wide consensus exists. In contrast with the managerial model that "manages" from the top down, the church operates as a community of believers that builds consensus from the bottom up.

We have seen much evidence that people in the polarized pews have rejected the top-down leadership of denominational officials who represent only one side. And denominational assemblies have been unable to "manage" by majority vote constituencies that are so sharply divided, with the minority never persuaded by the other side's victory. This has been made clear in the radical decline in financial support for denominational programs. It has also been seen in the rejection of denominational resources and curricula, as many congregations have turned to materials from parachurch agencies. The downsizing of central bureaucracies that has resulted has been the natural—and possibly desirable—outcome.

The rebuilding of consensus in pluralistic denominations will be a slow process. It must come through study, prayer, reaching out and learning in congregations and in face-to-face groups at other institutional levels. Here the mission of the church—love, concern and service—can transform top-down management, which has failed to build respectful community.

As long as churches are polarized between liberal and evangelical groups, it is likely that leadership will also be in some measure divided. But emphasizing the pastoral dimension of leadership, the elemental Christian calling to reach out to one another in love, at every level of church life may help the church find its way to healing and renewal. And a growing tendency to bring congregations into the decision-making process when a churchwide consensus on divisive issues is sought may aid the process.

We have noted that Roman Catholicism, with its strong hierarchical structure, is still faced with the problems of finding a "common ground" of shared, coherent faith and practice. In recent years the Southern Baptist Convention, which is thoroughly congregational in polity, has become riven by a top convention leadership takeover that affects all its widespread institutions. Changing from a moderate to a fundamentalist leadership has not been the "solution" for Southern Baptists insofar as learning to live together is their problem. Mainline denominations have had their determination to remain "connected" seriously tested over some of the issues discussed here.

The answer to developing leadership in today's environment does not seem to be to become more rigidly authoritarian at the top, else Roman Catholics would be simply reinforcing an already firm hierarchy. Nor does switching leadership from one dominant group to another solve our problems, as Southern Baptists have taught us. Can we simply abdicate leadership "from the top" in our denominational structures and leave local churches alone to develop their own consensus on important Christian theological and ethical issues today? Would it be wise to avoid making denominational judgments altogether, insofar as our polities allow?

A less drastic approach may be in order, and this is our third lesson. Perhaps we ask our national bodies to make decisions about too many issues in too short a time frame. Some denominations are developing elaborate mechanisms that allow for feedback from local congregations when they are studying issues that eventually must be decided together; this way study papers and statements receive extensive discussion and debate at the local level. Although this process has the disadvantage of drastically lengthening the time a denomination takes to respond to important current issues, it has the great strength of producing a much clearer reflection of the views of its members.

Furthermore, a more deliberative pace on issues that have no obvious biblical interpretation or traditional precedent is not only prudent but wise. How do Christians make judgments about cloning, genome mapping, privacy regulations or other human-reproductive decisions with heavy theological and ethical implications? Many of the concerns and decisions that face us today require profound, careful thinking in unexplored territory.

Precisely because there are so many facets to the decisions we must make as Christians, we need each other's insights. So much of the information and viewpoints in today's media-glutted society come to us from sources that have no obligation or commitment to shape our *Christ-centered* thinking. We benefit in a very special way when Christian laity with expertise in many fields contribute to our understanding through study papers and documents that can be used throughout our churches. Denominations have access to varieties of experience, background and knowledge beyond those available to local congregations. Although, as our interviewees have observed, such access can be abused, we would not want to eliminate the significant leadership potential of expert Christian laity at all levels of our churches.

Our denominational leaders and national staff may also serve us when they lay before our local churches concerns to which they believe we should all pay attention. Leadership can encourage us to see the broad, global picture in our local situations and assist congregations to do the "adaptive work" necessary for discovering God's leading in difficult, complex settings. Leaders do not have to push certain "answers" to every challenge in order to be faithful. But being willing to encourage Christians at all levels to look steadfastly at unwelcome or unpleasant realities in order to face them with Christian courage is true, faithful leadership. It can be practiced at all levels of church life.

Given the involvement of Christians around the world in one another's lives today, both at global and local levels, there is no immediate expectation that we can achieve consensus on many old and new differences, whether theological or ethical or social. As we shall explore in the next chapter, many people opt out of conflicts by dismissing denomination-wide efforts as being irrelevant to their personal lives. Others seek out like-minded congregations and thus avoid some of the major divisions of religious conviction. Still others quietly slip out of the pew altogether and become personal, but not institutional, believers. Today's church leaders need all the pastoral skills, some managerial skills and the humility to be leaders who follow where the Holy Spirit may lead.

13
. . . .
Do Denominations
Have a Future?

A t this point it becomes necessary to confront an issue that was not
part of the original design of this book but that has forced itself
onto the agenda.

A question often raised in our interviews was whether reconciliation
between polarized Christians is possible. This was not on the list of
questions we asked, but it surfaced repeatedly as we spoke with church
leaders. And the doubts they expressed were generally in terms of denominational viability. All believed that people in congregations could
find ways of getting along with each other on a personal level; in committees and other face-to-face groups success stories were frequent. But
there was grave question as to whether opponents could be reconciled at
the denominational level.

From the beginning of this study we assumed the denomination was
the framework of church life. We interviewed persons who were *denomi-*

national leaders: we identified them by the denomination to which they belong and the leadership position they hold within it. Denominational leadership, we assumed, gave them the credentials to speak wisely on church problems. Now we must ask whether or not our basic assumption about denominations is wrong. Will the kind of denominations Christians have known in the past continue to characterize the church landscape?

The denomination is largely an American institution, developed in the context of religious liberty and immigration. Every European motherland from which pilgrims and colonists came had its officially supported state church. America was the first nation in history to be founded on the basis of separation of church and state. Independent and self-supporting denominations became the American pattern. Churches accustomed to state support and officially recognized status elsewhere—even the Roman Catholic Church—became "denominations" here.[1]

Furthermore, immigrants found their grounding, their "home away from home" in denominations that nurtured congregations with a common language and culture as well as shared religious views. Several denominations have gradually removed their initial titles of identification by country—the Reformed Church in America is no longer the Dutch Reformed Church, and most Swedish Lutherans and German Lutherans are simply known now as Evangelical Lutherans, for example. But new groups keep coming, so there are several Korean Presbyterian churches that did not exist fifty years ago. In two more generations Koreans will be making the same tough decisions about national-cultural identification that prior denominations have made, because their grandchildren will likely and hopefully be thoroughly acculturated to American society.

Denominations, originally associations of like-minded people, become over time less homogeneous than their founders envisioned. Some maintain firm boundaries and a strong sense of doctrinal and moral consensus. Others seek to be open to all—a category into which most mainline American denominations fall. Although they are vessels for a common history, tradition and vision of the church, such denominations are increasingly "diluted" by the inclusion of members who join for many different reasons. Their mission intention to welcome all Christians is in tension with the will to conformity of belief and practice. Congregations in communities marked by economic flux and demographic variability may die if they depend on people of like race, class, culture and doctrine to fill their pews. Denominational loyalty becomes increasingly secondary to congregational survival. Local churches may stay in their founding denomination while being only minimally involved. Those who stay involved have an effect on the evolving nature of the denomination, especially as those changing local churches multiply.

What happens when a denomination loses its coherence, its like-mindedness? Can the level of contentious diversity that now characterizes these denominations be sustained? Does the steady twenty-year decline in membership of mainline denominations portend their gradual disappearance? A recent straight-line statistical projection of present membership trends in one such denomination had it disappearing by 2069.[2] Is this where we're headed?

The Issues Threatening Denominations Today
We have examined a wide range of issues on which liberals and conservatives, with varying levels of hostility, divide. The most intractable shoal on which some denominations today appear to be actually breaking apart seems an extraordinary one when seen in the light of church history. It is not the *filioque* of Nicea, or the *sola gratia* of the Reformation or any essentially theological matter. It is an issue that has never even surfaced as an ecclesiastical stumbling block in the two-thousand-year history of Christian discipleship. It is the question of whether or not self-affirming practicing homosexuals can be ordained as ministers.

In this question the underlying issue of biblical authority and interpretation is sharply confronted. Plausible, biblically based cases can be made on both sides of most of the single issues. The biblical argument for allowing women in leadership roles has been largely won, at least in theory, in the mainline churches. In the case of abortion, which almost all Christians oppose in other than extraordinary circumstances, both sides at least recognize that cases can be made from Scripture using examples of the taking of life in war or capital punishment or instances of choosing the lesser of evils.

On the ordination of homosexuals, however, as we have noted earlier, there appears to be no meeting ground. Liberals regard it as a matter of justice and inclusion under a gospel of love. They are unsure that the biological nature of homosexuality is even clearly understood: they ask, "Should gays be denied their sexuality if it is part of God's creation?" All

Christians are sinners—even those who are ordained. Is this sin so much greater than others that homosexuals must be excluded from ordination?

Most evangelicals adhere to the traditional position that homosexual practice is unrepented sin. The issue is not the rejection of homosexuals as persons. Many evangelicals have family members who are gay. Nearly all know some homosexuals personally. In congregations they treat them with personal respect and concern. They believe in a gospel of love, and they extend that love. But they see heterosexual marriage as the biblical order of creation. In terms of moral principle they stand firmly on what evangelicals regard as Scripture's plain, unambiguous condemnation of homosexuality. It is for them a biblical, not a cultural, issue.

Blurring of Denominational Identity

The precarious state of denominational unity in the crisis over the ordination of homosexuals comes in a period when a variety of cultural developments have weakened the personal sense of denominational identity once felt by most Christians. In an earlier chapter we examined as a case study the 1991 election at the General Assembly of the Christian Church (Disciples of Christ) in which Michael Kinnamon was narrowly defeated for the office of general minister and president. In later reflection on the incident Kinnamon spoke of the division between "what may be called 'denominational loyalists' and 'happen to be Christians.'" He said, "I frequently spoke about what we could learn about being Disciples from the controversies surrounding the nomination. It was quickly apparent, however, that for many the Disciples heritage was not only unknown but irrelevant to their reasons for church membership."[3] Denominational loyalists with an interest in their heritage are rare today. The impetus that once sent Methodists new to a community in search of the nearest Methodist church (instead of "the nearest church that meets our needs") is largely gone, at least for laypeople.

This is even more true of younger generations than of older. A U.S. Air Force chaplain, whose ministry is primarily with the "twentysomething" generation, spoke in an interview about the lack of denominational loyalty in young men and women serving in the air force. "If you talk to them they will deny any denominational affiliation," he reported. "'My Mom was this, my Dad was that, and I don't care.' This is the postdenominational era."

In a sense this weakening denominational identity is partly the result of a major emphasis of mainline denominations in the twentieth-century: the ecumenical movement they have nurtured has consciously transcended denominational identity. But there are cultural and societal roots to this trend as well.

Privatization of religion. In their influential book *Habits of the Heart* religious sociologist Robert Bellah and his colleagues focused on the "fierce individualism" of our times that undercuts a sense of community and the common good. "Today religion in America is as private and diverse as New England colonial religion was public and unified," they write.[4] Their now-classic illustration is "Sheilaism," a young woman's religion (she called it her "faith") that was so personal and private she had named it after herself. It was entirely free of any relationship to a church or religious community. Robert Wuthnow, in *The Struggle for America's Soul,* adds another case study, a hypothetical "Mabel" whose privatized religion is practiced before a television screen as she watches a variety of televangelists and religious shows "alone in her living room getting God by satellite."[5]

Even those who are closely related to and active in more conventional churches are still individualistic in their beliefs and involvement. Bellah and his coauthors cite Gallup's 1978 "unchurched American" study, in which 80 percent of Americans agreed that "an individual should arrive at his or her own religious beliefs independent of any churches or synagogues."[6] Even among Roman Catholics, according to the follow-up 1988 Gallup "unchurched American" study, 77 percent reported that they relied on their own consciences rather than on papal teachings when making difficult moral decisions.[7]

An extreme form of this privatization was identified by Stephen Carter in *The Culture of Disbelief* in terms of "God as a hobby." Religion, in the view of those who set the terms of public discourse, takes its place in the same category as stamp collecting or clog dancing, as a purely personal idiosyncrasy.[8] It is perfectly all right to believe "that kind of stuff," but it is not to be taken seriously.

Postmodern relativism. Accompanying the privatization phenomenon are other cultural developments. One is the postmodern relativism that dominates the contemporary intellectual climate and that rejects absolutes of any kind. It sees no objective truth, only many alternatives among which the individual person makes choices and celebrates his or her personal perspective while respecting, of course, the differing perspectives of others. Everything is relative. One belief is as good as another, and the guideline is "whatever works for you."

In *Vanishing Boundaries,* a close look at the religion of mainline Protestant baby boomers by Dean R. Hoge, Benton Johnson and Donald Luidens, the researchers found that the basic belief in religious authority and whether Christian teachings are exclusively true was at the heart of the matter.[9] The absence of a faith that commands a difference in one's life or that is theologically distinct from other faiths means going to church is optional (at best) for many baby boomers. Denominational loyalty or an interest in denominational concerns beyond the local congregation are almost irrelevant, and those adults studied switched from one denomination to another for largely pragmatic reasons.

Secularism. Closely related to the privatization of religion and postmodern relativism is another cultural phenomenon: the pervasive secularism of the times. Secularism is not, of course, a new development. What is new, however, is the present *alienation* of the public culture from religion and especially from Christianity. Stephen Carter describes a society in which religious voices and views are rejected in the public debate simply because they are religious. He discusses rules for public discourse based on "fact," which exclude "faith" as a way of knowing. "It is both tragic and paradoxical," says Carter, "that now, just as the nation is beginning to invite people into the public square for the different points of view that they have to offer, people whose contribution to the nation's diversity comes from their religious traditions are not valued unless their voices are somehow esoteric."[10]

In this secularized context denominational identification is no longer important to many. Surveys show that the number of Americans who identify with no religion at all is now approaching 10 percent. And among younger generations the percentage is much higher. Among the young men and women who make up the armed forces, as of June 1995, 18.25 percent listed no religious preference.

Changed perception of pluralism. Another factor is the changed perception among Americans of their nation's religious pluralism. America has always perceived itself as being a varied people. But through the first two hundred years of the nation's life this variety was seen as a denominational pluralism within a Judeo-Christian society, even though actual church membership was quite low early on. The American value system was derived from Western Christian civilization and acknowledged a national relationship to a just, righteous, sovereign God. Denominations were a way of identifying oneself religiously within this context. In the final third of the twentieth century this perception of denominational plurality has been replaced by that of a far broader diversity. There are increased numbers of Hindus, Buddhists and Muslims who have immigrated from Asia; and Black Muslims, who were originally a racial protest group, are now increasingly merging with orthodox Islam. The statistical change is still quite modest. Adherents of these non-Judeo-Christian religions constitute less than 1 percent of the American population. But the change in the public perception of religious pluralism is highly significant, especially in areas where these newcomers live. Identification with a particular Christian denomination becomes both more sensitive and less important.

All of these cultural developments—the privatization of religion, the relativism of the intellectual climate, the secularism of American life and the perception of a much broader pluralism—have created a cultural context in which denominational identification has lost its public relevance. Against this background, the decline in denominational loyalty and the casual shifting from one denomination to another are not likely to change. Denominational identity is no longer as significant a factor for Americans as it once was.

Do Denominations Serve a Useful Purpose?

Although they matter little to ordinary churchgoers, denominational structures still fill a needed role in church life. They provide channels for cooperatively achieving things that congregations consider important and cannot easily do apart. Classically these collective tasks have included mission. The sending of missionaries was one of the first tasks for which denominational agencies were formed. Initiated often at the congregational level, banding then into state groups, these world-mission societies rapidly became denominational. Now that flourishing indigenous churches exist in most areas where mission was undertaken, new relationships with those churches seems to American liberals to require different mission strategies from those of the past. The rapid growth of parachurch mission agencies, independent of the denominations, has provided alternative channels for evangelical mission activity. But mission remains a cooperative endeavor.

Other areas in which denominational structures once met widely shared needs include the development and publication of Christian education curricular materials as well as resources for stewardship, evangelism, church growth and other congregational activities. In all these areas an understanding of common mission has been made impossible by the liberal-evangelical split. Printed materials and leadership resources have been developed by independent parachurch sources to meet a wide range of preferences, particularly those of evangelicals. This is especially noteworthy with regard to Christian education curriculum, but it operates in other areas as well. It is entirely possible today for congregations, even those affiliated with particular denominations, to obtain their support and resources from other than denominational sources. Many do.

Yet congregations continue to need the broader relationships denominations provide. We have noted repeatedly the contemporary trend toward independent congregations, many of them thriving megachurches: Willow Creek Community Church, northeast of Chicago in South Barrington, Illinois, is a frequently cited example. Widespread interest in Willow Creek's "seeker services," its methods and approaches, has led to visits by interested clergy and the establishment of training programs. Other similar congregations with seeker services have been formed. The result is the Willow Creek Association, a rapidly growing network of congregations that seek to minister to the unchurched.[11] It is not a denomination in the full sense of the word, but it is moving in that direction. The Association of Vineyard Churches, which originated with one congregation in southern California and is spreading to numerous other locations, has become, by its own desire and will, a denomination. Southern California's Hope Chapel, still affiliated with the Foursquare Gospel Church, has a number of closely related branch churches. Calvary Chapel (centered in Costa Mesa, California) staunchly resists calling itself a denomination, but it has a network of associated congregations. A denominational structure seems to be developed for purposes of cooperation and mutual support, even by churches that begin independently.

Denominations and Clergy

A second and even more important role for denominational structures relates to the clergy. These structures provide an institutional base for ministers, particularly in those long-established denominations where clergy systems are fully developed. They offer professional support structures that help in many ways to define and govern the ministerial calling and can serve, in effect, as professional associations or unions for the clergy. They are the ministerial equivalent of the state bar for lawyers, the state or national medical association for doctors, the educational association or teacher's union for educators. They frequently establish and monitor minimum salaries, working conditions and job-related benefits for ministers. These structures also provide the mechanisms for job changes—often known as the "calling" system—for the clergy. The system may be highly structured and centrally controlled as in the United Methodist Church, where the power of the bishop in making ministerial assignments is very strong. It may be a localized system, primarily controlled by the congregation, as in Baptist churches. It may be a shared-power system, largely in the hands of the congregation but regulated by denominational structures, as in Episcopal and most of the Reformed family of churches. In all systems, however, denominational networks, standards and procedures are extremely important to the clergy in connection with calls and professional moves.

Clergy pensions and medical insurance, two crucially important professional support systems, are also handled by denominational structures. So is ministerial education, through ordination standards that are usually denominationally established and through the church-related seminaries. There are nondenominational seminaries, both university-related (Harvard, Yale, Chicago) and independent (Fuller, Gordon-Conwell, Union of New York), but for congregations of particular denominations their own seminaries are the usual source of clerical training.

It is, of course, possible for both congregations and clergy to operate without any of the professional supports ordinarily provided by denominational structures. There are growing numbers of independent congregations served by independent ministers, many trained by other ministers. The proliferation of such congregations is a striking trend in contemporary American religious life. Most American clergy, however, are ministers of particular denominations (this is their professional identity) serving in denominational churches. In considerable measure denominational identity may be regarded as a matter of basic belief. They are Baptist, Disciple, Lutheran, Pentecostal or Episcopal clergy for theological reasons, adherents of a particular denominational tradition because of deep conviction. As a practical matter, however, they are also shaped by and dependent on a particular professional support system.

For all these reasons, denominational identity is far more important to the clergy than to lay church members. A Baptist family can move to a new city and affiliate with a Lutheran congregation quite readily. If the new church seems to meet their needs and they ask to join, they will be welcomed. But for a Baptist minister to move into the pastorate of a Lutheran congregation would be a formidable task, difficult and time consuming if not impossible. Ties to the elaborate web of denominational supports, networks and pension and medical programs are not easily cut or readily established elsewhere.

Even if denominational structures are regarded by laypeople as largely superfluous, they are still very important to most ministers. And ministers have a dominant role in controlling church life. In episcopally organized church polities (Roman Catholic, Methodist and Episcopal) ministers' preeminent power is officially established. In polities that grant an equal or greater governing role to lay officers, clergy power is less direct but nonetheless real. Their leadership position in congregations gives them an aura of authority, although that is eroding. Their familiarity with church polity gives them an advantage in exercising control. Some lay officials become sufficiently active in denominational structures to become quasiprofessionals. Ordinary lay delegates to annual conferences and conventions, however, come and go, often at personal career cost. Clergy delegates are there year after year, for it is their "career." As in any other human organization, paid leadership tends to dominate.

For all these pragmatic reasons, the denominational structures that provide needed services to congregations and those that provide necessary networks and supports for the clergy are probably an essential part of church life. When they are not in existence, they are created, bringing new denominations into being, as we see happening with newer networks of independent congregations.

Central Bureaucracies

Denominational bureaucracies, however, are clearly in trouble. This book is crammed with evidence that programs at the national level in mainline churches and ecumenical agencies have been a major focus of tensions between liberals and evangelicals. Congregationalism avoids some of this tension, although the Southern Baptist Convention, with a heritage of independent, autonomous local congregations, has been ravaged by dissension in recent years. Interrelated and episcopally organized denominations are particularly subject to struggle over the appropriate activities and stances of denominational policy.

Different interpretations of biblical mandates, positions on issues, concepts of mission and role of national staff turn almost any initiative or policy into a battleground. During the affluent fifties and sixties, the program agencies of the mainline denominations expanded greatly, particularly as ensconced liberal leadership saw an activist role for the churches on many social concerns. The resulting bureaucracies were products of the twentieth-century managerial age, and management techniques were relied upon to make priority and goal decisions. But the managerial model was inadequate for resolving sharp polarities and a loss of consensus. Some staff were caught between opposing forces and attempted compromises, others took charge as "top managers" and manipulated the choices and decisions, and a few held posts where no major rifts occurred.

Now most such denominations are facing steep cutbacks in program staffing at various levels of their structures. They have experienced a decline in funding at the national level as well as increased designated giving to specific causes. Significant funding has been diverted to alternative and parachurch channels by both evangelicals and liberals when their views have not won the day. The routing of evangelicals' funds into more acceptable channels for mission (instead of into liberally tilted bureaucracies) has also been a strong factor.

From a sociological and organizational point of view, the central bureaucracies can be faulted for not meeting needs and concerns as many of their constituent congregations perceive them. While attempting to lead the churches into controversial areas of social concern, understood by liberals as faithfulness to the gospel, the bureaucracies have failed to attend adequately to the needs, diversity of views and protests of a sizable portion of their constituents. The polity structures that provide the directives to bureaucratic staff have also often been sharply divided—marching orders may be very weak, so some staff march to the beat of their own drum. Most mainline bureaucracies have addressed the concerns of their liberal wing and, indeed, have provided the liberal leadership in internal denominational struggles. They represent, in effect, only one part of their constituencies. Given all these factors, the heyday of large national headquarters and staffs seems definitely over. It is important, however, not to equate the future of these bureaucracies, which in their present form have existed for only the past forty years, with the future of the denominations themselves.

Is There a Future for Denominations?
It appears that denominations are likely to survive and to adapt to changes in church life. Their basic sociological function in a society based on freedom of religion is as voluntary associations of like-minded people. These groups come, of course, in a wide range of forms. At one end of the spectrum is the small sect with a high level of doctrinal and behavioral uniformity, enforced by a rigid discipline, that excludes all nonconformists. At the other end is the doctrinally and behaviorally diverse group whose like-mindedness consists of a desire to be open and accepting to all. At this end of the spectrum, however, the concern for diversity must be sufficiently strong *in itself* to provide the necessary cohesiveness. If such a group becomes polarized by deep differences over doctrinal and behavioral standards, as has happened in many of today's diverse denominations, that like-mindedness may be threatened.

The internal logic of denominations (to seek a like-mindedness sufficiently cohesive to hold them together) may take these divided groups in any of several directions, one of which is schism. Like-mindedness can be achieved by withdrawing and forming a new denomination. Quiet schism, as individual believers shift to more congenial denominations, takes place slowly. The other, most hopeful possibility is the gradual building or restoring of denomination-wide consensus. A necessary condition for such an outcome is a denominational leadership that is not identified with either side of the internal polarization. But whatever the organizational dynamics and the human processes involved, Christians' ultimate hope for a binding unity is found in the Lord of the church and the power of the Holy Spirit. The love of Christ is strong enough to overcome any human divisions.

As we have shown, denominations have had important utilitarian uses, but their most significant purpose has been to keep Christians in relationship with one another beyond the simple boundaries of local geography. We are "a people of faith." The spirit of that unity in Christ is expressed in colorful, even feisty terms by one eloquent writer in a church magazine:

> Even if "my side" loses, I will stay and will attempt to persuade others to do the same. . . . Throughout American church history, even down to the present day, when folks have disagreed, they have left the church and formed a new one so that they could "get on with being the church," so that they could be free of the distraction of fighting with one another. In that sense American Protestantism has participated in the "culture of divorce" long before the culture did. It is our history. We have seen contending for the faith not so much in terms of being called to a deeper sense of our unity in Christ and faithfulness to his church, but in abandoning that reality, frankly and candidly admitting our *lack of faith* in Jesus' reconciling power or in his call to us to share in his sufferings. . . . Apart from the fact that there are no pure [denominations] out there, the temptation to believe that we can create one or, at least, leave a worse one behind is more dangerous to our theological health than the mess we are already in.[12]

There is refreshing candor, common sense and basic loyalty in this declaration. Many a person born and bred in a particular tradition could speak similarly, although only a few tend to be under forty years old! This is not simply a statement of denominational loyalty, however. It is a recognition that God's people are bound together in a reconciling faith that needs collaborative expression, whether or not Christians find all their views agreeable.

We began this book with testimonials to our own positions and also to what we admire in one another's position as evangelical or liberal. Each has something important to offer; each can receive from the other emphases and essentials of the faith. In short, the church of Jesus Christ benefits from a richness of perspectives. Peeling off to form yet another denomination when differences arise or splitting the denomination into two separate movements, evangelical and liberal, does not strengthen the churches and their witness.

But other significant events are taking place that raise new possibilities for the future of denominations as we know them. In 1997 the Evangelical Lutheran Church, the Presbyterian Church (U.S.A.), the United Church of Christ and the Reformed Church in America entered into "full communion" with each other. This enables these denominations to exchange clergy, cooperate in missionary work and collaborate on social-service projects. The United Church of Christ and the Christian Church (Disciples) have joined together in even closer communion. The patient, diligent work of bilateral commissions is bearing fruit.

This church is in a time of transition and turmoil. It is quite possible that evangelical Christians could coalesce in one loose fellowship and liberal Christians in another, quite apart from denominational affiliations. Some of the signs point in that direction. Our "stories" as denominations, the theological and cultural distinctives and events that give each denomination its reason for being, might become less important. The weakening of denominational ties and the mobility of members may have positive aspects.

Faithfulness requires that we look for the working of the Holy Spirit in these difficult times. The church may well endure and even gain vigor by paying less attention to denominational prerogatives. Perhaps the presence of church members from many different traditions in our congregations and structures will have a leavening effect upon us. Maybe God is teaching us to consider a more Christlike way of joining hands in mission and worship. Rather than bemoaning the dilution of our denominational heritage, we might find ourselves enriched by the gifts that other traditions have to offer. Imagine the riches that could be explored by such a humble, open-hearted church! Our worship styles are already being influenced by traditions outside our own, and Bible study done ecumenically often reveals surprising new depths of insight. We do not have to give up in order to receive. While retaining some traditional denominational structure and key doctrinal elements, we might learn from

☐ the Quaker values of quiet contemplation, service to all in need and little distinction between laity and clergy

☐ the passion and attention given to the Holy Spirit by the Pentecostals

☐ the rigorous biblical study and intellectual diligence of the Reformed tradition

☐ the beauty and grace of the worship liturgy and the church architecture in Episcopalian and Orthodox churches

☐ African-American Christians' spontaneity and support for preaching the necessary word and their tradition of the "seamless garment" of gospel and social action

☐ the missionary zeal among various Wesleyan and Baptist churches

☐ the relaxed and warm fellowship, informal worship setting and effective outreach to young people characteristic of Calvary Chapel

☐ music, fine art, poetry and literature in many styles and cultures

The possibilities for renewal from one another are enormous, if we can receive these differences as gifts from God and not as obstacles to community. Of course we would each be uncomfortable in some styles of worship and with some behavior or polity positions we cannot accept for ourselves. Perhaps we would learn new ways of accommodating our differences, as seen among the orders in Roman Catholicism—each participates fully in the Catholic Church but has its own distinct fellowship. Protestant churches have never risen to that expression of "dwelling in unity," and it would be naive to expect some segments of Protestantism to respond. But, God willing, the slow crumbling of denominational structures could provide building blocks for a Third Great Awakening, the vision of which may not yet be apparent.

More important than the future of denominations is the future of the church itself, and about this we have no uncertainty. Liberals and evangelicals agree that the biblical message is clear. The future of the church is not in the hands of its human members, but in the hands of God. Denominations may come and go, but the church itself is God's, and the very gates of hell will not prevail against it.

An Episcopal bishop, when asked about the outlook for denominations, replied, "I'm not a sociologist, and I always want to bring in the Jesus factor, which is an unknown. Right after the Revolutionary War, all the mainline churches were in deep trouble. Thomas Paine predicted that in thirty years, at most, Christianity would disappear. And that was right on the eve of the Second Great Awakening. I think we're on the eve of the Third Great Awakening, which we'll see in the early twenty-first century."[13]

14

. . . .

Threads to
Strengthen
the Tie

In a divorce the children are caught in between and very often bear the scars. . . .
A church split affects how [people] view religion,
authority structures and the world in general. It is a divorce in the societal part
of their lives, and they are caught in between; but they have even less that they can do
about it. . . . It was too much to see people I had come to care about say
such awful things about one another. It was worst of all to see the people
I felt were closest to being "right" with their jaws set in place,
Sunday-school teachers arguing among themselves in class,
congregational meetings willy-nilly, full of eruptions. . . .
The whole scene made it difficult for me to trust being in a congregation again,
and it wasn't until a few years ago that I did. . . .
I notice that there are an awful lot of people in this world
who have never developed a level of trust in a congregation or a denomination,
many of them by being burned in similar ways.
PARTICIPANT IN AN ECUNET MEETING

Throughout this study we have been haunted by such testimonies as this one. The effectiveness of our witness as Christians to the love of God in Christ is inextricably related to our ability to maintain our unity and respect for one another in our churches. Jesus understood this as he prayed in John 17 that his disciples might be one "so that the world may believe that you have sent me." Our evangelism and our unity are interrelated. When we threaten to destroy our relationship with one another, we compromise our ability to convince others that we bear a gospel of love and forgiveness.

All the various issues, including the "single issues," that distance us from one another need to be weighed against our fundamental witness. When we allow different views on abortion, homosexuality or the appropriate role of women in the church to break the body of Christ, we make of that issue an idol—it displaces Christ.

In the eyes of the secular world we become caricatures of the gospel of love—hypocrites who talk of love to the society and express hatred against our own Christian brothers and sisters. As one of our interviewees puts it, "The world looks at the church and laughs! We're not riding the crest of the wave but the tail of a dinosaur."

We express the love of God for all humanity through our ability to hear and respond with empathetic concern and action to the demands for justice from the people in our society. For the church to be serenely and remotely intact—unruffled by the cries for fair treatment that emanate from both outside and inside the church—would be to provide another unpersuasive witness. Again, the charge of an unloving hypocrisy would beset the church.

Yet the urgency of unity, for the sake of both evangelism and justice, does not in itself eliminate differences. This project began with a decision by an evangelical and a liberal to work together on the problem presented by the evangelical-liberal tension. We set out *together* to look for ways in which the polarization can be reduced and reconciliation encouraged.

Neither of us "converted" the other. Though we have agreed on nearly all that has been said in this book, our basic beliefs and our respective ways of viewing the nature of the church and the gospel have not remarkably changed. We remain a liberal and an evangelical in a divided church, disagreeing on many issues that are quite important to us. Yet our trust in the authenticity and Christian commitment of people on *both* sides has been strongly confirmed, and our convictions about the essential unity of the church have been strengthened.

Beyond the many lessons we have ourselves learned and communicated to others in the pages of this book, our concluding observations reflect the "unity in diversity" that characterizes both the church and the authors. Each of us has different concluding observations, expressing what we regard as the most important things we've learned from this project. We present them separately—but with the important assertion that each of us agrees essentially with what the other has said! And this, perhaps, reflects a central characteristic of constructive unity in diversity: each side must allow the other to say what it believes, must hear what has been said and must affirm its significance to the other.

Before offering our concluding observations, however, we want to affirm some things we have personally learned while working together on this study. We knew from the beginning that our personal experience in working with someone from the "other camp" would be a central aspect of the project. And this has, indeed, been the case. We pass on our observations in the hope that they may be useful to others involved in similar activities.

Mutual Insights

Both persons' strong commitment to the church of Jesus Christ itself has been an important factor. Both of us believe the church to be a divinely established institution, necessary to the Christian life and worth taking strong measures to preserve. This also implies or includes commitment on the part of both of us to the authority of Scripture (though perhaps with different understandings of what this means), the classic creeds and confessional heritage (particularly the Reformed heritage) and the history of the church.

Commitment to the project itself was also a powerful motivator. Had we been simply discussing differences in a more general context we might have argued over our respective positions—trying to convince each other or simply airing our own views—indefinitely. But the necessity for completing our project forced us to work toward accommodation, mutual acceptance and something we could agree on. Differing groups or persons may find it helpful to work together with a specific goal or purpose.

As two moderates we discovered that even though we are in some ways and on some issues far apart, we are closer together than liberal and evangelical rhetoric might indicate. Each of us is in some ways attuned to and sympathetic with the more extreme positions in his or her camp. Dick Hutcheson, for instance, though recognizing its faults, reads with considerable appreciation (and allowances for its excesses) *The Layman*. Peggy Shriver, though deeply troubled by the 1991 human-sexuality report, appreciated the effort to break the silence over the issue. Dick's writings and speeches have met general acceptance in the evangelical community,

Peggy's in the liberal community. So we are in these ways quite far apart. Yet we both are essentially moderates, closer to the center than to those extremes (with whom we are occasionally sympathetic). This probably reflects the church itself, which is both sharply divided and at the same time essentially moderate. Though the extremes at each end are vocal and are heard sympathetically by large numbers in the respective camps, most are reasonably close to the center and most want to find accommodations.

When two people (or groups) try to reconcile differences, there may be many other factors at play in addition to the specific issue they are working on. These need to be recognized and accounted for. For instance, Peggy is a published poet and a skillful writer in narrative style. The stories of persons are important to her. Dick is a linear person, intent on pursuing a line of argument from a particular starting point, along a clearly outlined path and to a specific end point. Organization and logic are important to him. Neither is totally without the other style; Dick uses narrative, and Peggy follows an organization and logic. But the basic styles of writing (and thinking) are different. Sometimes it turned out that when we thought we were struggling over theological or ideological differences, our difference in style was the real barrier.

Process is not nearly as important as spirit, and methods are far less central than scriptural truth. In this context, though, we did learn about what works and what does not. The particular procedure we adopted for writing a book together may have usefulness to others engaged in a concrete, collaborative project. One person was assigned to write a chapter. The other person read it and made specific proposals, in written form, for modifications and changes. (We avoided simply critiquing the other's work in general terms and sending it back for a rewrite.) The original writer then considered the proposals and incorporated all those he or she could agree to. The modified chapter was then returned to the other for another read. Most disagreements were ironed out by this process. Those issues that could not be reconciled this way were worked out in face-to-face meetings. The solution of last resort (noting specific disagreements in footnotes or including two versions by different authors on a particular subject) was always available but was rarely necessary since a solution we could both agree on was usually reached.

We also learned from our process itself that disagreements are not always as hopeless as they first appear. When the writer of a chapter received suggestions from the collaborator, the first reaction upon reading a proposed change in isolation was likely to be, "This is impossible. I can't go along with that." But when the change was actually incorporated into the draft on a trial basis, minor modifications (often acceptable to the collaborator) made and the section examined in its entirety, it generally turned out to be something the original writer could live with.

The experience of writing a book together is not something to universalize as the best way of forging a binding Christian relationship, even though it has been greatly beneficial to us. Others could find they also grow in understanding by searching for at least one partner from a different "community of trust" (theological, social, ethical) and agreeing with that partner to keep in close touch. To speak about "the other side" with that partner in mind, as though she or he is present in every conversation, is a marvelous discipline to the tongue, the truth, the testimony of faith. We commend this idea to all who have fulfilled their own discipline to read to the end this book.

Concluding Observations (by Richard G. Hutcheson Jr.)

In the light of interviews with church leaders, conversations with Christians across the ideological and theological spectrum and other sources of data and insight, what can be said at the conclusion of this book to concerned Christians about addressing our differences? How can we summarize what we've learned?

Things on which we can agree as we begin. As we confront differences, there remain some things on which a large measure of agreement is possible from people on both sides of the divide. We stand on common ground to a greater extent than we, in the heat of our disagreements, often realize. Unanimity is rare, but in some areas there is a broad consensus, reflecting the position of an overwhelming majority of church members. Some of these areas of agreement are widely recognized; others are not so obvious. Any group, large or small, seeking to address the problems that divide us, might do well to begin by identifying what we can affirm in unity.

The starting point is our common faith in and commitment to the God revealed in Christ Jesus. All of us on both sides claim the name "Christian," and this is not an unimportant bond. The history of the church through two thousand years (as much as we may deplore some parts of it) is our common heritage of faith.

A second commonality, sometimes obscured because a difference of interpretation is frequently prominent in our squabbles, is the fact that all of us are, in some major sense, committed to the authority of Scripture. We are inescapably a people of the book. We differ in the ways we understand that authority and in the ways we understand its mandates. But its study, its interpretation and its liturgical and devotional use are central for all of us.

We recognize that there are a few among us for whom Scripture has only metaphorical significance, for whom it is nothing more than an evocative record of human striving to understand the universe. At the other extreme there are some for whom fixation on a rigid doctrine of verbal inerrancy makes the Bible a dividing rather than a reconciling force. But in most inclusive denominations the number of these extremists is negligible—even if their strident voices are not. We need to remind ourselves that in spite of our differing interpretations we are overwhelmingly united on the authority of the Bible.

A third commonality is our place in a culture by which we are inescapably affected. That culture, in our times, is itself sharply divided— engaged, even, in a "culture war" from which we cannot escape. Some of the ideological issues being fought out in the culture have religious roots. All of them have some religious dimensions. The political and judicial struggle in American government between factions we have come to designate as "pro-life" and "pro-choice" reflect, for many, deep religious convictions. So does the battle over homosexual rights or practice. Our love for our country, our attitudes toward military force, toward a free-market economy and toward a social-welfare system—all are shaped at least in part by religious convictions.

None of us seeks an exclusively "spiritual" religion that separates us from the world around us. But in a period of cultural battles over love of country, the market economy, abortion, homosexuality and political correctness, we all need a constant awareness of our relationship to our culture. There is a continuing danger of "baptizing" economic, political or cultural attitudes—whether liberal or conservative—into religious imperatives. All Christians both affect and are affected by the culture in which we live. Liberals must distinguish between Christian convictions and political correctness; evangelicals must distinguish between Christian convictions and cultural conservatism.

A fourth area of common ground is only now becoming fully apparent to both liberals and evangelicals. A shift in the locus of church life has brought us into an era marked by the primacy of congregational rather than denominational activity. Whatever is to significantly influence American religious life at the beginning of the twenty-first century will be focused primarily on congregations and less on ecclesiastical hierarchies or bureaucracies.

The larger church continues to be a necessary frame of reference for mainstream Christians. Certain middle judicatory, denominational and ecumenical functions continue to be essential. But no longer can American religion be chiefly envisioned in terms of denominational structures and the ecumenical councils they support. Pronouncements by denominational or ecumenical bodies no longer carry significant political or cultural clout. Americans are focusing their religious energies on (and spending their money in) the local communities of faith where they worship and serve. To the extent that a polarized church addresses its divisions constructively, the local congregation is the primary arena in which this will take place.

Some battles of the recent past, therefore, are no longer especially relevant because of changes already well under way. Denominational pronouncements that do not reflect a broad consensus matter less as issues are debated in congregations and fewer such pronouncements are made. Positions taken by denominational staff members matter less as staffs are radically reduced in size and function by financial pressures. "Stacking" of denominational study committees and manipulating outcomes will no longer matter so much as such committees cease to be the major instrument for decision making. The future of the church is in the hands of local congregational members and leaders, as persons on both sides of the divide now generally recognize. There is some loss to be lamented, however, because each separate congregation's voice will be heard in the culture and in Washington even less than the voice of denominational pronouncements.

Broad guidelines. This does not mean that there is no longer a place for intercongregational, regional and denominational conferences, committees or study groups. But wherever such discussions are held, the emphasis will be less on political maneuvering than on consensus building and growing the understanding of ordinary Christians in the pews.

We began this project with an assumption that such Christians *want* to find ways of lessening polarization and moving toward mutual respect and reconciliation. This assumption, too, has been generally verified by those we have interviewed and consulted. We are convinced that within congregations, and at times in broader settings, Christians will want to look for ways of confronting and dealing with their divisions. We looked above at some areas of agreement that provide a common base as such efforts begin. Beyond these, there are some broad guidelines for confronting differences that have emerged from our interviews, consultations and study.

A basic guideline is that we seek not to resolve all differences, but to live with them in a loving and constructive way. Biblically and theologically, as well as historically, we have learned that unity and diversity go together in the church. Neither precludes the other. The quest for truth goes on with the knowledge that God alone has absolute truth and that our human understanding of it is always limited and imperfect. Fixing the limits of diversity will always be a struggle, but accepting some measure of such diversity is part of the Christian life.

This being the case, a second guideline is that our objective, as we confront polarization, is not to win political battles or gain control, but to understand the other and, when possible, to persuade. Until understanding and persuasion produce consensus, majority votes on divisive issues risk broadening the polarization and should be used sparingly.

A third broad guideline, then, points to identification of those areas in which consensus exists and those in which it is (at least for the present) missing. The "single issues" such as abortion and homosexuality are particularly important here. In some congregations and groups, a broad pro-life consensus makes possible unified participation in activities sponsored by organizations such as Operation Rescue. In others, a similarly broad consensus on homosexuality issues leads to self-designation as a More Light congregation. In many congregations and groups, however, the absence of consensus on these issues must be identified.

A fourth broad guideline is that even as we confront differences with efforts to understand and persuade, there are in all congregations *some* common goals on which people with disagreements can work together. We have heard numerous stories of people who could not agree on abortion but were united in their efforts to bring about racial justice; people who had different interpretations of some passages of Scripture but who worked together on the scriptural injunctions to feed the hungry, clothe the naked, house the homeless and heal the sick. Every congregation or group can find ways of working together, and we have learned again and again that out of such common efforts has come the kind of unity that transcends differences.

A final broad guideline is to point polarized Christians to those resources of our own faith that compel us toward unity. Our unity is in Jesus Christ. At the heart of the Christian life are the commandments to love one another; to serve others; to bear one another's burdens; to live by faith, hope and love (the greatest of which is love); to engage in mission together; and to live in community with mutual responsibility for each other. As we worship and study together, providing nurture, support and opportunities for service and growth (whether or not we intentionally address our differences) we experience the reconciliation with one another that follows from our reconciliation with God in Christ. And as we intentionally address our differences, using these resources faithfully, we cannot entirely fail.

Specific ground rules. Persons can come together in groups with various structures for the specific purpose of addressing differences. We have heard stories describing many such experiences. Some are highly informal, some carefully structured.

There are no uniform ground rules for such encounters. But one important requirement is to adopt *some* ground rules to govern interaction. These rules may be drawn from the secular field of conflict resolution, which has much to teach us. Several examples have been given in this book. They may be borrowed from other church groups that have been intentionally brought together to address differences. But agreed-on rules about speaking, about listening and about what is off-limits are extremely helpful not only in structured groups but often in informal situations as well.

A final, specific ground rule for whenever contending groups meet is to identify ways in which the two groups need each other at some point of the gathering. The two authors of this book, representing in some measure the liberal and evangelical wings of the church, began their task by clarifying their own positions. But at the same time they spelled out ways in which each of them appreciated, and had been helped by, those on the other side of the division. That initial identification of things we appreciated about the other was helpful to us throughout the project. It reminded us both that despite our differences we are closer together than we sometimes think.

That is one of the hopeful notes sounded by this project. Most inclusive churches are churches of moderate believers rather than extreme ones. Our natural inclination is to live with our differences. And most important of all, we need each other. The church of Jesus Christ will never be of one mind on all issues—we are fallible human beings, and absolute truth belongs to God alone. But we all need each other within the rich diversity of God's earthly kingdom, which is the church.

Concluding Observations (by Peggy L. Shriver)

Down through church history it is evident that, despite the truth in Jesus' plea for unity for the sake of witness, there have been issues deemed important enough to fracture the church again and again. Sometimes the heaving of history has caused the church as well as the society to split apart—as in civil war. Other times there have been doctrinal differences sufficiently important in the eyes of some to separate parts of the body from one another, as in the Reformation. Differing interpretations of the Bible and opinions about its authority have split Christians into many camps. The *Yearbook of American and Canadian Churches* keeps track of only 240 fragments of God's community of faith!

What are the limits of inclusiveness? What in *God's eyes* is a legitimate breaking point with others who claim to be Christian? What is the importance of our witness and the peace and unity of the church in relation to numerous significant justice issues? Are there not some ways short of schism to accommodate different views within our churches?

We end this book with these questions hanging in the air, because the answers to them would reflect once again the nature of our disagreements in the church. But it is important that we keep asking them of one another. It is easy to answer them rashly, in the heat of argument, and to jump too quickly to "knowing" what God would have us do. Earnest Christians differ on what the burden of Scripture says about the ordination of homosexuals, for example. Is this our, or God's, "test case" for inclusion within God's family of faith? Which issues are worthy of rending Christ's body? Which simply replace Jesus with an idolatry of our particular righteousness?

Church history is, as one of our interviewees suggests, both a tutor to us and a discouraging reminder that we are all too human. Attitudes toward the revelation of God in Scripture and in the traditions of the church have been the cause of continual dissension. We cannot expect that all differing interpretations of the Bible can be readily reconciled, when for two thousand years they have not, but we *can* be reconciled to the *reality* of our differences. We can be respectful of different roads taken and at the same time be grateful that we walk on much common ground. As the United Church of Christ professor we interviewed encourages, we can be chastened by the long stretches of church history required to shape new thinking in our shared tradition.

Concurrently, we acknowledge that some of the most profoundly faithful Christians have been disrupters of the peace and unity of the church throughout its turbulent history. We do not counsel the silencing of a Martin Luther, a Galileo Galilei, a Sir Thomas More, a Joan of Arc or a Dietrich Bonhoeffer in the name of peace! The voices of prophecy and truth seem to ring with greater nobility and clarity as the centuries pass. The Holy Spirit's leading is often better appreciated in hindsight. The church in its resistance to such leaders bears the real responsibility for "disrupting the peace," although it still accuses the prophetic voice. The role of courageous Christians in confronting the evils of slavery, in recognizing the potential of Christian women to serve in broader ministry and in alerting the church to its complicity in numerous social injustices should be celebrated. Avoiding conflict in order to maintain a semblance of unity has not been the message of this book.

A rehearsal of gifts. Many of the people we interviewed spoke appreciatively of perspectives they could not fully share but that enriched or provided a helpful balance to their own. Our conviction that indeed we do need each other has only grown as the study progressed. A rehearsal of these gifts to one another, added to those we have already expressed, is a useful reminder as we conclude. Some key gifts have been helpfully encompassed in the article "What Can Liberals and Evangelicals Teach Each Other?" by my husband, Donald W. Shriver Jr.[1] Here is a brief summary of what, he says, liberals can learn from evangelicals.

□ *Humans hunger for elevated significance in their lives.* "People want to be saved from the undertow of sin, death and insignificance that so regularly undermines us. Evangelicals know this. Liberals, if they mean to be Christians, should know it too."

□ *What one believes, not what one does not, best defines a faith.* "Evangelicals are at their best when they are preaching a positive message of Good News to people mired in bad news. . . . There is a great difference between meeting God in an idea and meeting God in Jesus of Nazareth."

□ *Concrete love is the most powerful human truth.* "Religion is a communal fact. Its vitality springs from concrete human relations between people who visibly care about each other. In their individualism, liberals may have missed this fact."

□ *There is a witness.* "In their preoccupation with critical thinking, intellectual clarity and tolerance, some liberal Christians forget that their only access to this historic faith is someone else's testimony."

He further suggests evangelicals learn the following from liberals:

□ *Truth is as humanly important as meaning.* "Modern religious liberalism, with its roots in the scientific spirit of the 18th century Enlightenment, took science seriously because it took the Creator of the real world seriously. . . . At stake is the issue over which the Nicene Council struggled mightily: Does God meet us in the real humanity of a historically real Jesus . . . or not? Faith that ignores questions of reality will not long remain faith in the One to whom the gospel testifies."

□ *The worshiping congregation is indispensable to the life of faith, but faithful life in the world is equally indispensable.* "The withdrawal-and-return rhythm of the church's relation to the world is a rhythm of obedience, repentance and renewal."

□ *To worship God in spirit and in truth is to confess the inadequacy of our worship, spirit and truth.* "Religious right, left and middle become captive to human pride when their adherents forget that 'the sacrifice acceptable to God is a broken spirit' (Ps. 51:17)."

☐ *The freedom of God transcends every human freedom, and this truth is the hope of the world.* "Perhaps no major theological issue divides liberals and evangelicals so momentously as that concerning the relation of divine judgment to divine love. . . . Liberals have sought with some consistency to keep divine judgment and grace equally accessible to all."

If indeed we counterbalance and enrich one another in at least these respects, we need to find ways of acknowledging our indebtedness to one another and of nourishing a relationship that allows us both to receive and to give. Those among our interviewees who seemed most sharply alienated from their polar opposites were persons who had had the least association with each other. It is distressing that the increasing congregationalism of our denominations makes interaction and dialogue with differing views even less likely. Unless a congregation is purposefully open to diverse perspectives, it may lose its opportunity as a "safe space" in which to hear one another out on the issues we also tend to divide over in the broader culture, as we described in chapter ten. It is also vital that we join hands to become strong for the challenges that lie ahead of us in the next century. Our separate congregational voices will be weak in the face of those challenges.

A rock in a sea of change? The broader culture is washing over us in waves of growing ethnic and religious diversity, global economic uncertainty and international tensions over competition for jobs, the decline of the Christian church as the "established" religion of our nation, the degradation of our natural environment, unacceptable levels of crime and violence, the growing inadequacy of our education and health systems and the undermining of family life—all with a destabilizing undertow of social change. The "single issues" that so engage our attention in the church at present, which define the agenda of our so-called culture wars, may soon be swamped by other concerns. (It is even possible that our concentration on the "single issues" is a way of holding these other engulfing issues at bay. Perhaps we invest these personal issues with our anxieties and fears of the larger destabilizing changes we want to resist.) Yet riots in big cities like Los Angeles remind us that the churches have important roles to play in providing stability, justice and a compassionate presence among diverse peoples. We are having to learn at the same time, however, to live in an increasingly pluralistic religious community as our population shifts.[2]

Will we be so preoccupied with internal bickering, heresy hunting and "purifying" our church that these waves of change will leave us arguing in a stagnant backwater? Perhaps God is inviting us out of our family feuds and into the challenges of a world in which fax machines, satellite television, Internet computers and rapid transportation require us to live in the global church and the global village. We must learn afresh to speak the truth that is in us and to do justice, love kindness and walk humbly with our God. We must, says one of our interviewees, let world mission and justice issues, not infighting, consume our energies and "get on with a world burning down."

At the time of this writing the national headquarters of several mainline churches were being wracked by tough decisions, downsizing and drastic restructuring. Denominational trees are being pruned severely, especially in their upper branches. More and more it appears that local churches are keeping their resources under their own control. Local needs, lack of confidence in bureaucratic structures, conflict over priorities and postures, disinterest in denominationalism, fallout from culture-war skirmishes and a local shortage of financial resources all contribute to the diminishing of denominational structures and programs. This also means that ecumenical efforts that depend on strong denominational organizations and programs are severely weakened or curtailed.

However one views this shifting of the center of gravity toward the local congregation, some words of hope and caution are in order.

Remember the church's role. We must keep in mind that local churches can be places of welcome, where the human community is becoming knit together in recognition of one another's worth to their Creator and Savior and of their need for one another in building God's just kingdom. But churches can also simply become enclaves of similar people who lack the courage or will to include those who, for whatever reason, do not fit in.

Remember who we are. Christians are first of all *Christians.* We are also male or female, old or middle-aged or young, of a particular race or ethnicity, progressive or traditional, rural or urban, of a fixed or changing economic class and political party. Our identities and loyalties are multiple. When we ally ourselves with just one facet of who we are—be we liberal or evangelical—we leave some parts of ourselves in tension with the "party line" of that perspective. This is a healthy tension, and it keeps us open to hearing voices from our other loyalties. This is one source of our hope that we can be respectful toward other points of view and humble about our own positions. But our greatest hope for unity lies in our primary identification with Jesus Christ as we claim our heritage as children of God.

Remember that we are different parts of one body. Structures, both denominational and ecumenical, that link local churches into larger units serve to enlarge the vision and scope of a local congregation's experience and reach. Some churches are ethnically distinct; many new-immigrant churches begin that way. Others reflect a particular economic class. Some are organized around an evangelical or a liberal stance. We must preserve the key structures that beckon, even *require* us, to reach out in Christian collaboration to other Christians who differ from us in significant ways, lest we become comfortable and smug in our isolation.

Remember that we need one another. Our society is becoming more and more difficult to hold together as inner cities lose out economically, as pockets of immigrants stay in ghettos, as community interests become subordinate to individual interests and as the public becomes skeptical of its democratic processes. We live with the specter of a collapsed Soviet Union, of the disintegration of states like Yugoslavia into warring ethnic and religious factions, of India's religious warfare, of Somalia's ungovernable societal unrest—and other images that have come before us since this writing.

A fragmented Christian community, one that focuses chiefly upon its own distinct congregation, is ill equipped to bind the wounds of the larger society and to keep it whole. Strong local churches may function as important healing communities for individuals, an essential part of mission, but God also calls us into the *oikumenē*—the human community. Denominational and ecumenical structures have provided a skeletal framework for many parts of Christ's body to carry out their mission throughout the world human community. No particular organizational structure is a given, of course, but our connectedness to one another for the sake of the gospel is.

Remember to be fair. We cannot expect to *resolve* our differences over biblical

interpretation or over the many issues that grow out of those interpretations. But we can resolve to be fair to one another, to use at least the
common decency and courtesy we expect in other spheres of our daily
lives. Our interviewees recounted an uncomfortable number of instances
in which it was not apparent that even ordinary standards of fairness had
been met. Having a high religious purpose does not justify low standards
of behavior. Like most of their fellow human beings, many of those
interviewed gave the "benefit of the doubt" to those with whom they
shared similar views but remained quite suspicious of the intentions and
motives of others. (It even seems that secular sources of information are
often trusted by local congregations more than their denominational or
ecumenical sources: some liberal church leaders whom we interviewed
were still grieving in the aftermath of an assaultive episode of *60 Minutes*
or an attack in *Reader's Digest*, whose "truth" was readily accepted by
evangelical Christians.)

Change, whether welcome or feared, is upon us. Several thoughtful
interviewees documented the anxiety-producing pervasiveness of change as
we are forced into a social experiment in fluctuating times. Now is a time in
which the liberal openness to engage in pioneering creativity is to be valued,
but it is also a time in which the evangelical's deep roots of faith are needed
so that experiments do not simply wither and blow away. We need each other
for these opposite but valuable tendencies. In God's economy, neither talent
is wasted. But our gifts can be wasted if we use them to oppose, attack,
manipulate, stereotype or undermine each other.

Perhaps, therefore, the final word of this book should be about forgiveness. We want to trust one another, but we are all too quick to betray that
trust ourselves. ("Why do you call me 'Lord, Lord,' and do not do what
I tell you?") We want to love one another, but we are too eager to satisfy
our own friends. ("If you love those who love you, what credit is that to
you?") We want to live in peace with one another, but sometimes the
smallest differences ignite our animosities. ("So when you are offering
your gift at the altar, if you remember that your brother or sister has
something against you, leave your gift there before the altar and go; first
be reconciled to your brother or sister, and then come and offer your gift.")
We *do* need each other, but we need even more the merciful Lord who
"remembers our sins no more."

Notes

Preface
[1]The term *evangelical* is used today in a variety of ways. We use it to refer to the conservative (but not fundamentalist) wing of the church. A fuller discussion of our understanding of evangelicalism will be found in the latter part of chapter one.

[2]Cf. Peggy L. Shriver, *Having Gifts That Differ: Profiles of Ecumenical Churches* (New York: Friendship Press, 1989).

[3]Richard G. Hutcheson Jr., *Mainline Churches and the Evangelicals* (Atlanta: John Knox Press, 1981). The treatment of evangelicalism in this book reflects his present perspective.

Chapter 1: The Polarized Pews
[1]Robert Wuthnow, *The Restructuring of American Religion* (Princeton, N.J.: Princeton University Press, 1988).

[2]H. Richard Niebuhr, *The Meaning of Revelation* (New York: Macmillan, 1960). On pages 63-64, Niebuhr says that "the distinctions between the two types of history cannot be made by applying the value-judgment of true and false but must be made by reference to differences of perspective." Although the data of external history are impersonal—ideas, interests and movements among things—the internal history is personal, in which "the final data are not elusive atoms of matter or thought but equally elusive selves."

[3]Ibid., pp. 70-73.

[4]For a disturbing and challenging examination of the direction in which postmodernism is taking our society, see Kenneth J. Gergen's *The Saturated Self: Dilemmas of Identity in Contemporary Life* (New York: Basic Books/HarperCollins, 1991).

[5]Richard G. Hutcheson Jr., *Mainline Churches and the Evangelicals* (Atlanta: John Knox Press, 1981).

[6]Ibid., p. 33.

[7]This material is adapted from Hutcheson, *Mainline Churches*, pp. 33-35.

[8]Richard Quebedeaux, *The Worldly Evangelicals* (New York: Harper & Row, 1978).

[9]Bernard L. Ramm, *The Evangelical Heritage* (Waco, Texas: Word Books, 1973), p. 40.

[10]Richard Quebedeaux, *The Young Evangelicals: Revolution in Orthodoxy* (New York: Harper & Row, 1974), p. 144.

[11]Ramm, *Evangelical Heritage*, p. 122.

[12]Hutcheson, *Mainline Churches*, pp. 33-35. In addition to the works by Quebedeaux and Ramm cited above, I drew on the following books by evangelical authors in this analysis: Donald W. Dayton, *Discovering an Evangelical Heritage* (New York: Harper & Row, 1976); Morris A. Inch, *The Evangelical Challenge* (Philadelphia: Westminster, 1978); Robert K. Johnston, *Evangelicals at an Impasse* (Atlanta: John Knox Press, 1979); Harold Lindsell, *Battle for the Bible* (Grand Rapids, Mich.: Zondervan, 1976); Richard F. Lovelace, *Dynamics of Spiritual Life: An Evangelical Theology of Renewal* (Downers Grove, Ill.: InterVarsity Press, 1979); David O. Moberg, *The Great Reversal* (Philadelphia: Lippincott, 1972); Ronald H. Nash, *The New Evangelicalism* (Grand Rapids, Mich.: Zondervan, 1963); René C. Padilla, ed., *The New Face of Evangelicalism* (Downers Grove,

Ill.: InterVarsity Press, 1976); and David F. Wells and John D. Woodbridge, *The Evangelicals: What They Believe, Who They Are, How They Are Changing* (Nashville: Abingdon, 1975).

Chapter 2: Appreciation of the Other Side

[1]Lloyd J. Averill, *Religious Right, Religious Wrong* (New York: Pilgrim Press, 1990), pp. 162-63.

Chapter 3: Sociological Help in Understanding the Splits

[1]Peter L. Berger, *The Heretical Imperative* (Garden City, N.Y.: Doubleday/Anchor, 1979), pp. 60-61.

[2]Robert N. Bellah et al., *The Good Society* (New York: Alfred A. Knopf, 1991), p. 186.

[3]Wade Clark Roof and William McKinney, *American Mainline Religion: Its Changing Shape and Future* (New Brunswick, N.J.: Rutgers University Press, 1987). See also Richard G. Hutcheson Jr., *Mainline Churches and the Evangelicals* (Atlanta: John Knox Press, 1981) pp. 109-22.

[4]Among the factors affecting decline of mainline churches have been (1) the low birthrate among more highly educated people in the middle and upper classes; (2) the loss of members through regional transfers where historically no churches of that denomination exist; (3) the problem of retaining young people, especially in the sixties, among churches that seemed to represent "the establishment"; and (4) a modest church-outreach program domestically, related to a theology that does not impel missionary endeavor. Conservatives would emphasize the last point and would see liberals as having substituted a social-action agenda for evangelism. Claims that liberal church members are "deserting" to join conservative churches are not substantiated for the most part—far more move toward secularization. Furthermore, much of the "growth" among evangelical churches has been internal—geographic mobility, higher birthrate, recent immigration. James Davison Hunter concludes a thorough study of church growth and decline by saying, "Decline in the moderate and liberal denominations appears to have leveled off considerably, and conservative growth is not nearly as dramatic as it once was" ("American Protestantism: Sorting Out the Present, Looking Toward the Future," in *The Believable Futures of American Protestantism*, ed. Richard John Neuhaus [Grand Rapids, Mich.: Eerdmans, 1988], p. 35).

[5]Milton J. Coalter, John M. Mulder and Louis B. Weeks, eds., *The Presbyterian Presence: The Twentieth-Century Experience*, 7 vols. (Louisville, Ky.: Westminster John Knox, 1990-1995).

[6]Within the limits of its sociological approach the study is exhaustive if somewhat unfocused. (Each volume is a collection of essays by various researchers covering a wide range of specific subjects.) Volume one looks at "the Presbyterian predicament," most ably detailed in the opening essay by Robert Wuthnow. The five subsequent volumes examine in turn the Presbyterian pattern of decline, theological pluralism, pluralism in education and leadership, organizational issues and diversity of witness. The final and seventh volume summarizes the overall study and proposes an agenda for the future.

[7]D. Newell Williams, ed., *A Case Study of Mainstream Protestantism: The Disciples' Relation to American Culture, 1880-1989* (St. Louis: Chalice Press, 1991).

[8]Peggy L. Shriver, *Having Gifts That Differ: Profiles of Ecumenical Churches* (New York: Friendship Press, 1989).

[9]Martin E. Marty, "The Two-Party System," chap. 17 in *Righteous Empire: The Protestant Experience in America* (New York: Dial Press, 1970), pp. 177-87. In recent years some modifications to the two-party analysis have been proposed by a Lilly Endowment-funded study, "Re-forming the Center."

[10]Robert Wuthnow, *The Struggle for America's Soul: Evangelicals, Liberals and Secularism* (Grand Rapids, Mich.: Eerdmans, 1989), p. 178.

[11]Bellah, *Good Society*, p. 184.

[12]James Davison Hunter, *Culture Wars: The Struggle to Define America* (New York: Basic Books/HarperCollins, 1991). His later book *Before the Shooting Begins: Searching for Democracy in America's Culture War* (New York: Free Press, 1994) continues the same theme, with an emphasis on political processes.

[13]Hunter, *Culture Wars*, p. 161 (italics his).

[14]We differ in our appreciation of Hunter. Dick Hutcheson is especially impressed with Hunter's analysis in *Culture Wars*. He sees Hunter as urging the vast middle to "wake up and do something about it." Peggy Shriver is inclined to see Hunter as falling into the very trap he insightfully describes, so that voices in the middle get overlooked and muffled by him too. This adds to the sense of cultural polarity, she feels, frustrating and intimidating those who are trying to speak a word of moderation.

[15]Wade Clark Roof and William McKinney, *American Mainline Religion: Its Changing Shape and Future* (New Brunswick, N.J.: Rutgers University Press, 1987).

[16]Ibid., p. 26.

[17]Bellah, *Good Society*, p. 188.

[18]Douglas Jacobsen and William Vance Trollinger Jr., eds., *Re-forming the Center: American Protestantism 1960 to the Present* (draft version; Grand Rapids, Mich.: Eerdmans, 1998).

[19]Miriam Therese Winter, Adair Lummis and Allison Stokes, *Defecting in Place* (New York: Crossroad, 1994).

[20]Barbara Brown Zikmund, Adair Lummis and Patricia Chang, *Clergy Women: An Uphill Calling* (Louisville, Ky.: Westminster John Knox Press, 1998).

[21]A comparable analysis appears in an article by then Louisville Seminary Dean Louis B. Weeks and Synod Executive William Fogleman called "A Two-Church Hypothesis" (*The Presbyterian Outlook* 172, no. 12 (March 1990): 2-8). They suggested that their church consists in two related but presently estranged denominations, which they called the "local congregational Presbyterian church" and "the governing-body Presbyterian church."

[22]Jeffrey Hadden, *The Gathering Storm in the Churches* (Garden City, N.Y.: Doubleday, 1969).

[23]Summary of Hadden's three crises, based on ibid., pp. 3-30.

[24]Bellah et al., *Good Society*, p. 199.

[25]Ibid., p. 244.

[26]Excerpted from Barbara Wheeler's H. Paul Douglass Lecture, delivered at the 1995 annual meeting of the Religious Research Association.

[27]This thesis was first advanced by his book *The Noise of Solemn Assemblies* (Garden City, N.Y.: Doubleday, 1961), which has had a strong and enduring influence on American sociology of religion.

[28]Quotations in this section are from Peter L. Berger, "Reflections of an Ecclesiastical Expatriate," *Christian Century*, October 24, 1990, pp. 964-69.

[29]Tex Sample, *U.S. Lifestyles and Mainline Churches* (Louisville, Ky.: Westminster John

Knox, 1990).

[30]Ibid., p. 4.

[31]Ibid., pp. 57-58.

[32]John M. Gessell, "The Secular Side of Episcopal Traditionalists," *Christian Century*, July 29-August 5, 1992, pp. 715-16.

[33]Chapter by David Sikkink and Christian Smith in Jacobsen and Trollinger, eds., *Re-forming the Center*.

[34]Jacobsen and Trollinger, preface to *Re-forming the Center*.

Chapter 4: Biblical and Theological Help in Understanding the Splits

[1]James Davison Hunter, *Culture Wars: The Struggle to Define America* (New York: Basic Books/HarperCollins, 1991), p. 45.

[2]Philip Wickeri, "Making Connections: Christianity and Culture in the Sino-American Dialogue" (paper prepared for Columbia Theological Seminary in its "Christ and Culture: A Sino-American Dialogue" consultation, October 1992).

[3]The two documents being discussed are "Biblical Authority and Interpretation," a resource document received by the 194th General Assembly of the United Presbyterian Church in the U.S.A. (June 1982); and "Presbyterian Understanding and Use of Holy Scripture," prepared by the Council on Theology and Culture, Presbyterian Church, U.S., and published as a position statement of the Presbyterian Church (U.S.A.).

[4]"Biblical Authority and Interpretation," a resource document received by the 194th General Assembly of the United Presbyterian Church in the U.S.A. (June 1982).

[5]These findings reported by Richard John Neuhaus, "The Public Square," *First Things*, August-September 1997, p. 86.

[6]A classic treatment of this image of the church is Paul Minear's *Images of the Church in the New Testament* (Philadelphia: Westminster Press, 1960).

[7]Sallie McFague, "An Earthly Theological Agenda," *Christian Century*, January 29, 1991, p. 121.

[8]Milton J. Coalter, John M. Mulder and Louis B. Weeks, eds., *The Confessional Mosaic: Presbyterians and Twentieth-Century Theology* (Louisville, Ky.: Westminster John Knox, 1990), p. 23.

[9]Milton J. Coalter, in a presentation on *The Confessional Mosaic* given at Louisville Theological Seminary on October 12, 1990.

[10]Ibid.

[11]Midcentury events from which the renascence of American evangelicalism might be dated were the formation of the National Association of Evangelicals in 1942, the founding of Fuller Theological Seminary in 1947 and the establishment of the flagship evangelical journal, *Christianity Today*, in 1956.

[12]Westminster Confession of Faith (1646), chapter 1, VI.

[13]John H. Leith, *An Introduction to the Reformed Tradition* (Atlanta: John Knox Press, 1977), p. 105.

[14]Louis B. Weeks and William Fogleman, in their "two-church hypothesis," use different understandings of and attitudes toward evangelism as a "case study" to illustrate the estrangement within local congregations. See Weeks and Fogleman, "A Two-Church Hypothesis," *The Presbyterian Outlook* 172, no. 12 (March 1990): 2-8.

[15]Peter L. Berger, *The Heretical Imperative* (Garden City, N.Y.: Doubleday/Anchor, 1979).

[16]Ibid., p. 63.

Chapter 5: Snarls and Snags

[1]As quoted in *Presbyterian Outlook*, June 22, 1992, p. 5.

[2]"Homosexuality and Church Unity," *Christian Century*, March 11, 1998, pp. 253-54.

[3]"Presbyterians and Peacemaking: Are We Now Called to Resistance?" a 1986 Report of the Advisory Council on Church and Society in preparation for the 200th General Assembly (1988).

Chapter 6: Dialogue or Diatribe?

[1]United Church of Christ General Synod Pronouncement, "Christian Faith: Economic Life and Justice."

[2]The speaker noted that this incident is now recorded in the public domain through a book by W. W. Schroeder, *Flawed Process and Sectarian Substance* (Chicago: Exploration Press, 1990).

[3]Both polls reported in Richard John Neuhaus's "The Public Square," *First Things* 31 (March 1993): 59-60.

Chapter 7: The Goal Is to Win

[1]Michael Kinnamon, "Restoring Mainline Trust: Disagreeing in Love," *Christian Century*, July 1-8, 1992, p. 648. Other material used for this case study came from Ronald J. Allen's "Kinnamon's Defeat and the Disciples of Christ," *Christian Century*, December 11, 1991, pp. 1156-58; and "Disciples: Voting Abuses?" *Christian Century*, February 26, 1992, p. 217.

[2]"Presbyterian Panel Surprised by Support for Lay Committee," *Presbyterian Outlook*, October 22, 1990, p. 3.

[3]"Steps Proposed for Reconciliation with Lay Committee," *Presbyterian Outlook*, February 18, 1991, p. 3.

[4]Cf. the minutes of the 203rd General Assembly, Presbyterian Church (U.S.A.) (1991), part 1, pp. 419-24.

Chapter 8: Neighborly Ties

[1]Peggy L. Shriver, *Pinches of Salt: Spiritual Seasonings* (Louisville, Ky.: Westminster John Knox, 1990), p. 24.

[2]Tex Sample, *U.S. Lifestyles and Mainline Churches* (Louisville, Ky.: Westminster John Knox, 1990).

[3]These quotes and suggestions are taken from material prepared by Conflict Management Initiatives for use in negotiations. They were shared with the authors by Richard A. Salem, who, although a resident of Illinois, was encountered in Cape Town, South Africa, where his skills were much in demand.

Chapter 9: How Do You Love a Group As Yourself?

[1]Carl S. Dudley and Thomas Van Eck, "Social Ideology and Community Ministries," in *Yearbook of American and Canadian Churches 1992* (Nashville: Abingdon Press, 1992), pp. 7, 11.

[2]Roger Shinn, "Christian Faith and Economic Practice," *Christian Century*, July 24-31, 1991, pp. 720-23.

[3]We heard testimony to the positive, reconciling effect of Presbyterians for Renewal (a recent amalgam of two groups similar in views), which has conducted workshops and renewal conferences around the country. One pastor in New York City held a day-long retreat with his congregation's peace group and several national repre-

sentatives of Presbyterians for Biblical Concerns (one of the two that united). Although they achieved no consensus on peace issues, the discussion encouraged both sides to see the other as moving from a position of integrity, including concern for biblical understanding.

[4]These and the following quotations are taken from the statement "Called to Be Catholic: Church in a Time of Peril," available from the National Pastoral Life Center, 18 Bleecker Street, New York, NY 10012.

Chapter 10: Confronting Controversy in Community

[1]See James Davison Hunter's *Culture Wars: The Struggle to Define America* (New York: Basic Books/HarperCollins, 1991).

[2]Eric Hoffer, *The True Believer* (New York: Harper & Row, 1951).

Chapter 11: Moderates and Constructive Encounter

[1]James Davison Hunter, *Culture Wars: The Struggle to Define America* (New York: Basic Books/HarperCollins, 1991).

[2]James R. Kelly, "Religious Identity and Public Discourse: On the Importance of Common Ground in the Public Church," unpublished manuscript, 1997.

Chapter 12: The Leadership Question

[1]Ronald A. Heifitz, *Leadership Without Easy Answers* (Belknap, Mass.: Harvard University Press, 1994).

[2]"Episcopalians Elect Presiding Bishop," *Christian Century*, July 30-August 6, 1997, p. 687.

[3]This case is argued in an earlier book by one of the authors. See Richard G. Hutcheson Jr., *Wheel Within the Wheel: Confronting the Management Crisis of the Pluralistic Church* (Atlanta: John Knox Press, 1979).

Chapter 13: Do Denominations Have a Future?

[1]A classic work on the denominational pattern of American church life is Roman Catholic sociologist Andrew M. Greeley's *The Denominational Society: A Sociological Approach to Religion in America* (Glenview, Ill.: Scott Foresman, 1972).

[2]John P. Marcum, "Research Counting Down," *Monday Morning*, July 1997, p. 16.

[3]Michael Kinnamon, "Restoring Mainline Trust: Disagreeing in Love," *Christian Century*, July 1-8, 1992, pp. 646-47.

[4]Robert N. Bellah et al., *Habits of the Heart: Individualism and Commitment in American Life* (Berkeley: University of California Press, 1985), p. 220.

[5]Robert Wuthnow, *The Struggle for America's Soul: Evangelicals, Liberals and Secularism* (Grand Rapids, Mich.: Eerdmans, 1989), pp. 116-22.

[6]Bellah, *Habits of the Heart*, p. 228. Peggy Shriver was administrator of the "unchurched American" study.

[7]Reported in Thomas C. Reeves, "Not So Christian America," *First Things* 66 (October 1996): 19.

[8]Stephen L. Carter, *The Culture of Disbelief* (New York: BasicBooks, 1993).

[9]Dean R. Hoge, Benton Johnson and Donald Luidens, *Vanishing Boundaries* (Louisville, Ky.: Westminster John Knox, 1994).

[10]Carter, *Culture of Disbelief*, p. 57.

[11]David S. Lueke, "Is Willow Creek the Way of the Future?" *Christian Century*, May 14,

1997, pp. 479-83.

[12]Thomas W. Currie III, "Why I Am Not Going to Leave the Presbyterian Church," *The Presbyterian Outlook*, February 16, 1998, p. 9.

[13]Bishop William C. Frey, quoted in "The Spirit Hasn't Left the Mainline" (a forum including Frey, Roberta Hestenes and William H. Willimon, moderated by Tony Campolo), *Christianity Today*, August 11, 1997, pp. 14-20.

Chapter 14: Threads to Strengthen the Tie

[1]Donald W. Shriver Jr., "What Can Liberals and Evangelicals Teach Each Other?" *Christian Century*, August 12-19, 1987, pp. 687-690.

[2]The U.S. Census Bureau estimates that "minorities" will make up 44.4 percent of the U.S. population by the year 2050. In 1980 non-Hispanic whites (the "majority") constituted 84.5 percent of the population.